LOOKING AFTER

John Daniel

LOOKING
AFTER

A Son's Memoir

John Daniel

For Suzanne,
with many warm wishes

John

11/6/97

Oregon Book Awards

COUNTERPOINT
WASHINGTON, D.C.

Portions of this book first appeared in *Eugene Weekly, Hope, Northwest Review, Southwest Review,* and *Wilderness.*

Reprint acknowledgments appear on page 263.

LIBRARY OF CONGRESS CATALOGING-IN-PUBLICATION DATA
Daniel, John, 1948–
Looking after: a son's memoir / John Daniel.
1. Daniel, John, 1948–   . 2. Parent and adult child—United States.
3. Mothers and sons—United States.   4. Adult children—United States—
Family relationships.   5. Aging parents—United States—
Family relationships.   6. Caregivers—United States.   I. Title.
HQ755.86.D35   1996   306.874'3—dc20   96-18627
ISBN 1-887178-23-6

FIRST PRINTING
Book design by David Bullen
Composition by Wilsted & Taylor
Printed in the United States of America on acid-free paper that meets the American National Standards Institute Z39-48 Standard.
COUNTERPOINT
P.O. Box 65793
Washington, D.C. 20035-5793

Distributed by Publishers Group West

FOR JIM DANIEL
AND HEATHER DANIEL

I have become to myself a piece of difficult ground,
not to be worked over without much labor.

SAINT AUGUSTINE

I am as convinced as I can be of anything that this
experience of ours is only a part of the experience that is,
and with which it has something to do; but *what* or *where*
the other parts are, I cannot guess. It only enables one to
say "behind the veil, behind the veil!"

WILLIAM JAMES

I shall pass beyond memory to find you—oh, where,
where shall I find you, my truly good and serene delight?
If I find you without memory, I shall not remember you.
And how shall I find you if I do not remember you?

SAINT AUGUSTINE

The Dogwood Tree

In my mother's last years she ate her breakfast and lunch at a small oak table in our kitchen, by a window that looks out on the limbs and leaves of a dogwood tree. With ferns below it, the tree makes a small, dapple-lighted garden of that side of the house, screening us from Tom the neighbor's place next door. The pink blossoms gave my mother pleasure in the spring—though, like me, she preferred dog-woods that bloom white—and she also enjoyed the sparrows and finches and chickadees that came to the bird feeder with a mossy roof that hung from the dogwood's central limbs. My mother took a long time with her meals. She looked out the window as she ate, and sometimes the food on her plate seemed to surprise her when she looked down and saw it. She usually sat at the table long after I had finished my meal and gone out back again to write or off in the car on errands. My mother spent many hours with that dogwood tree.

I can see her clearly as I write this, and I can smell her, too. It's a fresh and musty smell of sandalwood and damp sweat, of skin cream and urine, and it's as vivid in my memory as her stooped back and curling white hair, as clear as her slow, flat-footed shuffle in bare feet or slippers, her hands flying out sporadically to a wall or table edge to steady her on her way. That smell of her old age is as sure in my mind as her quick scowl and sharp remarks, her laughter and childlike smile, her frowning concentration as she tried to listen with her bad ears, the look of her reddened eyes behind her glasses as she doggedly tracked lines of print across page after page of the books and papers and magazines she kept piled beside her on her bed.

Her eyesight, unlike her hearing, stayed sharp until the end. As we drove in the car she would sometimes speak out loud the names she read on street signs and billboards, as if to fix our location in memory—or maybe simply for the exercise, for the pleasure of forming words, for the happiness of being out of the house and in motion through the streets of Portland. Her eyes saw clearly the birds that came to the kitchen feeder, but she often asked their names. Sometimes she asked about the same bird at breakfast and again at lunch, sometimes at the same meal.

"What *is* that one," she would say, intently, "with the bright red . . ." She gestured at her throat with her long, purpled fingers.

"That's the finch," I'd tell her.

"*Finch*," she'd say. "That's what I thought."

A black tomcat, not ours, once in a while would rocket from the ferns and almost capture a finch or sparrow, upsetting the feeder in a spray of millet and sunflower seed. My usual response was to charge out the back door and throw a stick of firewood at the fleeing cat. My mother would watch through the window, looking at me and the wobbling feeder as if the scene had never occurred before and was as delightful as anything that had ever happened in the history of the world. And sometimes a particular image would come to her, a known shape of words, a recurrent visitation from the mists and shadows of the past.

"Do you remember," she would ask, in that way she had of giving each syllable its full enunciation, "when the cat brought a poor bird to the door, and I scolded it? And you were there, all of six"—she'd be smiling now—"and you said, 'Mother, it's a cat's *nature* to hunt birds.'"

"I remember," I'd tell her, though in truth I didn't remember saying it so much as I remembered hearing her tell the story about me. I remembered being remembered. But I cherished those moments, brief and infrequent as they were, when the two of us could pause together in the shared light of each other's recall. In those moments we were all at home—me, my mother, the family and friends we spoke of. I felt myself resting then, relaxing from some continuous effort I hadn't known I'd been engaged in and would shortly resume.

Sometimes when she brought up a glimpse of the past, I would try to draw her out, to enlarge the landscape of her recall. But memory for my mother was a thing of moments, as mutable as the lightplay in the dogwood tree. What I searched for with my questions usually wasn't there. She knew the names I spoke—my father's, my brother's, the places we had lived—but much of the time the names had come loose from their moorings, like boats adrift on the sea. If I told a family story she would recognize it with pleasure, but my mother in herself had few stories left.

In the hot summer months the dogwood leaves curled on the tree, and then as fall arrived and the light turned pale, the leaves took on a tinge of red—a subtle red, nothing vivid—and began to drop and gather on the ground. The gray Northwestern season that starts in mid October and lasts through late spring was hard on my mother's spirits. In the spring she could watch the dogwood twigs hopefully for evidence of buds. In the fall she could only watch the tree unleaving itself. By late November of her last autumn the branches shook in the wind with only a smattering of leaves still clinging, and there came a morning when only one was left, on a lower branch near the window at my mother's end of the breakfast table. She pointed it out to me, and again the next few mornings. "Still there," she said, smiling as if with a secret we shared.

One morning as I heard her feet begin to shuffle from her bedroom, I glanced at the window and saw that the leaf had fallen. I pointed as I poured her coffee. "It's gone," I said.

She gazed blankly out the window.

"The leaf is gone," I told her. "The last leaf."

"Oh," she answered vaguely. "The leaf."

Because it was absent from her present sight she had only the faintest memory of it. The leaf was profoundly gone for her, and soon would be absolutely gone, but in my own mind it still hangs on. I can see it now, I can't stop seeing it: a dark curled form infused with red, a beautiful ghost that by chance or willfulness still holds to its place in the world. In memory I circle and circle that leaf. I watch it much more carefully than I watched it before. I want to know what makes it hold on in the cold wind, how it somehow emerged out of sap and fiber and grew in the sun and remains now only by habit, by a spell of nature, by nothing at all. It's only memory that holds it now, and memory, at last, that lets it go.

CHAPTER ONE

It's October, the last clear days before the rains. The sun is warm and bright but paling, already retiring toward winter. There's a trace of wood smoke in the air. Crows have gathered in the park, as they usually do in the fall, poking around in the grass, raising querulous hubbubs as I walk by. I squish through a scatter of fallen plums, breathing in their sweet rotting aura, breathing it out. The birches lining the streets are yellowing, their leaves collecting in small drifts in the oil-stained gutters. Some of them scatter as the wind comes up, then settle to the street again.

I've been talking with a psychologist, and I'm gusting with memories. Or not whole memories so much as pieces, random leaves swirling, patches of bright color I haven't seen since childhood. Where have I been all my life? *Who* have I been? It's odd to think it, even odder to write it, but I don't feel whole. I'm a hodgepodge, a motley crowd I hardly know. This *me*, this whatever it is that I am, was passed one to another in a makeshift relay race, a race with no destination that happened to wind up here, me, walking the gridded streets of a North Portland neighborhood, three thousand miles and forty-five years from my birth. The others just drifted away once they'd carried me a while. They lost themselves in my memory's terrain.

But it's not them—*I'm* the one who's lost. I'm lost from them. Is this a midlife crisis? It feels too gray for that, too dull and sluggish. I'm not inspired to leave my wife or dump my career. How could I dump my career when I don't have one? I don't have an itch to bungee jump or hole up with video games or seek a guru in Nepal. And I'm glad, because that kind of thing is undignified for a man in his forties. It's the kind of thing Bob Bourgeois might do, if he had the courage. Bob's one of my selves who stuck around. He's the one who actually enjoys mowing the lawn, who worries that he should paint the rain gutters with Rustoleum, who ambles docile and well scrubbed through the cavernous spaces of Costco or Home Depot, gently henpecked by his smiling wife. You can see Bob's face on every sack of Kingsford charcoal briquets. He's a basket case, a swamp of quiet desperation. Let *him* have a midlife crisis.

Whatever's happening to me, I prefer to think of it in Dantean terms. I've lost the way in a dark wood. I've lost the way, I don't know where it was going, I don't think I ever knew. You get up in the morning, you drink your coffee, you read the paper, you set yourself in motion. You put one foot in front of the other and do what's next. You go ahead through your life like that and suddenly your life's half gone, and more than half. You're over halfway to those stars of no return.

My doctor says I'm suffering from depression, which is depressing in itself. What do you do about depression, give smiling lessons to your lips? Read *The Power of Positive Thinking*? My doctor prescribed pills, little red traffic cops to direct the chemistry of my brain. I take them dutifully, and maybe I feel better, but I think I need to do more than recalibrate my chemistry. That's why I'm seeing the psychologist. If I'm depressed there must be something I'm not seeing, or lots of things, things I need to understand. It's only in the last year, since my mother died, that I've been able to glimpse my depression, let alone see inside it. It's a gray weather that I've come to take for normal. I walk inside it for days or months and never see it, then the sun burns through and it slips out of me. I see its dark form, shaped like me, then the mist again.

Drinking lightens it, then makes it worse. Exercising helps, and so I take these fast walks with weights around my wrists and ankles, like some prisoner in a hurry. There's only one reliable medicine, and it's not here. It's out beyond the end of the road, in wind and rivers and ponderosa pines, silently offering itself in every leaf and stone. The gospel of the good sweet world, the beauty beyond all human moods. It never fails me, but I can't seem to bring it home. It fades like the colors of a caught trout. When I return, it's always to myself and my gray weather.

Power poles march next to me, two or three to a block. The dull-colored houses sit behind their fences, lawns clipped and edged, flowers weeded, roses mulched. So much care in keeping things in order, keeping things enclosed. Blank windows, shut front doors. I have a wild urge to stride in my shorts up a walkway, any walkway, and pound on the door with my weighted right hand until someone answers. Twenty-five years ago, frazzled by methamphetamine, I did just that . . . Someone's looking at me from his window. I imagine a gun in his hand. I wave and keep walking.

At the end of the block I turn left onto Willamette Avenue and there's Mount Hood, dark and streaked with old snow, floating in the southeast like a figure from a dream I can't quite recall. Not far from here, somewhere on this bluff above the river, William Clark looked south two centuries ago. He saw no bridges, no cranes or dry docks, no tankers or tugboats, none of the clustered oblong spires of downtown Portland. In the continental quiet he looked at wooded hills, the river surging in spring flood, maybe the huts and smokes of an Indian camp. Mount Hood floating in the distance as it floats for me. It thrills me to imagine what he must have felt—to have traversed the wild heart of North America to stand in that great solitude, to look upon a vista no man of European ancestry had ever seen.

It was for some tiny semblance of Clark's Voyage of Discovery that I used to climb mountains, and it's for that semblance that I now hike desert canyons and old-growth forests—always outward, away from the human world into the sanity of nature. But this time, I know, it's a different kind of journey that I need. I have it in my head that "crisis," in the Greek it comes from, means separation. So maybe this is a crisis. I'm separated from my life and whoever's been living it. From myself. From my selves.

There's one in particular who keeps calling me, one who's been hidden a long time. My psychologist says it might do me good to get to know him again, and I think she's right. I can't see him clearly, the boy I was, but I can smell the breeze on his face as the Appalachian Trail steepens beneath his feet, leading him to a rocky promontory where thick hardwoods give way to sparse pines, where nothing but distance obscures the view before him, a view he has glimpsed through trees but not seen in its wholeness until now. The brown Shenandoah River meanders through patched farmland and forest below him, and beyond the river valley the blue Allegheny Mountains range away, ridge after ridge, into the hazy West.

I wish I had the poem the boy wrote there. I know it sang with all the lonely passion of his fourteen years. I know it sang of wanderlust—that word was in the poem. It sang of the perfect peaceful looping of the Shenandoah, the blue grandeur of the mountains, and the pure formless possibility of that far distance where the mountains disappeared. I had traveled out there with my family, clear to the Golden Gate, but that had been motels and restaurants and the car. That had been my parents and their arguments. This was me, my life, and I absolutely knew that someday I would live out there. I sat for a long time with my arms around my knees, watching with a wild exaltation as the wind called in the pines and called in me.

It's crazy, this living of a life. You're never quite sure where you're going or what you're doing, and in the rearview mirror the most it makes is a chancy kind of sense. The boy was right. I did go west, and now I'm looking east across thirty-some years for that kid who looked this way with all his longing. We meant to stay together, but we got split up somehow. He got lost or I got lost and now he's back there on that Blue Ridge promontory, and I'm walking the circular squares of these Portland streets. This wasn't in the poem he wrote. This isn't what he had in mind when he looked west. And so I'm going in this time instead of out, I'm going back to find that boy, to find others if I can, to find anyone who might be me. If you've lost your way in the forest, how can you find it again except by going back?

CHAPTER TWO

*F*ailing is the term
we use. Failing health. Failing mind. As if life were a series of tests,
and we have to keep our grades up right to the end. And failing
whom? Oneself? Or those around oneself, those family and friends
who know a person in certain ways and hope and expect that she will
continue in those ways forever? To fail is to disappoint, to prove unreliable. When a bank fails, it proves unworthy of everyone who had
faith in it. It ruins people—and behind the scenes, we suspect, someone got rich. "Fail" comes from the Latin *fallere,* which means,
among other things, to deceive.

It's hard to say when my mother began to fail. My wife and I, and
my brother too, were living in California during the 1980s, a continent away from my mother's home on the coast of Maine. Failings
tend not to show in letters or phone calls, or even in occasional visits,
especially to those who aren't looking for them. My mother had long

been a vigorous and independent woman. In her twenties and early thirties she was a labor organizer, like my father, and later in life, after my brother and I had left home and she and my father had separated, she became a nomadic adventurer and seeker. She sailed on steamers, lived in a lakeside cabin in British Columbia, spent two years in the Findhorn spiritual community in Scotland. In her seventies she became a devotee of the Indian avatar Sai Baba and made two pilgrimages to his ashram, staying several weeks each time, sleeping on a thin mattress on a concrete floor. She had always gone her own way. She was tough as lobster shell, solid as New England granite, lively as the wind.

And she was living in her old age exactly where she wanted to be, in the same region of the central Maine coast where she had spent long stretches of her girlhood. Her father, a Unitarian minister, kept a modest summerhouse on Hancock Point, near Acadia National Park, and with her two sisters my mother did much of her growing up there. Tides and fogs and the clangor of the bell buoy became part of her being, as did the inland lakes (which New Englanders call ponds) where her father took the family on camping vacations. I have a photo of the teenaged girl who would become my mother as a Sea Scout, standing on the bowsprit of a two-masted schooner, one hand on the headstay, hair and bloomers flapping in the breeze. That is a true portrait of her spirit. The salt wind drew her back to Maine throughout her life for visits and vacations—my brother and I too did some growing up there—and in 1978, tired of roving, she settled in to stay, it seemed. She rented a plain wooden house in Brooklin and lived simply there, keeping a garden, reading and writing, working as a proofreader for *WoodenBoat* magazine.

In 1980, when she was seventy-two, my mother's Volvo station wagon left the road and almost plunged her into Blue Hill Harbor. She escaped with only a broken left arm, a lucky outcome that we too readily interpreted as another sign of her reliable durability. She didn't know or wouldn't say how the accident had happened. Two

years later she passed out at the wheel of her car in her younger sister's driveway in Needham, Massachusetts. Only then did she go to a
doctor, who immediately put her on a drug to control her high blood
pressure. My mother's attitude toward illness was a simple one: she
denied it. A friend who dropped by on an early spring day in 1983
found her sick with flu and chilled to sluggishness, too weak to keep
a fire in the woodstove. She had a telephone but had called no one. I
remember talking with her on the phone while she was recuperating
with friends. She seemed baffled, mystified by what had happened—
and, it occurs to me now, a little scared.

Such incidents put us on alert, I suppose, but she seemed to recover quickly and go on with her life. She was white-haired now and
a little stooped, weaker in her left arm, but still Zilla Daniel, still my
blithe mother. My father had died at seventy-two, and given what he
had done to his body, he had been lucky to live out his biblical span.
He smoked four packs of Chesterfields a day and was a hard-drinking
alcoholic for four decades of his life. My mother had quit cigarettes
long before and no longer drank heavily. She ate healthy food, and
the same willfulness that caused her to deny illness filled her sails
with an indomitable spirit. I remember when Marilyn and I saw her
off at San Francisco Airport on her second trip to India, in the fall of
1986. In pants and sneakers and canvas vest, water bottle dangling
from her belt, my mother resolutely pushed her baggage cart up the
rampway of the international entrance, waving good-bye with her
ticket in an upraised hand, looking back not once. We laughed at the
wonder of it.

When she returned two months later, though, she seemed subdued and peaked. For the first time she fully looked her age, which
then was seventy-eight. It turned out that she had brought home a
well-developed staph infection in her leg. She had to stay with Marilyn and me in our tiny cottage, gradually regaining her strength as
the antibiotics took hold and beat down the bacteria. She slept and
rested in our bed; we flopped on a pad in the living room or in a tent

on the gravel patio out back. I had a talk to give in our old hometown in Oregon, but she wasn't well enough to travel with us, so Marilyn had to stay home with her. This wasn't a happy alternative—Marilyn and I had been looking forward to the trip together—but there was nothing else to do. A new responsibility and a new kind of tension had entered our lives, a harbinger of what was to come.

My mother got well slowly in the weeks after my Oregon trip. When I was done teaching for the day I would drive her to the nearest almost-level road—we lived in the foothill country of the San Francisco Peninsula—and we would walk there, slowly, a little farther each afternoon. She breathed hard from the exertion. For the first time in my life my mother was leaning on my arm for support, and I wasn't comfortable with it. I had a life to live, things to do, little accomplished as a writer and a lot to prove. I didn't like the drift. Zilla Daniel was supposed to be strong. She was supposed to take care of herself. She was supposed to be leading her independent and presumably happy life three thousand miles away on the coast of Maine—where I could visit her once in a while, where we could feast on scallops and lobster together, where we could drive to Acadia Park or row in her boat off Naskeag Point and talk about those things we were able to talk about. Where, in our oblique ways, we could affirm our love for each other. And I could leave, knowing that my mother was living the life she wanted to live and was doing just fine.

CHAPTER THREE

I want to say that my first moment of awareness occurred in my mother's arms. The sense of the memory is vague, but I seem to remember the warmth and gentle pressure of arms and breast. And I seem to remember a voice speaking to me, drawing me out of myself into the world—I hear it murmuring like a stream moving easily over smooth stones, the words all dissolved now in the lilt and whisper of their flow. Maybe it was her heart and blood I was hearing, maybe it wasn't words at all.

But it's the stars that I remember most clearly from that moment, or that I think I remember. It's the stars that were my first seeing. Maybe my mother was talking about them, crooning about them. I saw, I think I saw, a scatter of light above me, and it was in seeing that scatter of light that I first distinguished a world separate from me and a me separate from the world. I think of it as my second birth, as profound as my first—more profound, because it was the birth of consciousness, of the point of view that I would come to know as myself, more *me* than arms or legs. And, of course, it was also a death. In that instant of seeing I fell from the cosmos I was born to and had been securely and unknowingly part of.

There are other details of that first experience that I want to say I remember: that the night air was warm and soft on my face, that the stars looked cold somehow, that crickets were sounding, that a dog barked. But how could I at two years old or less have been aware of anything I could identify and remember as the sound of crickets? A dog's bark, maybe, because we had one and I knew she barked, but crickets? And what did I know of the sensation of cold that I could identify it and extend it to the stars? Surely my mind has invented those details, remembering them *into* the memory of voice and warmth and scattered light. I'm a writer, after all, and I have a writer's instinct for artifice. I want to make the scene immediate for the reader, and that artifice of language is only an extension of a deeper, preverbal artifice. Something in my psyche wants to make the scene immediate for *me*, the me who distantly remembers it. Memory itself is a fabricator, a spinner of yarns, a poet and a liar.

Scientists for decades have been trying to discover the site or sites in the brain where memories are stored. Now, at last, they seem to have found the answer: there are no such sites. When we remember an experience, the brain does not somehow retrieve a record of it from storage, as a computer retrieves information from its memory banks. There is no record. The brain *re-creates* the experience, conjuring the image out of vast, labyrinthine loopings of neurons firing in a pattern similar to the one evoked by the original experience.

Similar, but not the same. The re-creation is not a photocopy. According to neurobiologist Gerald Edelman, there are ten billion neurons in the human cerebral cortex, and more potential connections between those neurons than there are subatomic particles in the entire estimated physical universe. It is a system of near-infinite complexity, a system that seems designed for revision as much as for replication, and that is what occurs in memory. Details from separate experiences weave together, so that the rememberer thinks of them as having happened together. The actual year or season shifts to a different one. Some details are lost; others are freely invented. We tend to remember in ways that suit the present self, not the self of ten or twenty or forty years ago. And even the fresh memory, the "original" memory, is unreliable. It happens all the time that two eyewitnesses to the same recent incident give widely divergent accounts. We remember not the story of what happened but always *a* story, not the truth but a version of the truth that fits our present understanding of the world and helps us get on with our lives. That story is subject to revision over time. The latest draft becomes for us *the* story, the clear and certain memory we would swear to.

And so how do I proceed? My memories are me, they live exactly at the center of who and what I think I am. If I can't know them to be true, how can I know who I am? How can I write a memoir if I can't trust memory? It disturbs me to acknowledge, as I must, that my recollection of seeing the stars from my mother's arms may be entirely fabricated. Like the cat and bird story, it may be an instance of remembering myself being remembered—my mother may have told me, when I was older, that she had carried me into the yard one night and I had seemed to take an interest in the stars. I may not have been in my mother's arms at all but in the arms of Nanny, the woman who helped with housekeeping when my brother and I were small. Or I may never have seen the stars from anyone's arms. It may all have come from stories, from songs, from who knows what or where.

It's even possible, I believe, that the memory I call my first may have come with me into the world. We are from the stars, after all. Every particle we are made of was formed in their unimaginable fire. The matter that we call ourselves and our world, the matter of our brains and bones and the eyes we see with, has been gathering, dispersing, and drifting the distances of space for billions of years before materializing in these familiar forms. Our nature and all of nature is a story of fire strewn through darkness, and that story must some-how be inscribed in us. To see the stars for the first time may be more an act of recognition than of learning, a dawning into consciousness of what in some sense we have always known.

But what I have, regardless of its origin, regardless of its veracity, is the memory. The image. I looked up from my mother's arms and saw the scattered stars in the black night sky. I have carried that glimpse for over forty years, and there are other glimpses I have car-ried nearly as long. The stars were on my mind as a young boy. When I was five or so, my mother was trying to explain the West Coast to me, a place called Oregon. I got it that the land went on from where we were and ended far away in Oregon, but for some reason I didn't see an ocean beyond the land. I saw trees and mountains, a last solid shore, and then the void of starry space. *Oregon.* And there was a re-current nightmare I had throughout my childhood, my most terri-fying experience. There was no story to it, just an image. I felt myself floating among icy stars, a dead and disembodied soul lost forever from my life. I would cry out until my mother came in to turn on the light and comfort me.

I still have an acute fear of death. It's liable to well up suddenly in any circumstance—in classroom or concert hall, talking at a party, alone at my desk, in bed with my wife. It isn't a fear so much as a cer-tainty, an ultimate despair. It says: *I will die from this sweet world. I will vanish among the stars in the cold abyss of eternity. I will be noth-ing forever.*

I've sometimes thought that the glittering sky I saw from my mother's arms somehow burned me with a fear of death, but it makes no sense. Why would that moment have been fearful? What danger could I have sensed? What was death to the *I* who had just been born beneath those stars? My fear must have come later, from some other source that memory still withholds, something that subverted my original vision and turned the stars cold, turned them into emblems of extinction.

I don't recall any frightening experience involving the stars, but fire and bright light were threatening in a different context. In the late fifties and early sixties we lived in Glen Echo, Maryland, a semi-rural suburb of Washington, D.C. The firehouse was just down the street, and its siren was loud, an implacable shriek. When it went up and leveled off at its highest pitch I would stop everything and wait for it to go back down, because that would mean it was signaling only a fire. If it didn't go down it meant the worst. It meant that Russian missiles were on the way and nothing could be done to stop them and along with Congress and the president and my family and friends I would soon burn instantly to nothing in a blinding flash. I would be standing in the center of my blue-papered room, my Rand McNally world map on the wall, all my familiar things around me—and then I'd be gone. When the siren seemed to stay too many seconds at its top screaming pitch, I closed my eyes and *willed* it to go down, then pleaded, beating my fists against my thighs.

Light and dark, to be alive, then suddenly not even a body—is that what gave me the nightmare? Is that what caused me to see a terrifying brink at the end of America? I don't know, and I don't suppose I can know. But maybe it's enough to realize that the starry dark is a primary image for me, a riddle of my being—and so it makes sense that my memory should work and worry it, shape scenes and stories from it, tease it into words. There is something there to be discovered, some shape that memory both hides and wants to body forth from its darknesses. Something I need to know, and the only way to find it or let it be born is to follow this pencil, this circling, stuttering, scratching pencil that might know more than I do. I can't be sure that everything it writes will be true, but I can hope to approach the truth only by following it.

And by following my mother. It's she who stirred this up in me, first by living here and then by dying. Until she came, I had never thought much about my past or anybody's past. The past was past; I believed in now. But when she came, her memory falling from her like sediment from a slowing stream, I began to gather my own memory, gleaning the past as she let it go—as if I could save it for her, as if I could save her sense of self from its slow dissolution. And then she died, over a year ago now, and I haven't been able to stop grieving. I cry frequently, suddenly. I tell her how sorry I am. I miss her intensely despite my vivid memories of how hard it was to have her with us.

It's as though she has something still to teach me. She comes in dreams occasionally, and in one of them, a recent one, she asks to see the leafless tree. I take her to the deck behind the house where I live, where she too may live, though it's not our Portland house. I'm assisting her, but she doesn't need it—she's agile, steady on her feet, the Zilla of twenty years ago. She's wearing a navy blue sweater. She holds her cane vertically in front of her, grasping it just above the middle, raising it high and marching after it in high spirits. We pass two trees I've never seen before, a lemon and a grapefruit, both with glossy leaves. The tree we came to see is the third one, the last one. I suspect I was wrong about it, it might have leaves after all, but I can't bring myself to look at it. I don't know if my mother looks or not. She says she'll walk to a stream that runs through the forest behind the house, she'll walk to a pool in the stream and wet a handkerchief there. "You'll need help," I say, but I know that I'm the one being guided now. I'm the one who lives in the house but doesn't even know what's behind it—a stream in the forest all this time and I never knew.

CHAPTER FOUR

It surprised us when my mother, after recovering from her infection and flying home to Maine, began to ask for money. She had never had a lot, and what she'd had she hadn't tried to save, but she lived cheaply. Between Social Security and Medicare and what she earned at *WoodenBoat*, she always seemed to have enough. When she didn't, her sisters helped her out. Now her letters were saying that she was a bit short this month, could we spare fifty or seventy-five or a hundred dollars to tide her over. She had a car payment due. She owed the dentist. The Bar Harbor Bank was dunning her about her VISA account.

We were concerned about the health of both her body and her finances, and so I flew to Maine in December of 1987 to spend Christmas with her. She was pleased—relieved, it seemed—to let me go through her bills and checking records. I found that she had enough income to cover her expenses, barely, but that she had been writing redundant checks. She had paid her rent twice in a month, made two car payments, and the like. Her checks were bouncing from Blue Hill to Bangor, and at the larcenous rates that banks charge to cover bad checks, or not to cover them, she had dug herself a sizable hole.

"Oh!" she said, in self-disgust, when I told her what the trouble was. "How absolutely *silly* of me."

"It's no big deal," I said. "I'll get you a record book to help you keep track."

"I shouldn't need one," said my mother, still scowling at herself.

I bought the record book and set it up for the year ahead, listing the checks she needed to write each month. My brother sent some money to get her out of the red, and things seemed squared away. But I remember, walking the bright snowy streets of Blue Hill—my mother had taken an apartment there—an inescapable knowledge dogging me: *My mother is old.* And I remember my discomfiture as I talked to the bank teller about my mother's account. I lowered my voice and leaned close over the counter, wishing other customers weren't around. My mother's check-bouncing was a sign of mental deterioration, of senility—at least *I* knew it was—and somehow that was shameful.

Her staph infection had caused me no embarrassment. Most bodily illness carries no stigma; the afflicted one is a victim, an unfortunate, a brave spirit let down by her flesh. But mental lapses, mental illness, mental *failing* are different. We don't extend the same sympathy and support. There's a suspicion that the failing one could do better if only she would try, that will or discipline, rather than health, is what's wanting. I felt it right away, and I would feel it again when I came back to Maine the following fall and saw that her entries in the record book had tailed off over the winter and disappeared in the spring. Her finances had bollixed up again. It's not her fault, I thought. And then I thought: All she had to do was follow the list.

I realized during my Christmas visit that my mother would eventually need to come west and live with Marilyn and me. Eventually, and maybe soon. Some of her many friends, most of them much younger than she, told me that the time was coming or had come, and her frailty was evident enough. She walked slowly, at moments a bit unsteadily. Her white head seemed too heavy for her neck, bowing of its own weight. But it was her way of getting groceries to her second-floor apartment that revealed her decline most graphically. I can see her now, coming in from the snow in her mackinaw and L. L. Bean boots, a bright wool cap on her head. She sets the grocery bag on the third step, hoists herself up two steps with the handrail, then lifts the bag ahead of her again and in that way follows her groceries up to the landing, where she hefts the bag with an effort and lugs it into her kitchen.

I felt a sharp prick of guilt that her life had become so hard and I had been so oblivious to it. She had never complained, of course. Her fierce willfulness had sustained her, and her devoted friends checked up on her, helping her as much as she would allow. She got the groceries up the stairs. She got by—and isn't that what parents are supposed to do? Parents care for you, not you for them. They raise you, they help you and hurt you, they see you on your way. They look on as your own life comes to the fore, and they recede gracefully, loving you, of course, as you love them. They are prudent and realistic. They plan for their old age. They take care of themselves.

But my mother, ever the nonconformist, didn't do what parents are supposed to do. Like me, she never planned very far ahead. She lived from day to day, from year to year, trusting in fortune and the gods. There was no retirement home awaiting her, no efficiency apartment reserved and paid for, no senior-citizen Elysian Fields of group dinners, organized activities, and medical staff at the ready. She had no money for such a thing and no desire. She would have hated it. She would have preferred to fail on her own and call it happiness, and maybe happiness is what it would have been.

"How would you feel about living out West?" I asked her on Christmas Eve, at dinner in a Blue Hill restaurant.

She took a long time to answer. "Well, I don't know," she finally said.

"It's pretty hard for you here."

"Oh, it's not hard. There's no need to talk about it now."

It wasn't easy for either of us to speak of personal matters. There's no tradition of it in our family. As I was growing up, personal discourse between my parents consisted often as not of shouted accusations and recriminations, followed when the liquor had worn off by grim silences. My brother and I learned to be little Stoics, novitiate monks in the Daniel Way. And my mother, in the two decades after her split with my father, had followed her own compass and kept her own counsel. She was not accustomed to discussing the course of her life with anyone. I don't know to what extent she discussed it with herself, but I do know that she frequently consulted her pendulum, a small steel weight she dangled from her fingers on a chain, watching for it to swing one way or another in answer to her questions. It was a practice she had learned from New England dowsers. And I do know that she, like me, subscribed to the vaguely Taoist sixties notion that not to decide is to decide. That things have a way of working out.

We went on to talk of subjects we were easier with—her friends, my brother and his daughter, the weather. Snow was drifting down in the lighted central street of Blue Hill. There was a candle set in a wreath of holly on the table between us. Talk and laughter and the smells of good food flowed warmly in the restaurant, and suddenly I felt an upwelling of Christmas as a child—the snugness and happy expectation, the tree with its bright lights, candle chimes whirling and tinkling in air that smelled like coffee and brandy, my mother and father genially drunk by the fire. A sense that all was well and would be well . . . I suppose we slip into childhood all the time, hardly aware, when circumstances trigger it. The restaurant cast a powerful spell. It was my mother who snapped me out of it. Not anything she said or did, but her face—her truly beautiful old woman's face, wreathed in white curls, smiling at me in the candlelight exactly like a child's.

Marilyn flew in a couple of days after Christmas. She agreed that my mother needed to live with us in the West, or near us at least. There was nothing to be done about it at the moment, since my mother couldn't possibly afford a Bay Area apartment even if she wanted one, and there was no room for her in our 470-square-foot cottage. But Marilyn and I were looking for jobs in Oregon, where both of us had lived before marrying and moving to California, and we decided that when we moved north we would ask my mother to join us.

If we had any doubts, they were extinguished at the Bangor air-port, early on the icy morning we were to fly home. I had driven the three of us the sixty or so miles to Bangor in my mother's little blue Dodge, and now, after our farewells, my mother was setting off back to Blue Hill. Her stooped frame looked too small in the driver's seat, her jauntily capped head barely clearing the wheel. We watched from inside the terminal as she eased the car back and nudged the bumper of an empty sedan behind her. Then she swung the wheel and crept ahead, working for maneuvering room, and bumped the car in front of her not quite as gently. Suddenly I noticed the many small nicks and scrapes on the body of her year-old car. At last she swung it clear and steered slowly away, the rear wheels tossing up lit-tle spumes of snow behind her.

CHAPTER FIVE

I was thirteen, I think, when I announced to my parents that I would attend the University of Oregon and study forestry. Forestry, because I liked the outdoors and because an aptitude test in school had shown that I should be a forest ranger. Oregon, because I had never been there, because I'd been reading Bernard De Voto on Lewis and Clark and the westward expansion, and because I liked the name (which at the time I must have pronounced ARE-uh-GAHN). I no longer believed that the world ended there, but even with an ocean beyond it instead of the starry void, Oregon had the allure of an Ultimate Place. It was more enticing than any of the foreign countries arranged in soft pastels on my Rand McNally World. I've never much cared about other countries, but I've always had a passion for America.

I got it right and got it wrong. In the late summer of 1966, eighteen years old, I did indeed steer the rattling blue-and-white Jeep my mother had given me across the country to the great state of my imagining. I had been turned down by Harvard, a stinging slap at the time that I now see as a fortunate fall, and had chosen Reed College over Cornell and Wesleyan. It wasn't a hard decision. I'd gotten into Reed on my good grades, a decent short story I'd written in lieu of an application essay, and the sheer force of my desire. At the end of my application I wrote, "Every train whistle in the night seems to pull me toward the Pacific." The admissions committee might have wondered how many train whistles one is likely to hear on Connecticut Avenue in Washington, D.C., but how could they refuse such eagerness? My brother had gone west the year before, to George Air Force Base in the Mojave Desert, and now it was my turn.

I cried as I drove away from the apartment my mother and I shared in D.C. I cried, and I was intensely happy. I had America and my whole life ahead of me—and, though it wasn't in my mind at the time, in the life I was leaving there was much I was glad to leave. Living with my mother had become a little strained. By my mere presence in a small apartment, I was interfering with her relationships with men. What's more, in my last two years of high school I had banged up one car and totaled another, her favorite, a black Studebaker station wagon with a sliding roof panel. The accidents were due partly to bad luck, partly to inattentiveness, and partly—the big wreck in particular, which could easily have killed me or the other driver—to my new and enthusiastic appreciation for beer and other forms of drink. I'm amazed my mother could still afford insurance. One night during my senior year when I once again came home late and loaded, she looked up from the book she was reading in bed and told me, scowling behind her glasses, "I'll be glad when you're gone."

Drinking was, of course, a tradition of the Daniel Way, and though my mother drank her share while I was growing up in the fifties, the standard setter was my father. When he was home—his work for the AFL-CIO took him frequently on the road—he was often drunk. He had an enormous capacity for beer and bourbon, and up to a point his drink made him wonderfully amiable, a delightful companion for playing cribbage, listening to Beethoven on the hi-fi, or watching the hapless Washington Senators on our black-and-white TV. With a ball game to absorb us, we could talk easily. We could laugh and groan, exult and brood, lean forward in tense anticipation. My father took great pleasure in my command of pitching and batting statistics, gleaned from books and baseball cards. He liked to show off my memory to his friends, and I was gratified to please him.

Franz Daniel was six feet two and two hundred twenty pounds, handsome in a full-faced Teutonic way, and invested with a charismatic past. He had started out to be a Presbyterian minister but found a more compelling religion in the late 1920s—the uplifting of industrial workers through the American labor movement. He followed that calling through a dedicated, tumultuous, and sometimes dangerous career, and liquor fed his zeal. As early as the 1930s, my mother once told me, he was drinking as much as a quart of bourbon or white lightning a day. He spent time in a sanatorium in the late thirties and at Menninger's Clinic in 1965. Though the father I knew was mostly affable in his drunkenness, at any moment he might do something that embarrassed me in front of my friends or the neighbors. He might stagger or slur a sentence or not have his bathrobe all the way closed. You never knew. And, I learned early on, he might at any time do battle with my mother. I lay awake listening more nights than I want to remember, rigidly alert to the rhythm of rising and falling tension, the urgent lowered voices and sudden curses, a hand slamming a table, my father's heavy footsteps on the hardwood floor.

After the split-up—they legally separated in the mid-sixties but never divorced—my father went to live with three of his sisters in Springfield, Missouri, in the country where he had been born and raised. In the summer of 1966, when I was setting out to Reed College, it happened that he had an assignment to organize oil workers in the Four Corners country, so I picked him up in Springfield and we chugged west together in the Jeep. My father had bourbon and water with dinner each night, and in the motels he sat on the side of his bed drinking beer as he read, chin propped on his thumb and a cigarette between his fingers, the ash growing in a long sagging curve and falling to the floor without him noticing. A few weeks after I left him in Farmington, New Mexico, he wandered down to the hotel lobby in his underwear, cursing and wrestling the alcoholic demon that wouldn't leave him be. I think that was his last drinking binge. After drying out in a New Mexico sanatorium, he started going to Alcoholics Anonymous meetings back home in Springfield and remade himself in the last ten years of his life.

But I was through with my father's drinking, through with family pain and acrimony, through with my past as I drove south from Farmington, hit U.S. 66 in Gallup, and turned west again. I was on my own at last, barreling along in a vibrating capsule of engine noise and exhilaration. The southwestern landscape wasn't beautiful to me then—to my eastern eyes it seemed bleak and glary, the vegetation too sparse and not green enough—but it was vast and open, and I was free. I sang Bob Dylan's "Mr. Tambourine Man" over and over, shouting the lyrics above the Jeep's blatting roar—the final verse especially, that extraordinary ode to pure ecstatic solitude.

I was on my way to see my brother in the desert and then to the Pacific Coast, to Big Sur and San Francisco, over the Golden Gate and up through the redwoods and on to Oregon, on to college and the future and the life, whatever it would be, that was supposed to be mine. It makes me smile to see him, that boy I was. He's got a hand on the wheel, a hand on the death's-head gearshift knob, a bucket of coins beside him from a summer of waiting tables, and he's singing himself without memory or fate down the hot asphalt ribbon of Route 66 that stretches ahead of him forever. Is he really me? He seems more like a son than like myself, a son who's reached the age where I don't know him anymore. I don't know him any better than he knows himself. But he's on his way to Oregon, I do know that, and Oregon is where I'm waiting, where I'm writing this spell to speed him on. I haven't seen him for a long time. I need him. But I fear him, too. I can't help feeling that all his hope and blithe enthusiasm should lead him to more than what I am. I can't help feeling that I've let him down.

CHAPTER SIX

In the spring of 1988 Marilyn got the job we'd been hoping she would get, with the Oregon Department of Environmental Quality, and we moved to Portland. My mother agreed—readily, it turned out—to come west in the fall and join us. Marilyn and I rented a green Victorian house in the Irvington district with an extra bedroom for my mother, should we need it. Our plan, though, and her preference as we understood it, was that she would live in an apartment in the neighborhood where we could watch after her without unnecessarily cramping her independence. Hunting a place for her was fun. We thought about how many steps she'd have to climb (it had to be none or few), how far she'd have to go for groceries, what kind of view she would have, what sort of people she'd be living among. And it had to be cheap enough that she could live and feed herself on her Social Security check.

We settled on a two-room efficiency in an older brick building only two blocks from our home. Its only drawback was the view, which was mostly of the blank, olive-drab siding of the house next door. Otherwise it seemed perfect—hardwood floors, breakfast nook, little flourishes of trim we knew she would like. She flew to Portland in September, and while I was driving west in a Ryder truck with her goods and furniture, the little Dodge in tow, Marilyn showed her the apartment. My mother didn't speak. She stared at the window, trying to put on a brave face, but clearly shaken. Her apartment in Blue Hill had looked out on spruces full of birds. Everywhere she had lived she'd had a view. And now not only had she been uprooted from one end of the continent to the other, from a landscape and community she loved to a place she knew nothing of, but for the first time in twenty years she was living in a big city.

Yet it was more than that. My mother, as she stood in that bare apartment, was more disoriented than we knew. I can say with some certainty that in that moment she probably couldn't have named the city she was in or what direction it was from the home she had left. She probably couldn't have given the date or day of the week. She would have had a hard time saying, except in very general terms, where her son Jim lived or what her son John was doing at the time. If asked by a stranger why she was there in that apartment in a strange city, she might have said she didn't know. She might not have remembered talking with her son and daughter-in-law about moving west. That new apartment, we know now, was barer and the view blanker than my mother could tell us, or even tell herself.

But with her familiar bed in place—it had been made for her by a friend from planks and timbers seasoned by seacoast weather—and whatever else of her furniture that would fit, she seemed tolerably content. I visited most days to help her arrange her nest—hang a picture, move a table, plug in a new extension cord so that a lamp could go in a different place. I took her grocery shopping, found her a doctor, got her registered to vote. Sometimes we walked a few blocks of the neighborhood. My mother hooted at the Lutheran church's open belfry—"It looks exactly like a *gallows*," she remarked—and she appreciated, as I did, the old maples and horse chestnut trees that had filled their enclosures and buckled the sidewalk slabs with their roots.

Occasionally for lunch we walked to the closest restaurant, the Metropolis on Broadway. It was a small, busy place with good salads and other light fare. We got to know the waitresses, who soon welcomed my mother happily when we appeared. The big black man who bussed dishes, always wearing a brightly colored African cap—bright like my mother's own eclectic clothing—would often stop at our table to talk. My mother's ears were pretty bad by then and she often missed what he said to her, but it didn't matter. She liked him, and she smiled at him, as at many people she knew only slightly or not at all, with a radiant childlike energy. She smiled utterly, from deep within herself, as if words were extraneous to that truer speaking of the spirit. No one who received that smile could fail to be moved by it.

When I see her smiling that way in memory, it's always someone else she's looking at—the dish busser, a doctor, a visitor in our house. Or else I see her delighted at a dog, a dandelion in a sidewalk crack, a robin splashing in a puddle, or something else in the natural world. I don't see her smiling that deepest smile at me, and I suppose I didn't give her my fullest smile either. When I was a baby and a toddler we must have exchanged in that way, but the truth is there wasn't a great deal of warmth between my mother and me as I was growing up. She was not a particularly tender or affectionate mother. I recall her as intense, frank, and aloof, given to gaiety and effusion usually with friends rather than family and usually under the limbering influence of liquor. I don't think I ever doubted her love for me, but she was not a mother—and we were not a family—much given to the demonstration of love.

Of the many things my mother taught me in the last years of her life, that deep smile of the spirit may be the most important. Or not the smile itself, which can't be taught or learned, but the need for it, the poverty of its absence.

But the first thing she taught me—and maybe it's prerequisite to the smile—was patience. The lesson is still far from complete, but my mother got me started. In the Metropolis she would close the menu and pick it up again, not sure what she had decided on; she'd open and close it, pull out her glasses and put them away again. And she would still be eating, glancing around the restaurant with a full fork suspended in air, when I had finished and was tired of drinking coffee and wanted us to be on our way. In Nature's, the grocery market, she dithered over the vegetables, poking among them with one hand as she held on to the cart with the other. And every time she prepared to leave the apartment with me, she would paw through her handbag to be sure her glasses and Kleenex were there, take a sip of cold coffee, look through the bag again, make her way to the bathroom one last time, and finally consent to put on the coat I held for her and walk out the door, her face still wondering if there was something she'd forgotten.

I suppose I had expected my mother to resume her capably independent existence once she had settled in to Portland and her new place. I found, instead, that I was spending considerable time each day taking her on errands and attending to her needs. I tried, not always successfully, to contain my irritation. She didn't know anyone in Portland, after all. She had left behind a loving and loyal band of friends. What's more, she couldn't walk far—especially if she was carrying a burden—and Marilyn and I had resolved that her driving days were over. When she spoke of using her car again, we pointed out how busy the streets were, how fast everyone drove, how different it was from little Blue Hill. "My dear," she sternly informed me, "I have been driving my entire life."

"Well," I told her finally, "to get an Oregon license you'll have to take a written test, you know." I gave her a copy of the driving manual from the Department of Motor Vehicles. She kept it at her bed-side, immersing herself periodically in its plaguing complexities, and after a while she let the issue die. On the surface, at least.

What I saw was my mother losing her powers of judgment, along with her hearing and her strength. What my mother saw, and proba-bly felt more keenly than Marilyn and I appreciated, was the loss of her independence. Of course she wanted to keep driving. To her the little blue Dodge meant freedom, release from her viewless apart-ment in gray and dreary Portland. It was her most tangible link not only to the life she had left in Maine but to her life in its entirety, the life that was slipping from her memory. This was a woman who had spent much of her sixties roaming North America in a Land Rover. A woman who fifty years ago, when the law was after my father for union agitation in Tennessee, had driven him on an eighty-miles-per-hour getaway attempt down a winding highway, pursued by a carful of sheriff's deputies brandishing guns. My father told her to pull over when he saw the deputies aiming at their tires. *"Like hell,"* my mother said. He had to coax her into slowing and then stopping the car. As they took my father into custody, the sheriff of Roane County, Tennessee, said to Zilla Daniel in honest admiration: "Ma'am, you are the best woman driver I have ever seen in this county."

I'm certain it injured my mother to give up driving. And I'm equally certain that she and her nicked and scraped-up Dodge wouldn't have lasted a week or even a day on the streets of Portland. The city would have eaten her alive. And so, the child now more pow-erful than the parent, and the parent acting like a child, I enforced my will and tried to make it as palatable as I could. And vowed to myself that I would recognize when I should no longer drive. And knew I probably wouldn't.

My mother couldn't talk about the loneliness and disorientation she must have been feeling. She couldn't talk about it directly, that is. Her way of expressing it was to say flatly, "I think I'll go back home soon. You know, back where I came from."

"Mother," I'd tell her, "you live here now. All your things are here. You're a Portlander."

"But I don't *live* here," she said one day. "I'm only *staying* here."

"Mother, you live here. I know you miss Maine. Maybe we can go back for a visit next year."

"Oh, I don't miss it," she said, frowning her don't-be-silly frown and turning away. I could almost always count on her to deny any feeling I attributed to her, and sometimes that played to my advantage.

But she wasn't happy, I was running myself ragged, and she wasn't getting by very well. I found chicken in her refrigerator cooked on the outside and raw in the middle. When I came over, which usually wasn't till noon or after, she often was unsure if she had taken her blood pressure tablet. Undoubtedly there were days when she took several and days when she took none. I marked the bottle "Take One Every Morning" in big letters, but it didn't seem to help. She was sick a lot that fall, an easy mark for West Coast viruses she hadn't been exposed to before. In December she was so ill that Marilyn slept over in the apartment. Independent living wasn't working.

One evening around Christmas, after dinner at our house, my mother said again that she was ready to go back home.

"Well, Zilla," said Marilyn, "here's another idea. We have a room upstairs. Would you consider living with us?"

"Why *yes*," said my mother. "Why didn't we think of this before?"

CHAPTER SEVEN

In January we moved
my mother into our house. And in January Marilyn said to me, "I
feel as though I'm carrying a little ball of light."

I remember lowering the *Atlantic* I'd been reading, looking at her
in the glow of what she'd spoken. As I went to her I saw through the
window the outspread arms of Douglas firs two blocks away, stirring
fluidly, soundlessly, against the pewter sky. And later, on the way to
the store to buy something for dinner, I drove slowly, splashing leisurely through puddles in my mother's car, my usual impatience
with traffic entirely abolished. Let others rush if they needed to. I
was slowing the world from within myself. What hurry could there
possibly be? In such happiness, what hurry?

We'd been trying to have a baby for four years without a hint of
luck. After the first year, as it became evident that merely forsaking
birth control was not going to do the trick, we gave ourselves up to

the techniques of fertility. We scheduled love for biologically propitious moments, developing a nuanced eye for the gradations of blue
by which ovulation-detection kits measure the female cycle. For a
time we relinquished the task of insemination to a nurse named
Ruth, who capped Marilyn's cervix with a dose of semen I produced
at home and Marilyn kept warm between her legs as she drove to the
clinic. "Here's hubby!" chirped Ruth as she did her work. Back at
home, smiling sweetly, my wife quipped that she and Ruth would
make a lovely baby together.

To find out if her fallopian tubes were open and functioning, Marilyn first endured a procedure that shot her full of dye, and then a la-
paroscopy, in which a doctor actually pokes around the reproductive
system with seeing-eye equipment, ascertaining firsthand the inner
conditions and snipping away any troubles. Marilyn's system was
fine, but she was left miserably nauseated by the anesthetic. For my
part, I rendered samples on demand, learned a new word—"motil-
ity"—and had the satisfaction of knowing that my little swimmers
had proven themselves capable of penetrating the ovum of a ham-
ster. But my sperm count was marginally low, and so I switched to
boxer shorts and had a varicosity removed from my scrotum. (Too
much blood warmth kills sperm.) In the course of the operation I
needed two additional shots of spinal anesthetic, and even with those
I could feel the surgeon pressing and tugging as he discussed California wines with the anesthesiologist. Neither of them noticed, but I
did, when the music system piped in Willie Nelson singing, *"All of
me, why not take all-l-l of me . . ."*

Each new step in the process seemed to promise success, but the
magical microscopic union never happened—or if it did, it didn't
prosper. The experience was intensely frustrating. The gift that most
couples receive merely by rolling over in bed was being withheld
from us, like the fruit of Tantalus, even after we had engineered ourselves into the most efficient reproductive machines we could be.
Marilyn had children already, two boys near adulthood by her first

marriage, but I had none. In my twenties I had wanted none, but now, in my late thirties, married and at last with a sense of vocation, I wanted a child passionately. I felt aggrieved, unjustly denied. Most of my friends had children, my brother had a daughter, the streets of Portland were filled with laughing kids in bright clothing. I had the irrational sense that I'd been reduced to a cipher. Life comes of life, said the emotional logic—if you can't produce a life you aren't alive.

One night, in our third year of trying, I had a dream. A certain few of my dreams have a numinous presence by which I understand that something of primary value is being revealed. They usually occur soon after I fall asleep, and usually they are composed not of a narrative sequence but of a single image. I think of them as sleep visits, or visions, rather than as dreams. This was of that kind. I saw a baby with upraised arms, cradled in darkness, glowing with a soft light and loosely wrapped in glowing strands. When I woke—I wake immediately from these visions—I took it as a sign that a child was on its way to us, but instantly I doubted that interpretation. I had a troubling sense that my desire had awakened me too soon, a moment before the vision was fully born. I didn't know if it boded well or if I merely wanted it to bode well. The light around the baby might have been the holy spirit; it might have been the subdued glare of a hospital ward. It might, I felt for some reason, be radiation. The glowing strands could have been drawing the new life to this world. And they could have been the tubes and wires of life support.

And so, after four years of hope and frustration, in a new home in a new city, with my mother newly arrived in our household, we learned that we would have a child. Marilyn, who was forty-two at the time, knew the risks—Down's syndrome, spina bifida, the possible necessity of a late abortion. I knew them too, in my mind, but my excitement overwhelmed all worries. I was giddily eager. I read *A Child Is Born*, poring over the photographs of embryonic and fetal development, astonished at what happens as a conception evolves through fish and amphibian and reptile to the human. I bugled the news to all our friends and family. I hadn't been so happy since I was a boy. It felt as if I were on the threshold of completion, as if my family, fractured in my childhood, were verging on a rebirth into wholeness. I wished my father were alive, and almost felt he was.

I was cheerfully evasive in breaking the news to my mother. "Now that you're living here," I said one night at dinner, "how would you feel about more family moving in?"

"Jim?" she asked.

"No, I don't think Jim can leave California. Someone else."

She puzzled, looking at her plate and out the window, her jaw set.

"Someone new," I said. "Someone little."

"*John Daniel,*" said my mother. "Don't be coy."

"You're going to be a grandmother again," I told her. "Marilyn and I are going to have a baby."

Her mouth opened. "You aren't," she said, looking back and forth between the two of us, smiling her deepest, childlike smile.

"We are," said Marilyn.

"Oh, that's wonderful," my mother said, lowering her eyes to her plate and eating again. Clearly she was touched, but I also felt a hesitance in her response, a joy withheld or absent—as if she didn't completely comprehend what we had told her, or as if she understood it all too well, as if she had glimpsed a future that I couldn't or wouldn't allow myself to see.

We couldn't see the baby's heartbeat when we went in for the first ultrasound examination, but the technician and the doctor weren't disturbed. It was nothing unusual. But then Marilyn began spotting, then cramping, and on Valentine's Day we lost the child. "The blood ran out of me," Marilyn would write in her journal. "A steady stream for a while—stop—a cramp and another stream. Soon I could feel the distorted rhythm of it. My late child. My Elizabeth slipping from me. February 14, 1989."

It's best she wasn't born, of course. It's best he wasn't born. Something was wrong in the making, something was flawed in the seed, something ended the life at six weeks. I dwell on possibilities. I think of the sixties propaganda about LSD damaging chromosomes and how I scoffed at it. I think of x-rays, of radiation from a thousand sources. I think of coffee, whiskey, tobacco, marijuana, pesticides, chlorine, all the billions of molecules that have entered my body and perhaps done nothing, perhaps done harm. And of course I remember that nature itself is flawed and lives by its mistakes. Nature itself is extravagant with conceptions, stingy with achieved lives. The story of an offspring that isn't to be is the commonest story in the world, a necessary story, a story that has to be true so that other stories, happier stories, can also turn out true. I know all that, but I also know what *nature* means. It's from the past participle of a Latin verb, and the verb means *to be born*.

We told my mother when we got home from the clinic. She reached out her hands, one to each of us, and we sat linked together in silence. I was feeling a kind of numb grief, but something else more strongly. It overcomes me whenever I suffer a major disappointment. It's the most debilitating feeling I know. It's not really a feeling at all but a lack of feeling, a repudiation, a cold mockery of feeling's failure. *This is the truth,* it tells me, *this is reality. Your hopes and expectations were foolish. You have deluded yourself again. Others may achieve their desires but you will not achieve yours, simply because you are you. You will not succeed because you are not worthy. You are not worthy. You are not worthy.*

CHAPTER EIGHT

It was in the late 1930s that my mother and father began to think of having children, or at least my mother did. They had been married since 1934 and had been involved with each other for another four years before that, but throughout the thirties they had lived together only intermittently. Both had been leading rootless, independent lives as labor agitators and organizers in the East and the South, constantly on the move from one unionizing campaign to another. My father had transferred his religious passion from Union Theological Seminary in New York, where he had studied with Reinhold Niebuhr, to the social gospel and the streets of working America. A man of books and opera and philosophical argument, his hands and body bore the scars of numerous fights with scab workers and company goons. His greatest gift, by all accounts, was as a speaker. Whether soapboxing to a few uncertain workers on a street corner or addressing a rally of two thousand, he could bring the brotherhood of man to life in his words. He was a catalyst, a pinch hitter, a man the union chiefs called in on their hardest campaigns and those that needed a shot of new fervor.

My father was a Socialist party organizer in Philadelphia when my mother met him, and she fell hard both for him and for the union cause. A descendant of Pennsylvania suffragists, she attended Kent Place School for Girls in Summit, New Jersey ("Where Manners Maketh Man," the motto went), and Vassar College, where she majored in English. After graduation she became interested in the labor movement and took a job in the necktie sweatshops of Philadelphia, at six dollars a week, to see what working-class life was like. She taught at Highlander Folk School in Tennessee, then as now a beacon of social activism, and along with my father she took up the challenge of organizing clothing and textile workers in the South. She would go into little mill towns in Tennessee and the Carolinas, frequently alone, and quietly make contacts, feeling out the chances for unionization. Decades later, when she was interviewed for an oral history called *Refuse to Stand Silently By,* she said that she hadn't been afraid for herself but for the workers, who risked being fired for the least taint of union activity. "So I tried to be careful and to be honest about it," she told the interviewer. "I was asking them to take a big chance. . . . The company almost owned many of them. Often there was a company store and they always owed something, so their pay was always goose eggs: zero, zero, zero. Week after week after week."

Her one great success came in 1933, at the Liebovitz plant in Knoxville, Tennessee, where she succeeded in organizing the first Amalgamated Clothing Workers local in the South. For the most part, though, her work could not overcome the very long odds against it. On several occasions she was arrested and jailed. Once, when she called for a union election in Greenville, South Carolina, crosses were burned on the lawns of local activists. And on an organizing mission in Anderson, another South Carolina town, my mother was fired on in her car by deputies with shotguns. *That* scared her. "My knees shook so much on the way back, I wasn't sure I could keep my foot on the accelerator," she told the interviewer. "But I think you can't function if you are going to allow yourself to be fearful. I didn't give it any thought because fear is a negative emotion."

My mother and father had no home base in those years and didn't organize together. They spent what time together they could, a week here and a day or two there. He had told her before they were married that the labor movement would always come first, and it did. In a letter I found recently, my mother mentions two abortions. She doesn't say when they occurred, but it must have been during that intense activism of the thirties, when caring for a baby would have been unthinkable. I have no idea where she went for the operations, who performed them, or how. Abortion was illegal then, very likely dangerous, and almost certainly a wretchedly degrading experience. My mother's letter gives no sense of how she felt about ending two pregnancies that way. My guess is that she saw it as part of the price one had to pay to be involved in a mission of grand idealistic purpose with a man she loved and admired, a man who expected her to be emotionally self-sufficient and all for the cause.

Soon after she turned thirty, though, my mother realized—or resolved—that she wanted to have children. It took her a while to convince my father, but in 1940, while he was troubleshooting for the Laundry Workers Union in New York and they were living in Greenwich Village, she became pregnant and quit the labor movement. The pregnancy ended in a miscarriage, and she fell into a deep depression—from losing the baby but also from losing her freewheeling labor career. "I remember being so depressed I sat in a chair and couldn't get out of it," she told me years later, when she was sixty-nine. A doctor recommended electric shock treatment, but my father vetoed that. His rising star in the labor movement carried them on to New Orleans, where they rented a second-floor apartment in the French Quarter with a wrought-iron balustrade and bedbugs in the mattress. There they lived happily in a circle of progressive intellectual bons vivants. "All those lovely bars," my mother recalled. "I just decided I'd try every one of them."

Before long she was pregnant again, and before long they were back in Philadelphia, where my father worked as a city organizer. George Hawes Daniel was born in the early morning of September 29, 1943, after a long labor during which my mother, as she would write to my father's sister Margaret, "raised a terrific ruckus. For once I lost all inhibitions, and kicked and howled and even bit my arm." The impatient obstetrician finally ended it by hauling little George out with a pair of forceps, raising a temporary knot on his head for which my father almost killed him. For a couple of days, every time the nurse brought George to my mother, she and he promptly fell asleep. It had been well worth the siege of labor, she wrote Margaret, to have produced a fine, blond-haired baby who resembled nothing so much as a small suckling pig.

The little pig grew into a happy and healthy child who delighted his parents. My mother's letters over the next few months give off a glow of satisfaction in the minutia of baby tending, and my father, for his part, absolutely doted on Georgie. The tough labor fighter rocked his son on one arm as he made formula, my mother wrote, and laughed with pure joy when the baby cracked a toothless smile. My father was not quite forty and in his prime when George was born. It's both lovely and a little painful, as I read his and my mother's letters, to imagine him dandling his child, cooing at him, showing him elephants at the circus, ducks and sheep in the Pennsylvania countryside. By the time I had arrived and was growing up, my father was turning fifty, an aging warrior nursing his many emotional wounds. He was reserved and remote, given to long brooding silences. I never knew—or at least I don't remember—the young fatherly zest, tender and a little goofy, that little George drew out of

him. I don't think Jim knew it either. My mother once told me that
George was the only human being my father ever loved absolutely,
without stay or condition.

I love him too, in my own way. I think about him often; I think I
might owe my life to him. I carry his picture in my wallet, as if he
were not my brother but my son. And there are times, like tonight,
when I get out all the pictures, all the curling, creased, black-and-
white snapshots I'm grateful to my father and mother for taking. I
spread them on my desk and try once again to see through their
aging glossy surfaces into the boy himself, this golden-haired child
who is not me, not Jim, but a whole other blending and reforming of
my mother and father, a whole other Daniel starting out in his life,
picking up the kindling my father splits and piling it into his wagon.
It's fall and he has just turned three, he is wearing a light canvas
jacket and a dark watch cap with his hair flowing down on his forehead almost to his eyes. His striped t-shirt is rumpled, one strap of
his overalls is loose, his eyes are downcast and he is smiling a slightly
off-center smile as if he has finished a long day's work that he thinks
of now with both pleasure and pain. He is only a boy of three years,
but there is something about him as old as anything alive.

He is loading his wagon in front of a white tenant's cottage in the
country near Wellford, South Carolina, where his parents have
moved from Philadelphia with him and his baby brother Jim—
Jimmy Dan'l, as George likes to say—and a hound dog called South
Caroline. They arrived in August and now it is fall. Oak leaves lie
strewn on the ground, there must be a chill in the air as his father in
a sweater splits kindling and he gathers it up. It's the end of October
now, and in just a few days or perhaps today little George will cough
and run a slight fever. He's fine, the pediatrician will say, he's fine, but
four days later, on November 4, he will start to choke. His father has
taken the car to work, there is no phone in the cottage, his mother
will scream for Mrs. Ponder up at the big house and run there with
George in a blanket, choking, and they will drive as fast as they can

to a doctor ten miles away but always, every time she relives it the rest of her life, her firstborn child will die in her arms before they arrive.

Laryngeal tracheal bronchitis was the cause of death, as my mother remembered it. A common infection that in some few cases achieves a critical mass, an exponential explosion that rapidly overwhelms its host. A fulminating infection, one doctor called it—meaning, literally, an illness that strikes like lightning.

The doctor they had reached too late was the local mill doctor, and he refused to sign the death certificate. My mother and father had to find George's pediatrician for that. Numb with shock, they made phone calls to family and friends. The next day they arranged for a small service at a funeral home in Spartanburg. Labor friends drove down from Philadelphia, my father's sister Berthe arrived. Neighbors who despised my father's work came by with gifts of food. The local preacher stopped in several times and was very kind, my mother recalled, but mostly she remembered two things from the aftermath of George's death. She remembered sitting on the porch for hours at a time with little Jim in her arms, rocking and rocking. And she remembered the train. My father was out drinking with his friend Wes Cook, balming his pain in his usual way, when the train left town with George in his small coffin, bound for Atlanta and the crematorium. My mother knew what time it would leave, she heard it pass, and in that moment she felt herself collapse inside—she felt void, she said, just utterly void, as the train whistle sounded and died away.

CHAPTER NINE

I t's like sleepiness without being tired. My eyes don't close but my awareness does; it folds up the way some flowers do at night. All it knows how to do is play the carousel of doubts and second-guessings. I'm forty-five years old. I have gray hair. I wear jeans and t-shirts as if I were a kid. I don't have a child. I call myself a poet, a writer. What have I written? I make less than twenty thousand. I weigh too much. I'm a writer but not a great writer. I don't know who I am. I wasn't patient enough with my mother. I didn't help her enough. I don't know what I feel. I sleep too late. I don't have a real job. I don't get enough done. I don't spend enough time with my wife. I don't have a child. I don't know what I'm doing. I have gray hair.

I'm angry at an editor for turning me down, but even my anger is dampened, dulled by a low gray sky. I'm sunk down inside myself. A chickadee takes a sunflower seed from the feeder, holds it against a birch limb, hammers it with his bill. I watch, but there's some screen, some invisible smoke between us. He lives on the birch limb, but he doesn't live in me. He takes another seed, hammers it, flies out of the window view. The chickadee is what I was. As lively. As gone.

Thoreau says in his journal that he values his melancholy moods. "Be as melancholy as you can be," he says, "and note the result." He says there's a "certain fertile sadness" that he seeks, a sadness that saves his life from being trivial. Well, fine for you, Henry. Mine must be a different kind—an infertile cross, a mule of a sadness. It makes my life seem trivial and nothing but. It's certainly not melancholy. It has nothing of the music of those four syllables, the minor-key chant they make in the mouth. It's flat, just plain flat and heavy. Old snow specked with dirt.

My psychologist has been asking about the part of me that doubts and second-guesses, that tells me I'm not worthy. Who's saying that, she wants to know. *I'm* saying it, I told her at first, and what's wrong with it? I hold myself to standards. Self-criticism helps me get things done, helps me do things better. But I knew the lie of it even as I said it. It's when I'm *happy* that I get things done, because I love doing them. This mood only dulls me. It leaves me slouched in my chair.

Listen to that voice, she says. How does it come to you? Whose voice is it? Well, it's a male voice. And it's someone older than me, someone in authority. Not my father, not any teacher or boss I've had. No one I've known at all. He's a stranger, and yet he knows everything about me. The more I pay attention, the more military he seems. (That's one of the things he nails me on: I never served, never proved myself in battle.) He's not a drill sergeant, not a general. Not even active duty—he's retired. Only a retired man would have so much time. He's always watching me. He observes, he remembers even the smallest things I've done wrong, or may have done wrong. Last night I lay awake till 3:00 A.M. watching a Halloween party ten years ago at Stanford University. The night was well along, I was two or three sheets to the wind, I climbed over a raised kitchen hearth to get around a clog of partiers to the living room. My sneaker hit a blue-and-white bowl, and glancing back, very quickly in my drunken hurry, I couldn't tell if I had broken it or only rattled it.

Why do I lie awake ten years later worrying—*worrying*—about a bowl I may or may not have broken at a party? Because I didn't go back to check, as I should have? Because I was drunker than I should have been? Because I need to learn that when I'm wildly happy I'm careless, and things get broken? Or what? The observer who insists I remember doesn't tell me why I should remember. He doesn't even know if I broke the bowl (or does he?). He only says that I was wrong, I was wrong, and he'd be derelict if he didn't call it to my attention. It's not his *job,* exactly. He doesn't work for anyone. But it seems to be his discipline, his preoccupation, his self-appointed office. It's what he does. I think I'll call him the Inspector.

The chickadee is at the feeder again. He has his own preoccupation, but his is natural and right. His gives him sustenance. The Inspector only wears me down.

But it's not the Inspector I want to think of now. I'm sitting at my desk in Henry Thoreau's spirit, trying to see if my sadness might be fertile after all. To see if it might grow something. What's coming to me is a winter afternoon by the Potomac River, near one of Washington's memorial parks. I think it's the Jefferson. I'm a senior in high school. My friend is taking pictures for the yearbook, of which I'm editor, and I'm watching the dark river with my hands in my pockets against the cold, watching the gray sky with its pale glow of late sun in the west. My face—*his* face, that boy of seventeen's face—is smooth and unlined. His curly brown hair is my hair, and there is no gray in it. His lean body is my own, thirty pounds lighter, and I know the familiar way it feels in the cold, the way it firms and tenses, scrotum tight, how shivers turn its tension to a shaky warmth.

I know some things about that boy. I know he reads a lot, he does his homework, he gets straight A's. His way of life is to please people, older people, and he's good at it. He cherishes the praise of teachers

and fears he'll disappoint them, fears they'll see into the emptiness
he covers with words and smiles. He smokes cigarettes, even though
they made him sick at first. He's lonely. He doesn't talk much except
when he's excited or drunk. He drinks at parties, dances in the warm
melee with no one in particular, sometimes stumbles out to sprawl
on the grass as everything spins and his stomach heaves. He's had a
few dates but never had sex. He envies his friends who have, or who
act like they have. If asked, he might tell you he wants to be a histo-
rian. Inside he wants to be a writer, but he worries he has nothing to
write about. If he has a deep desire he doesn't know what it is. He has
always been in school and assumes he'll go on in school, reading
what he's told to read and bringing home the A's, riding the escalator
his parents put him on when he was five—the escalator that surely
is taking him somewhere, that surely will deliver him in the fullness
of time to the life and career of a man who knows what he is doing and
belongs in the world.

I know these things about the boy, but I don't know what he's
thinking as he stands on a walkway above the Potomac in the wan
light of a winter afternoon. I don't know whether he's happy or sad,
whether he's content to be waiting as his friend takes pictures, or else
bored and restless and wishing he could leave. But this is what he
does. There is a figured stone parapet between him and the river, and
his gaze lights where a little skiff of snow has caught in the carving.
One shape of snow among several, unremarkable. But he stares at it.
He stares harder. What he sees takes on a strangeness. Why should
that shape of snow be just the way it is? He wants to burn the image
into his memory, to photograph it. He wants to have it always, exactly as it is, just so. He feels a flood of light within him. He stares
longer, his eyes watering. He wants to be absolutely sure the image
is his, a part of him forever, exactly as it now lives in the world.

Why? Why did he want that? Why did that image glow so intensely for him? Why was he so concerned with clarity and perma-
nence, perfection of memory? It's as though he had a message to

send, and he could only send it coded in a clear image, perfectly pre-
served, through years and decades to the adult he could not know but
knew he must become. But what? What was the message? He relied
on me to understand, but I'm failing him. I'm standing there above
the river, I'm staring at the parapet, the snow. I see tones of white and
gray, snow and stone, I see the quality of light, I think, but I've let the
image go out of focus. I don't see the exact shape of the little drift, I
don't see the specific figuring of the parapet, the texture of the stone.
It's murky, mocked up, like the scenery in a dream if you look at it
hard. I have only a blurred estimate of a thing the boy wanted passionately to secure undiminished, undiffused.

Is it inevitable to lose like that? Does memory give up its clarity
the same way hair gives up its color, skin gives up its moisture, mus-
cle and bone give up their green resilience? Is memory losing focus
as my outward vision has, forcing me to wear these twelve-dollar
reading glasses that Bob Bourgeois bought at the drugstore, that
keep slipping down my nose as I write and blurring the entire world
when I look up from the page? What I want to believe is that the soul
builds itself from the experience of life, that it makes a thing of last-
ing wholeness, a monument unseen from without, and memory is
what we see from inside it. But what I feel isn't a building, it's a wearing down. My memories lie scattered in pieces. If it's a monument it's
in poor repair, and the city where it stands is deserted.

I started noticing lapses about the time my mother came to live
with us. I'd walk into the kitchen or my study and forget for a moment what I'd come for. I'd forget to tell Marilyn that her father
called. I'd make a list and forget to take it to the store. I suppose memory does decline with age; I suppose it must, like everything else.
And then, for some like my mother, it plunges near the end. And
what about the end? Can all that living, all that accumulated seeing
and doing of a lifetime, can it all go dark—lights out, gone? Surely
there's at least a zone of fade, the mind slowly going dim like the light
in a dying animal's eye. And maybe memory comes back at the end,

maybe it's all restored, everything—but dissolving into gray form-lessness, a sea of shaped particulars melting down, moving vaguely with what was their life as all light ebbs away. Fog. Final fog, and nothing. And where then is this soul I want to have? Where does the monument stand? And what can it be made of?

A light rain is falling, slanting without sound. The chickadee's back, perky in his black cap. He takes one seed again, always one. He has a leisurely way of cracking it, a patient hammering: *tap . . . tap-tap*. The sparrows and finches feed in gangs, standing in the tray and spraying seed as they scratch and peck. I like the chickadee. He's a loner. He comes to the tray for one good seed, and that's enough. I did keep a promise to myself. Thirty years later, I did remember. The boy got through to me, and maybe it sounds a little silly, but I feel a kind of awe at that, and gratitude. The shape of snow on stone hardly matters as much as he does, and though the image of what he saw has weathered in memory, the boy is true. Snow melts, stone wears away. Everything, including me, is made of time. But the boy stands faithfully by the dark Potomac, filled with a brilliant clarity, as intent and changeless as a god, pouring himself into the passion of his seeing.

CHAPTER TEN

Dinner was the one meal that my mother and Marilyn and I usually ate together, and it often began with a Sanskrit food prayer my mother had learned in India. We held hands as she sang. The prayer began with a long *Om* that started deep in her chest and slid up the scale to a soft, wavering height that she held as long as she had breath. After four short verses in that higher range the song ended with another *Om*, sung the same way, and then *Shanti* three times, the last syllable of the last *Shanti* taken up a tone, then trailing downward to silence. We held the peace of that silence a few seconds before squeezing hands and opening our eyes to dinner.

Though in her last years she forgot much of the life she had lived, many of the people she had known, and most of what she might have read an hour before in the newspaper, my mother never forgot that song of prayer. She never faltered in singing it. It seemed that she had taken it into her deepest being, and there it rested unassailable. I think that song was the culmination, the fruit and final harvest, of the spiritual journey of her life.

I don't know as much about that journey as I would like to know, but I did understand something of it as she was living it, and I've been gleaning more from her letters and writings. Her father being a minister, she must have grown up in at least a thin atmosphere of Christian spirituality—though Unitarianism, as I experienced it in the occasional services and Sunday school sessions my parents took me to, seemed more of an intellectual coffee klatch than a religion. My mother would eventually tell an interviewer that she had found it arid and uninspiring. As with my father, who was a confirmed agnostic, some of her spiritual energy went into the labor movement of the 1930s, but unionism didn't remain for her the all-consuming, millenarian mission it was for him. I think that she, as I would later do, followed her hunger outward into the natural world. For my father, nature was primarily the scenic backdrop to the drama of human history. For my mother it was a balm, an excitement, a mystery.

In 1953, the year I turned five, my father's work took us from Charlotte, North Carolina, out to Denver. My mother, then forty-five, had never seen the West before. I remember her driving Jim and me to the open amphitheater at Red Rocks for shows of one kind or another, and sometimes she took us up toward Loveland Pass for a dinner cooked in a cast-iron skillet and eaten under the stars. I remember, or I think I do, the pleasure she took in sandstone pinnacles and mountain vistas. If the coast of Maine was the first landscape my mother loved, the Colorado Rockies were the second. She told me once that the years following my birth in 1948, with Jim and me healthy and the awful grief at George's death subsiding, were the happiest of her marriage. To then come to a place of such sublime natural splendor must have made her joy complete.

But it wasn't to last. We had been in Colorado for not even a year when my father was appointed Assistant Director of Organization in the newly merged AFL-CIO, and we picked up and moved to Washington, D.C. My mother practically had a breakdown, she told me years later. She wept as she packed and wept as we moved, until my father finally told her to buck up because he didn't want his friends to see her that way. He made the same demand on several other occasions during their marriage—he was going through a difficult time, he would tell her, he was under a lot of stress and needed her to be strong. In my own memory I have a faded image from our Denver house of my mother leaning against a doorway, crying. The first harsh words I remember them exchanging came at that time. I didn't know then what the arguing was about. I only knew that they both were angry and my mother was sad.

She would return to the Rockies, though not to Colorado, nearly two decades later, after the marriage had foundered, Jim and I had left the broken nest, and she had reached the age when she could retire from the union work she had resumed but cared little for by then. The late sixties had a liberating effect on my mother. Unlike the many of her generation who reacted against the tumult and excesses of the counterculture, my mother learned from it and in her own way joined in. "If I have a cause these days," she wrote to my brother in 1967, "it is the young. We have nowhere to go, unless we follow your paths." When I told her, in the middle of my first year at Reed, that I had been taking LSD, she was intensely interested in my experiences. I don't think she ever took a psychedelic herself, but I think she may have smoked some grass along the way—though not habitually—and she was looking in the same direction we drug takers were looking. "I'm going to read *The Doors of Perception*," she wrote in a letter. "Opening those doors has attracted me for a long time. I try in many ways."

One way she tried was in writing poems. She read poetry throughout her life and worked at her own verses now and again for several decades. Her efforts didn't satisfy her, and few drafts remain. One that does, written probably when she was in her forties, ex-

presses in uneasy union the passion of a sensualist and a spiritual
seeker's yearning for transcendence:

> [My blood] runs with the grace of a mountain stream
> and my breath at dusk is a smoke of balsam
> to one whose arms are sinews of my love,
> whose hands know how to bless a thousand ways,
> whose lips are sweet and [illegible]
> in the blue-flamed candle melting time's deep fog.
>
> And so I cry with laughter at the clumsiness
> of death's bravado
> when a pale gold scimitar dangles above my window
> in a sea-green sky,
> for I have ample warmth for others
> but only a spark to fire the fences of my blindness,
> and in the beauty of their burning learn, perhaps,
> it is not death to die.

After retirement my mother took a long voyage on a freighter—
to Africa, I think—and vagabonded around the U.S. and Canada in a
Land Rover she called the Green Seal. In 1970 she settled for what
would be five years in Kaslo, British Columbia, on Kootenay Lake in
the Canadian Rockies. For two of those years she holed up in semi-
seclusion in a small cottage accessible only by boat. I know she read
and studied Carl Jung's collected writings during that time—"hard
going," she wrote my brother, "and will become much harder because I intend to pursue it until I find the Self." In the handwriting of
her letter, "Self" was first written with a small s, then corrected with
a capital. The voyage of self-realization she saw herself launching
was at the same time an act of self-reformation. Her reading of Jung
persuaded her that the masculine side of her psyche, because she had
refused to accept it, had been acting itself out in rebellious and sometimes spiteful behavior throughout her life, perplexing her relation-

ships with men—her father and husband especially. She vowed to soften her hard edges and tame her angers, a quest she would follow, with mixed results, the rest of her years.

Solitude, her reading, and no doubt the glory of her surroundings seem to have opened a mystical awareness in my mother, or at least set off a mystical seeking in words. The rebellious Vassar intellectual and gritty union organizer was now, in her sixties, meditating, reading the Upanishads and other sacred literatures of the East, and writing verses such as these:

> If I see something I dislike
>   let me look deeper
> if I hear something displeasing
>   let me listen with my inner ear
>
> for the Heart of all Being assumes
>   forms inconceivable to us
> and beats with an almost imperceptible
>   gentleness.

In 1975 her evolving religious imagination led her out of solitude to the Findhorn spiritual community on the north coast of Scotland, where she prepared meals, cleaned the Sanctuary, and worked in Publications—"with Boris the binder (who screeches) and Guinevere the guillotine paper cutter." I don't know specifically what attracted her there. She may not have known herself. I do think she was interested in reports that some individuals at Findhorn had communicated with the Devas, or nature spirits. And I think she probably felt a need for a church, a fellowship, some kind of shared structure for her religious feeling.

My mother's early letters from Findhorn teem with a thrilled excitement in the community and its setting—she was living near the sea, on a sparsely settled coast something like Maine's—and with a sense of inadequacy in the company of persons she considered more spiritually advanced than she was. The feeling of inferiority seemed to pass, though, in the course of group meditations she found enormously powerful. She wrote, "I sort of watch myself developing in unexpected ways, and wonder, is this *me?*" Her new sense of wholeness, she wrote, "is not a passive state and cannot be experienced alone, but a positive, irradiating process of entering into others and interweaving with them in daily acts which thereby become fulfilling; a process of discovering cracks and knotholes into openings of communion with other realms."

A photograph in a 1976 issue of the Findhorn newsletter shows her kneeling in a simple shift with a group of gardeners, both hands on her spading fork, an easy laughing smile on her face. She looks more relaxed and content than I remember ever seeing her. Typically, she is older by twenty or thirty years than anyone else in the picture.

On my birthday that year, my mother wrote a card in which she thanked me for choosing her and my father to be my parents. She would express the same idea in various ways the rest of her life. Nothing, she came to believe, occurs by chance, and each of us is responsible for everything that happens to us. Human existence is a school that the Self puts itself through, and the Self creates the curriculum it needs for its own advancement. Little George came and died, my mother now believed, to teach her humility and acceptance. Because of her rebellious willfulness, the lesson had to be harshly dealt. George had the look of age in his young face because he was an old soul, a soul capable of enduring the wrenching transition of entering and quickly departing the flesh. He had reincarnated into the world, my mother was advised in a spiritual reading. She would very likely meet and recognize him, and when she did she must say nothing.

A skeptic might argue that my mother had merely contrived a shelter of spiritual trappings to help her endure the ongoing pain—a pain that must have contained much guilt—of Georgie's death. It may be so. But even though I don't believe in reincarnation—not in

any coherent way, at least—I find her view of the Self and its education compelling. Not illuminating, but compelling. I was twenty-
eight in 1976. Within three months of my birthday and my mother's
card thanking me for choosing her as my parent, I crushed my right
ankle in a rock-climbing fall, my father died, and a five-year relationship with a girlfriend ended abruptly and painfully. What did I
need to learn, I wondered, that required such devastating lessons so
closely bunched? What in my education was I being a bonehead
about? Something to do with loss, obviously. Something to do with
limits. Something—if there's any lesson at all—I still don't see.

My mother, ever restless, returned to the States in 1977 and traveled for most of two years. "Will it ever end?" she wrote. "I am pro-
pelled, or drawn, and it is as it is. Innerly I'm beginning to create the
little place 'to be.'" Findhorn friends and the power of her first love
led her to the Maine coast in 1978, and there she settled. There, from
my ample distance, she seemed to have found the wholeness of living
that had been eluding her. Village life suited her independent disposition, yet she was part of a community of friends who loved and respected her. She worked at *WoodenBoat*, raised a garden, read much,
wrote some, and rowed among loons and seals in her skiff, the *Lully
Lulay*. She became ordained in a New Age church and performed
wedding ceremonies for friends. In her letters she began to refer to
herself as a Wager of Peace, and, inspired by a John Gould column in
the *Christian Science Monitor*, she sometimes signed them "yr. Es-
teemed Old Geezer, Mom Zilla."

Spiritually, though, she was still seeking. She went to dowsers'
meetings in Maine and Vermont and took up some of their techniques, including the use of a pendulum to receive guidance from energies transcending the personal. For a while—I don't know if this
came from the dowsers or from a different source—she wrote me
about "entities," or alien presences, that she had discovered and was
clearing from her mind and also my mind and my brother's. Though
I've known since the 1960s that I have plenty of strange things in my

head, I had a hard time relating to this direction of her quest. It seemed too technical and negatively focused. My own diffuse sense of spirituality acknowledged no need for cleansing, no threat of anything alien. All of nature, all of being, was my church. What could be alien? Her talk of "entities" sounded like science fiction to me.

I had a hard time in the mideighties, too, when Findhorn folk told my mother of a holy man doing good works in India and she decided she must go to him. My own religious inclinations tilt away from gurus. I don't feel I need an anointed human to show me the sacredness of life and things, and I don't trust the fanatical devotion that arises around some gurus. Humans distort truth, sometimes deliberately, sometimes for gain. Nature distorts nothing. I'd sooner take a river or a Douglas fir for a spiritual teacher, and I had thought my mother felt the same.

But Sai Baba seemed to answer a hunger in her that nothing else had. She believed him to be a true avatar, a perfect realization of the Divine in human form. He was her final resting place, the end of her journey. Twice in her late seventies she traveled to his ashram, near Bangalore in southern India, and each time she stayed several weeks, living a monastic life. She and a traveling companion were granted a personal interview with Sai Baba, an infrequent occurence. Upon her return from each pilgrimage she wrote a series of remarkable devotional meditations, some of them in the form of letters addressed to "Satya Sai Baba" or "God" or "SSB." She thanks him, in some of the writings, for the help of his love in her efforts to make pure her "imperfect, flawed self." The flaws she notes have to do with prejudice and self-superiority, her tendency to respond to differences between her and others rather than to commonalities. But other meditations, such as this one, are psalms of pure joy:

Dawn outlines the window of my worship room. I go downstairs, and as I watch the sun come up and turn the bare trees into pillars of light, it comes over me, "He does this, the sun circling, the stars and galaxies in their courses." The flames of the fire begin to leap up, also His, warming the room where intriguing frost patterns, never two the same, are slow in fading from the window—His also. It is overwhelming, and I am awestruck, that mankind should be so fortunate, living on his parent-planet, to have also been created as the most perfected of animals, because You were lonely and needed an activity of this immensity to throw Your immeasurable energies into. It is unfathomable, but I make no attempt to even try. It is simply so. Furthermore, You made me with my own measure of Godhead, inscrutably estimated from my innumerable lives, for which infinite gratitude fills me with Your Love, which I humbly accept as Your most wonderful gift of all.

Until my mother became too weak, she attended meetings of Sai Baba's devotees in Portland. She read and reread her books of his talks and sayings, underlining passages in pen. She kept pictures of him in her room and in her wallet. She kept a vial of *vibhuti*—sacred ash from Sai Baba's ashram—in her purse, where it frequently spilled and made a mess; sometimes she placed a dab of it on her forehead between her eyes. And she sang her blessing song at dinner, surely, beautifully, from deep within.

My mother found something, something she needed. One night when I picked her up after a song session with other devotees, she was extraordinarily relaxed and effusive. I asked her what it was in her religion that gave her joy. "Oh," she answered happily, "we don't have to pretend God is something he isn't." In that kind of happiness, the happiness of her deepest smile, she seemed not only at peace but overflowing with spirit. She was ready to face anything, death included. But at other times she was agitated, at loose ends, discontent in ways she couldn't express, impatient with her failing body but fearful of dying too. She thought she ought to see the doctor for one thing or another. She worried that she'd had a stroke or a small heart attack. She seemed to be clutching at a world that no longer had a place for her, a world she was afraid to leave.

In the four years that she lived with us, my mother spent most of her time reading in bed. She read the *Oregonian* (Portland's daily newspaper), the *Monitor,* various magazines she subscribed to, appeals from conservation and social action groups, junk mail of all sorts, and stacks of books—not only her sacred texts but books of all kinds. She understood what she read, and I assume, from underlined passages I found after she died, that she found solace in some of it. But most of her reading seemed only to fill time for her, to take up hours every day that she had no other way to spend. Often I saw her pick up a book she had only recently finished and start it again, and usually when I asked her what she had been reading she couldn't talk about it—the pages she'd been immersed in only an hour before had turned virtually blank in her mind. The stillness I sensed in her most of the time seemed less like peace and more like vacancy, an emptiness into which her memory was dissolving, a void that swallowed her words and interposed itself between her thoughts and turned them in recurrent circles.

And so I don't know. Did she find the Self she had set out in search of a quarter century before? Or did she lose, toward the end, what sense of self she had? Did she leave with wind in her sails or merely drifting, becalmed on an empty sea?

CHAPTER ELEVEN

One night in 1966, home at Christmas from my first year at Reed College, I became aware of myself sitting on a sofa with a matchbook in my fingers chattering incessantly at a dark-haired girl who had been listening with smiling interest that now had changed, I thought, to clinical detachment—the face one wears in the presence of the mentally disturbed. I *was* mentally disturbed. I was wearing a gold paisley short-sleeved shirt I had never seen before, I was fidgeting on a sofa tearing a matchbook to shreds, I was babbling everything that came into my head or came out of my head at a young woman who understood none of it because I was insane. I had once been a regular person—I *knew* this girl—but now I was crazy and wouldn't come to my senses again, if I ever did, until I was white-haired and toothless and my life was over. Maybe that's what I already was. Maybe I'd always been crazy.

Then three friends came into the room and I remembered we had all taken big hits of LSD. The girl was Debby, the sister of one of my friends. It was their house we were in. The four of us left her and drove around the neighborhood for a while, doing what teenagers in the suburbs had always done, just differently intoxicated. We ended up at Dulles Airport in northern Virginia. It was new then, a technological whizbang. Maybe we wanted to see with spaced-out eyes where the world was going, but really I don't know why we went there. If I had the sixties to do over, I would be more selective about where I went and what I did on psychedelic drugs. We sat at a little table in the terminal, and we may have had coffee. My friends seemed in perfect command of the situation, psychedelic connoisseurs, cracking jokes of uncontainable meanings that kept them rollicking and kept me worried. I was spooked by the disembodied announcement voices resounding through the terminal's vast bright spaces, and I was pretty sure the security guards knew all about us. About me, at least. Why else would they keep looking? And what were we even doing there?

On the way home from Dulles, near dawn, the car skidded on a patch of ice, spun, and smacked the guardrail. This was surprisingly undisturbing, except perhaps to the friend who had just crunched the fender of his parents' Volvo. No one was hurt. The car was drivable. What's a fender bender to young men with open minds? As the unlucky driver and another friend worked at clearing crumpled metal away from the front left tire, John Sterne and I drifted off a ways on the empty highway. We had known each other since junior high school and now were attending Reed together. With silent snowy fields around us we looked at the stars, the brightest ones shimmering like pools of liquid light, and after a while we glanced at each other in glad wonderment, as if to say, *Can this be us?* Sterne's spectacled scholar's face was tilted back, half smiling, his dark hair haloed with stars. *Yes,* said his eyes, *this is us, and this is the world we never knew.* We stood there laughing like two lords born to the realm, nothing between us and the infinite sky.

I've often wondered if my sense of fragmentation, of being separated from myself, came from LSD and the other drugs I took in the sixties. Sometimes I feel it's taken me twenty-five years just to gather myself together after bombing my brain with psychedelics. I put myself through some terrifying times, moments in which my normal sense of self broke up in a riotous sea and left me—whatever *me* was—desperately clinging to a piece of wreckage, certain that I was lost forever from my life. Those were moments of true insanity, the kind of insanity that caused one friend who had taken acid with me to crouch down and pound his head on the sidewalk and run away shrieking down Connecticut Avenue one overcast Friday afternoon in Washington, D.C.

I've lost touch with that friend, but I've heard from a reliable source that he is now a psychiatrist. Somehow we survived our self-induced insanity, most of us, and got on with our lives. The car was damaged but drivable. And maybe the only damage LSD really did was to show us, too suddenly and too vividly, the actual volatile complexity of the human psyche. Maybe I had always been fragmented and hadn't known it. A brain scientist I've been reading, Robert Ornstein, says that what we call mind, as if it were one thing, is really a loose tribe of many minds, many selves that shift into and out of control all the time, mostly without the knowledge of the conscious self. He thinks consciousness is a secondary phenomenon, not very strong and not very active, that comes to the fore only when the body is threatened or the tribe is in conflict about what to do. We experience a more or less consistent sense of self because the conscious self is mostly unaware of the others, and because the entire menagerie shares at least a weak sense of group identity.

So maybe psychedelic drugs only introduced me to my personal tribe—introduced and abandoned me to be devoured raw. It would probably profit me to get to know better my various selves. I do know a few of them, vaguely at least—Bob Bourgeois, the Inspector, the

boy I used to be—but the self that interests me most is not of that
tribe. It's a self that brain scientists don't believe in, but I do. I have
discovered it more than once. It's a deep and calm and undivided self,
the self I was in that moment at dawn with John Sterne, the self my
mother sought and wrote with a capital S. That Self is utterly at
home in the universe it was born to and shares in its numinous perfection. It is both immanent and transcendent, within and without
the wraps of ego and personality, always newly born and thrilled
with the adventure of being. It was to be that Self again, if only for a
moment, that I kept taking psychedelics and enduring the insanity
they wrought.

On my first acid trip, a month into my freshman year at Reed, I
felt as though my mind had flowed forth from the cave of its confinement and now was infusing my body. It *was* my body. I was a field
of conscious energy aflow in the world. I couldn't stop smiling. The
sunny Reed lawn was clearly itself and completely transformed.
Each tree, each blade of grass, shone with its own being—familiar,
elusive, beautiful beyond words. I was walking in the first field on the
first day. I climbed a tree, the smooth firm limbs approving the fit of
my hands, and at the top I shouted laughter like a two-year-old. Later
I lay in the grass, my eyes closed, and whatever I was opened up inside, opened deep and far as time itself. I felt some ancient presence
within me, moving like a long slow wind, the father of all things. Delight deepened into awe, and I was trembling.

On LSD I was often unsure who I was, but when I was outdoors
and alone, I always knew where I was. I was in the world, the luminous, palpable world itself, and what I felt was the mystery of its being. Among native peoples there are cultural means by which
adolescents seek a guiding vision from beyond the realm of normal
consciousness. Our own culture offers no such means. It does its
best, in fact, to enforce the idea that there is no meaningful realm beyond, nothing to be learned that can't be taught in school or church
or everyday experience. I believe that I and a lot of other young
people in the sixties were trying to invent, mostly unaware, what

our culture failed to provide. In our bumbling and haphazard ways, we were initiating ourselves into the sacred.

As a child I knew sacredness mostly as a vague aura around Christmas. My father would read in his baritone voice from the Gospels, which he still appreciated as literature, and the carols we sang and heard on the hi-fi—"Silent Night," "Away in the Manger," "O Little Town of Bethlehem"—seemed to confer a glow of holiness that meant as much to me, until Christmas morning anyway, as the presents beneath the tree. Then one Christmas Eve I stood on the open roof of the side porch of our Glen Echo house and watched snow come down in the light of the one street lamp. A white Christmas had been more than I dared hope for, but now it was here, the snow drifting down out of darkness to glint and waver as it settled to the street. I'd meant to stay only a minute, but something held me there, and the longer I stayed the stranger it seemed that all warmth and comfort and sacredness should be sealed in below, in our living room with its music and bright tree, while all the infinite universe was darkness and cold glinting light. The best-ever Christmas of my life seemed suddenly a paltry thing. I needed it to take in the night and the snow, the untold mystery that wouldn't let go of me, and I knew it couldn't. When I went downstairs to the fire, I was shaking from more than the cold.

What I started to see with the help of psychedelic drugs was sacredness in no enclosure, unless the enclosure of earth and sky, a sacredness more common and more precious than I had known. Some version of that realization was occurring to many of us in the sixties, but there was no ritual, no institution—except for the kind that recognized only the insanity—to interpret and validate our experience. We were lucky to have a few books for guides. *The Psychedelic Experience,* the five-dollar hardback by Leary, Metzner, and Alpert, based on *The Tibetan Book of the Dead.* Aldous Huxley's accounts in *The Doors of Perception* and *Island.* Alan Watts's books, William Blake, a few others.

Mostly we had ourselves for guides. In my small dorm at Reed there were six or seven of us who were experimenting, and it still moves me when I think of how we looked after one another. My friend Michael, whom I'd known only a few months, once sat with me for what must have been hours when a whole tab of Owsley acid had melted my body and left me a mass of disturbed protoplasm on the dorm-room floor. I can still see his smile, the friendly interest in his eyes as I talked at him, probably with little coherence. I kept saying the word *remember,* seeing for the first time what it meant: to put the pieces together again, to rebuild the familiar house of the world. Michael's narrow Irish face was boy and man and old gray listener, continuously shifting as it stayed the same. I recognized the Michael who lived upstairs in the dorm, and I recognized the one who wore Michael's being, an ageless and undying friend.

All of us knew a little of the wilds we were exploring, and we made sure that everyone who entered them came back out. We came out, and we went back in. The flaw in our ad hoc initiation through LSD was that it led only to itself again. We were dilettantes, mere tourists of the sacred, buying tablet or blotter square time after time for the big transformation ride, complete with horror show—conveniently located right on campus, right in the dorm, right in the mystery of our own minds. No preparation, no effort required. The wonder of a psychedelic drug is that it shows you the authentic Self—but it shows you the Self whether or not you are ready to see it, and always it takes the Self away, with no clue how to find it except by the tablet or blotter again. In one of the Grail stories, the boy Parsifal discovers on his journey a mysterious fire in the woods with a salmon roasting over it. He reaches for the salmon, burns his fingers, and thrusts them into his mouth. He wasn't ready for what he desired. The mystery was too strong for him. Like Parsifal, I was left with a taste of the sacred and a lingering hunger.

Timothy Leary visited Reed in the spring of 1967, and probably three out of four of us who came to hear him were on acid or mescaline. I had taken a small hit, just enough to feel along my spine, enough to loosen the gridwork I carried in my head but not enough to dissolve it away. Leary, dressed in white with a mandala pendant, sat among vases of flowers and paisley tapestries on a small lit stage in the darkened Old Commons. He smiled the knowing smile of the acidhead, and as he talked along in his sonorous way, his voice returned again and again to six carefully cadenced words he delivered with a dance of his hands: "Turn on . . . . . . tune in . . . . . . *drop out.*"

I didn't need much encouragement. I had begun to realize, with the assistance of my chemical education, that all my reasons for being in college were actually other people's reasons—my parents', my relatives', my high school teachers'. I liked my classes well enough, but I couldn't see that they pertained very much to my life, and besides, I'd been working hard in school for many years. I'd been locked in a house of words, it seemed, looking out at life instead of living it. In the fall of 1967 I came back for my sophomore year, but I knew I wanted out. In November I went to Dean Dudman's office and told him I needed a leave of absence, and I suppose it was only fitting that I was high on mescaline when I did.

I cringe at the platitudes I must have spoken to explain myself. I probably told the dean that I was my own best teacher, that real learning couldn't happen in a classroom. Probably, like a million other teenagers in those years, I used the word "irrelevant." But still, though my thoughts were simplistic and unexamined, I was doing what I needed to do. I was in no shape for the academic rigors of Reed College, and I had the vague but sure sense that great adventures awaited me outside. In the spirit of openness that I had decided would characterize my new life, I told Dean Dudman that I was on mescaline. The dean, a good and generous man, showed immediate concern.

"Have you been treated?" he asked. "Have you had medication?"

I looked at him and smiled.

CHAPTER TWELVE

I never looked for-
ward to helping my mother with her shower. She wasn't the least
self-conscious about baring her body in my presence, but something
in me shrank from it. To be with her in her nakedness seemed too in-
timate for a grown son. And some other part of me, the child who
wants always to be cared for and never burdened with responsibility,
felt put upon and put out. Why was I having to do this? It seemed an
indignity, and it touched an open wound. I had no child to bathe, to
make faces at, to splash and laugh with. Most likely I never would.
What I had was a frail and failing old woman who couldn't take a
shower on her own.

Talking her into it was the first challenge. "Oh, I don't need a
shower," she would say. "I just had one yesterday, didn't I?"

"You haven't had one for a week."

"But I don't *do* anything. Why do I need a shower?"

It wasn't only bad memory and lapsing judgment that made her resist, of course. It was also that the shower was strenuous for her, and she didn't want to acknowledge, or couldn't, that she needed help with anything so simple. In her own mind, the mind I believe she inhabited most of the time, she was perfectly capable of taking a shower by herself if she wanted to. In this mind she was still the woman she had been five years ago, a woman who came and went and drove a car, a woman who lived on her own on the coast of Maine and was only temporarily exiled in a distant place. This woman was honestly perplexed when we bought her a cane and asked her, over and over again, to use it. What need had Zilla Daniel for a cane? Somewhere inside her she was not only an able-bodied woman but still a Sea Scout, climbing the rigging in a bright clear wind.

But in her present mind she knew, whenever she leaned far forward in a chair and tried to stiff-arm herself to her feet, whenever she steadied herself with a hand on the wall as she shuffled to the bathroom, just how incapable she had become. She knew, and she hated it. How could she not have hated it? And if she had to bear it, she didn't want me or Marilyn or anyone else to have to help her bear it. She wanted to carry herself on her own stooped shoulders. I can still hear her making her way to the toilet with her left hand pulling her nightgown tight behind her, disgustedly whispering *No, no* to her bladder that could not hold back what it should have held back. As if she were castigating an unbroken puppy, but without the tolerance she would have granted an innocent thing.

It's easy to see, watching my mother from this remove, how much I resemble her. George and Jim inherited straight hair with a slight wave; I got my mother's curls. I got her long, slender fingers rather than my father's thicker ones. I got the Hawes nose. But just as surely, just as strikingly, I got my mother's Inspector. She didn't drill it into me—she didn't play Inspector as a mother any more than most parents—but somehow it just appeared in me, along with the hair and fingers and nose. The irritability, the spites and sulks, the impatience and the sharp tongue—and never sharper, of course, than when directed inward, aimed at herself, aimed at myself, aimed at the only failings and shortcomings in the entire human world that absolutely cannot be forgiven.

Standing for any length of time was hard for my mother, and so the shower was a kind of siege. She would grip the soap tray with both hands as I got the water temperature right—*"Aaant!"* she would holler, "too cold!"—and soaped a washcloth to scrub her sway-spined back. Even the soap met resistance.

"Sai Baba says not to use soap," she informed me early on. "It's just one more thing that has to come off."

"Well, it does come off," I answered, peeling open a bar of Dial. "It rinses off."

"My dear, it leaves a *residue*. Plain water is enough."

"Mother, for God's sake. This isn't the ashram. You need soap to get clean."

"Yes, Father," she said with a scowl.

Eventually we worked out a mulish compromise. We used Ivory, which we both agreed was the most natural. I washed her back and buttocks with a soaped washcloth; she held the cloth a few seconds in the shower spray before washing her front. One hand on the soap tray for support, she briefly swabbed her sagging breasts, her abdomen, the thinly gray-haired pubic region from which I once emerged, and the smooth, still-young skin of her upper thighs. Then I helped her down to the bath stool, where she rested a while and washed her lower legs and feet. The skin of her shins was dry and papery, perpetually blotched with dark purple—not impact bruises but bruises of age.

As I lathered shampoo into her wet white curls, her head would bow from the pressure of my fingers. I'd ask her to hold it up and she would for a second or two, then it would slowly sink again. It must have taken a major effort just to hold herself as upright as she did in her last years. All the while she was slowly bending, slowly folding, curling toward the fetal comfort of the grave.

She squeezed her eyes shut as I rinsed her hair in the shower stream. She scrunched up her face, stuck her lips out, and sputtered through the soapy runoff. It was in that recurring moment of her life with us, her hair flattened to her head, darkened a little with the soaking spray, that I could almost see my mother as a girl—swimming the cold swells off Hancock Point, splashing and laughing, shouting something toward shore, laying into the water with strong even strokes that would take her where she wanted to go.

She would let me stop rinsing only when she could rub a bit of her hair between finger and thumb and make it squeak. Then I would steady her out of the shower stall, her two hands in mine. It felt at moments like a kind of dance, a dance that maybe I knew how to do and needed to do. Who was that, doing the dance? Who was it who allowed himself those moments of pleasure helping his mother from the shower? Bob Bourgeois, I suppose. Bob has time and patience for things that only irritate me. He enjoys them. But it was someone else, too. When I look back at that scene in the bathroom, I see a boy in my place. A solemn boy with a bit of a smile, a boy attending his mother out of love and duty blended as one. The boy was there, and he was there now and then at other times in those years my mother was with us. He was there when I'd let him be there.

I helped my mother down into a straight-backed chair and left her in the bathroom with towels, clean underwear, and a little space heater to keep her warm. She took her time, as with everything. Often it was half an hour or longer before she emerged in her dressing gown, her hair beginning to fluff, her face smiling. No matter how hard she might have resisted the idea, a bath or shower always seemed to renew her. Soap or no soap, the old woman came forth cleaner of spirit.

"She was pure as the driven snow," she usually quoted, gaily, then a pause: "But she drifted."

I guess I came out of the bathroom cleaner of spirit myself. Soap or no soap, whatever the tenor of our conversation, I appreciate now what a privilege it was to help my mother with her shower. I wish I'd seen it more clearly at the time. We don't get to choose our privileges, and the ones that come to us aren't always the ones we would choose, and each of them is as much burden as joy. But they do come, and it's important to know them for what they are.

One morning as my mother came out of her shower she paused at the bottom of the stairs. I was reading the paper in the living room.

"Do you feel them sprouting?" she said, smiling in her white gown.

"Do I feel what sprouting?"

"Your wings," she said. She stood there, barefooted and bright, smiling right at me and through me, smiling as though she weren't feeble of body and failing of mind but filled with an uncanny power that saw things I could only glimpse.

"Mother, I don't have wings," I said.

But she was still smiling as she headed up the stairs, gripping the banister hand over hand, hauling herself up fifteen carpeted steps to her room and her bed made of sea-weathered posts and boards, where she would read for a while, gaze out her window at sky and treetops, then drift into sleep.

CHAPTER THIRTEEN

I'm standing with one hand on the red brick wall at the bottom of the stairs, peeking around the corner to the left into what we call the recreation room—the cool and musty basement that holds the TV set, a foam-pad sofa and a chair or two, a few bookshelves, a file cabinet, and my father's safe. Behind me there's a door I can open and walk through into the morning of a bright spring day, but I haven't sneaked down the stairs for that. I heard something, and I've come to see what. Why am I even home? It must be a weekend. Or maybe it's summer, not spring, summer vacation after third grade. It doesn't matter. Baseball, mess around in the yard, go across the street to Bobby Bradley's, whatever I was planning to do before I heard a repetitive sound and started down the stairs, none of it matters.

My mother and father are in the room. They aren't speaking. My mother, in gray corduroy pants, is facing three-quarters away from my father, looking down, her hands clasped in front of her. Is she crying? I don't think she's crying. My father, stubble-cheeked and cold sober, his face drawn flat and gray, is wearing his bathrobe and brown leather slippers. He is taking a step with his left foot, swinging his right leg free of the bathrobe and kicking my mother's rear end. She doesn't move, except with the impact. She stands there, just stands there, as he steps back and forward and kicks her again, and kicks her again, the two of them together like a windup toy somebody started in the basement and nobody knows how to stop—certainly not me, not the boy staring through the mortar joints of the brick corner unable to stop staring, certainly not him.

I still can't stop it. The toy plays on and on, a perpetual-motion machine in a sealed glass chamber where nothing disturbs it, nothing interrupts the perfection of its motion. My father with his lips pursed tight, his right leg pale and sparsely haired, the creased brown slipper flopping slightly as his foot leaves the floor. My mother with steel gray in her dark curling hair, her eyes dark and downcast, her face contracted in something like anger, something like sorrow, something like resignation. I see them as if they stood in front of me now, and I see myself too, I see myself watching—my torso skinny in a white t-shirt, my hair curly like my mother's, brown with sun-bleached glints, my fingers on the brick wall narrow and delicate like hers. I see my closed mouth. I see myself crying.

But I don't know what I'm feeling. I know the boy, I know what he must have been feeling, the way I know what he looks like from photos, but I don't feel it inside me now. It's not inside me. It's inside him. It's clamped behind his skinny ribs, behind the flat wall of his belly. He's holding it, molding it to his familiar form, so it won't fly loose where who knows what it might do. He's trying to hold it where he can take care of it, keep it from scaring him, like the big flying beetle he used to keep in a coffee can punched with little holes.

The boy must have been afraid, of course. I must have been afraid, and in a new way. Their arguments always scared me, but they composed a kind of weather that had come to seem normal in our household. I could almost predict the storms and how bad they would be, but this was different. This was crazy. This had no words, shouted or whispered, to clarify it. No tears or slamming doors. This was silent and dead sober. It felt as though I'd stumbled upon a secret ritual of marriage, a ritual of hatred—and that's the missing word, isn't it. Hatred. In that moment I think I hated my parents. Hated my father for kicking my mother. Hated my mother for standing there, for letting him do it. I hated the stupid secret craziness they had made of our family, without even whiskey to explain it now, a shameful, rotten craziness at the heart of our home.

Gradually, over weeks and months, I learned enough to make some sense of what I had seen. I learned it all indirectly, of course, the way I gathered all my intelligence—overheard conversations between the two of them, between them and their friends. The word "affair" wouldn't have meant anything to me at the time, but I learned that my mother had done what husband and wife do with a man named Guy Pfoutz, and my father had found out about it. Most likely, knowing what I know about my mother's personality, she told him about it. Probably tossed it in his face, just as she had tossed her radical politics and liberated lifestyle in her father's proper Unitarian face in the 1920s, just as later she would choose a dinner party as the occasion to announce to her husband that she wanted a divorce. She probably told my father all about her affair so that she could feel honest if not pure and hurt him for the weeks and months she had spent alone, for the career she'd forsaken to traipse the country in the tow of his, for the Cause that was his highest love and the whiskey that was his closest friend, and for everything I don't know about and never will.

She hurt him and stood there taking the hurt back, the hurt that part of her felt she deserved. She hurt herself through him, he hurt himself through her, and so the broken toy of their marriage cranked on and on.

There must have been a time, I keep thinking, when it wasn't so.
A time when their love for each other was full and fine and sufficient.
Maybe the Carolina years of the late forties and early fifties, those
summers of barbecues and homemade ice cream, friends flowing in
from everywhere, scratchy seventy-eights of Verdi and Beethoven
loud on the record player, the wound of Georgie's death healing and
two lively boys running in the grass. And a few years earlier, too,
when my mother was pregnant with George and confident at last
that she wouldn't miscarry again. She wrote my father nearly every
other day when he was on the road, and in all her letters her tone is
never more tender. "You first, darling," she writes. "I especially love
to hear from you 'en route' anywhere: the whir of wheels underneath, country racing by, something new ahead. It's a fine feeling."
"Darling," she writes, "to have you set a date for coming is enough. I
am tremendously excited . . ."

And they had their first years together, that time in the early thirties when they were new and fresh to each other and saw themselves
as nothing less than revolutionaries, committed to a huge and impossible mission that maybe was possible after all, because the passion they shared with their fellow organizers was so intense and
boundless. When Franz Daniel was a charismatic zealot from the
seminary with an eloquence that made factory workers cheer and
weep at rallies, that made Zilla Hawes weep in meetings, where she
sat sometimes literally at his feet. And when Zilla Hawes herself was
a daring firebrand of patrician manners whom one male friend described as an Athena from New England, a woman, if not beautiful,
of such vibrant and virile intensity that she made him and many men
feel like inarticulate clods.

My parents wrote their own wedding ceremony, and they incorporated this verse from a poem by Ralph Chaplin:

We shall be faithful though we march with Death
And singing storm the battlements of Wrong,

For life is such a little thing to give.
We shall march on as long as we have breath—
Love in our hearts and on our lips a song.

Their marriage, early on, was a comradeship as much as a romantic union. I don't know if they would have called themselves happy in that tumultuous era. What they craved, it seems, was not happiness but *action*—they wanted to storm and sing to the utmost limits of their souls. Through most of the thirties, as they shifted independently around the South and East on various strikes and organizing drives—both before and after they were married—they explicitly granted each other sexual freedom. My own parents, it turns out, were experimenting with Free Love a full thirty years before the hippie culture of the sixties made it a catchphrase and a sporadic way of life. It didn't work out any better for them than it does for most who try it. My mother did indeed experiment—and my father, when he found out, raised holy hell in spite of their agreement. My mother, in later years, wasn't sure if he had had other relationships. She thought not, but a woman friend who lived with them in Philadelphia in those days tells me he certainly did.

"Franz and I never really gave ourselves a chance," my mother said to me in the 1970s. Their personal lives were so consumed in the cause that they didn't even take a honeymoon after their wedding— they threw a house party on the Maine coast instead, carousing with labor comrades, and then plunged quickly into work again. They hardly knew what it was like to spend long periods alone together. My mother was philosophical about that, and wistful, when she and I talked. I could feel her sadness, and though my father never spoke to me directly about their marriage, his sadness loomed enormously. I can't think of them as a couple without feeling sadness myself. They were powerful people, yet very nearly helpless to steer their own way together in the turbulence of their lives and times.

But their sadness, and my sadness for them, is not what I meant to write about. Sadness is not what I felt as I watched their windup toy in the basement when I was nine. And it was something more intense than sadness I felt later that year, or the next year, when they called Jim and me into the living room one night and told us they were going to divorce. I walked toward my father in my underwear, crying "Don't go." And later I lay awake a long time, staring out at the ceiling light in the hall through the bedroom doorway that I'd asked my mother to leave open. *This happens to a lot of kids*, I remember thinking, my head cocked on the pillow. *This happens all over America*. I stared at the light and kept thinking and thinking—already generalizing, already abstracting my pain, already withdrawing to a watchful distance where I could sit by myself, sit quiet and still, feeling not too happy, not too sad, and maybe—if I was quiet and watchful enough—maybe safe.

CHAPTER FOURTEEN

On a little bookcase not far from her bed, my mother kept a small framed black-and-white photograph of my father. She may have taken the picture herself, from the stern of a rowboat—her father's green-painted boat, probably, on a Maine lake or the easy tidal waters of Frenchman's Bay off Hancock Point. My father, in a sweater, is handling the oars. He is forty-something—possibly younger than I am now—and he's smiling. He looks as happy and easy as I ever saw him. Surely that's the reason my mother chose that picture to keep near her: it shows the joy her husband was capable of, the joy, maybe, that *they* were capable of. The remembered joy, intact and still alive in the wreckage of their marriage, that had made her wistful in 1977, a year after my father's death, when I asked her to talk about him and their life together.

I recorded those conversations, with my mother's consent, and

I'm glad I did. Those tapes, along with the interview in *Refuse to Stand Silently By* and her letters that I've been able to gather, form the basis of what I've written so far about her marriage and labor career. To her present mind, as she was living with Marilyn and me, very few of those memories were available—and then only sporadically, randomly, occasional leaves wavering briefly through the sundown light of her psyche. There were days when she knew the given name of the man she had spent half her life with, but there were many days when she didn't. *Your father,* she would sometimes say, after struggling in vain for the missing single syllable full of consonant sounds she must have spoken ten thousand times in the course of her life: *Franz.*

How could his name have vanished from her? How could *he* have vanished to the extent he did, the man she had worshiped and slept with and partied with and borne children by and betrayed and been kicked by and hated and pitied—and loved deeply, abidingly, through all of that and beyond?

Sometimes when I barbecued I remarked to my mother how Franz had taken great pride in his steaks.

"Oh yes," she would answer, smiling, taking a sip of her Scotch. "He called his basting sauce his Persuader, remember?"

"Why yes, John, that's right," she'd reply, and on like that, as if my words ignited some light in her mind, a pleasurable glow, but there was little there for the light to illuminate, little to offer back in kind. There was recognition in her, but little recall.

What was missing in my mother as we conversed was not intelligence or caring and certainly not language ability. She retained an extensive vocabulary to the end of her life, she rattled off nursery rhymes and snatches of poetry, and she spoke her words with an elaborate precision. Her enunciation had always been clear, but in her last years she took even greater pains to form her syllables carefully and completely, practically sculpting them in their saying. She seemed to taste and savor her language as she spoke it, as if in that way at least to forestall the formlessness expanding within her, to enact upon her life in the world the one exactitude that still remained to her.

What was missing was her part in the *interplay* of human talk, the ready resilience we mostly take for granted that absorbs another's words and returns—ingeniously, without planning and often without thought—words of one's own that answer or expand upon or deflect from or turn in a new direction the language received. That, I can see now, is a substantial part of what irritated me, what tried me in a way I didn't understand. It was unusual for conversation with my mother to *go* anywhere. She would sink it or shut it off, as if weary of the subject. One of the phrases she spoke most frequently, held in mind sixty years from her undergraduate days at Vassar, was *Questo non far niente. This really doesn't matter.*

In her first year with us, before we understood her affliction, I thought my mother was being purposely evasive. I wanted to hear about her labor work, her college life, stories about me and Jim and George, her final thoughts about my father and the life they had shared. What I got instead, most of the time, were repeated comments and questions about the appearance of trees she spent hours looking at through the windows, about the arrangement of the furniture or the placement of a picture, about the food we ate. When was Jim coming to visit? What was the little bird with a black cap? What *good* strong coffee I had made. The remarks and questions recurred with maddening frequency, but it wasn't only the repetition that annoyed me. If she wasn't purposely withholding herself, it could only mean that she had no self to share. It's both baffling and an outrage when mental failing occurs in a loved one, because the ailment can't be located in leg or heart or liver. It's not the body but *she* who is failing, the person inhabiting the flesh, the one we have loved and trusted and thought we knew. When a loved one loses her health, it is a sadness. But when she even begins to lose her mind, it is a sadness and a betrayal, an emblem of our deepest fear.

It was usually while we were walking that my mother remembered my father, and it almost always was a dandelion that provoked the memory. The natural view of her old age, because of her stooped back and bowed head, was toward the ground. She noticed bugs, kids' chalk marks, the stamped imprints of the sidewalk makers, and all the flowers along our way. The small, low-lying blooms were her favorites—violets, saxifrage, others that neither of us could name—and none delighted her more than dandelions. She liked their plain bright faces; she liked the way they pop up anywhere, including sidewalk cracks; and she liked them, I think, because they're so commonly scorned. I can't count the times she told me, not spitefully or ruefully but still returning the dandelions' yellow smile, "Your father, you know, could not *abide* dandelions. He had to rid the lawn of every one."

I don't remember that myself, but it fits. Perhaps because of the German in him, my father did like to keep the yard well mowed and orderly. But I don't think my mother was remembering a mere fact of my father's lawn-tending habit. As she made the same remark many times over the months, I got the strange but certain feeling that all their bitter arguments through the years and decades, all the painful wrenching and tearing they inflicted on themselves for so long, that all of that—very little of which my mother specifically remembered—had distilled and resolved in her present mind to a difference over dandelions. It may have been a kind of oblique coming to terms, the best she may have been capable of as her past receded into what must have felt like a dream to her, a dream lived by someone who was and was not her, and the present—pain in her bones, a bird in the tree, the shining flowers—drew her deeper and deeper into its sheer unspoken mystery.

She wanted no part of argument in her life with us. At dinner sometimes, infrequently, Marilyn and I would bicker about one thing or another—an issue in the news, something that did or didn't need doing around the house—the kind of disagreement that generates a little heat but quickly passes. My mother couldn't stand it. She stared into her dinner, chewing hard, clanking her fork on the plate. *"Please,"* I remember her saying once in complete disgust. "Would you *please* behave yourselves." Looking back now it occurs to me that my mother didn't know, because she hadn't experienced it, that a husband and wife could argue casually. She didn't know what a healthy marriage was, what strains and turbulence it might absorb without suffering harm. Also, of course, she had been on her own for twenty years, living in the quiet of her own company—and, in recent years, absorbed in the teachings of her religion, which frowns on disagreement with others.

Dinner was difficult for all of us. My mother, because her hearing was bad and her new hearing aid, her first, remained semi-incomprehensible to her, had a hard time tracking Marilyn's voice, which is softer and projects less well than my own assertive foghorn. And so, to make herself understood, Marilyn had to speak directly at my mother in loud forced syllables—not exactly what she felt like doing, first thing home after a long day of office and meetings and bus. She wanted to talk about her day, but she and I couldn't converse in our usual easy way without my mother feeling left out. She would interrupt to ask us to repeat what we had said, sometimes reprimanding us for our rudeness. I would ask her to turn up her hearing aid, if she had it in; she would do it and complain that she heard herself chewing. Irritation flared in all of us. Conversation lurched in fits and starts. I felt very much in the middle, wanting my wife to enjoy herself, wanting my mother to enjoy herself, wanting the two of them to enjoy each other and the dinner I had made, wanting the peaceful aura of my mother's Sanskrit prayer with which the meal had begun.

Dinner, of course, was the social highlight of my mother's day. Usually, unless we went out to lunch or to an appointment with a doctor or on some other errand, she saw no one during the day but me. Often I didn't either, but that was by choice; I could break off writing or reading and leave the house any time. My mother was marooned in a comfortable but silent home without work to do or friends at the door, no coming or going except with me, few travels except out the window with her eyes and wherever she journeyed within herself. Sleep and wake, the same books and magazines beside her, the bathroom and back to her bedroom, drifting along with the changing light until maybe a walk in the afternoon, then a drink in the living room or in the kitchen as I fixed dinner.

Marilyn and I tried to find ways to get other people into my mother's life. I took her to the local senior center a few times, but she resisted from the beginning and clearly didn't care for it. She was a misfit among the bingo players and TV watchers. I felt like a parent forcing a reluctant child to attend day camp because it would be good for her. We arranged with a senior outreach program for a volunteer "friend" to come over now and then to visit with my mother. For a few weeks this seemed to please her, but she was well aware of the artificiality of the relationship, and both she and the visitor lost interest after a while. Her most satisfying friendship was with a colleague of Marilyn's, a young Socialist and labor activist, who occasionally took her to breakfast on a weekend. And she did attend her Sai Baba meetings, but only once in a while. When the evening of the meeting arrived she frequently didn't feel up to it. Because of her physical weakness, any outing, even the most pleasant, had a dimension of ordeal.

Worried about her isolation, her listlessness and lack of initiative, in the spring of 1990 Marilyn and I asked a psychiatric social worker who worked for the county mental health service to evaluate my mother. She came twice, asking questions that left my mother slightly but pleasantly bemused—any visitor perked her up. Marilyn and I had suspected that she was depressed, but the social worker thought not. Lonely for sure, somewhat resentful over having been moved from her home and having her car taken from her, but not medically depressed. The social worker thought she had detected something else, though, and referred us to a clinical psychologist.

My mother spent two long sessions in the psychologist's office, performing verbal and visual tests with names like the Pfeiffer Short Portable MSQ, Hooper Visual Organization Test, Porteus Maze, Trail-Making Tests A and B, Wechsler Memory Scale Subtests, Familiar Faces Test, Boston Naming Test, and the Geriatric Depression Scale. She emerged from the sessions fatigued but in a good mood. She liked the psychologist, a warm and sympathetic woman, very much; and the psychologist, like so many who encountered my mother, was instantly and thoroughly taken with her. She was nearly in tears as she told Marilyn and me that the test results pointed clearly to a primary progressive dementia probably of the Alzheimer's type. Another possibility was multi-infarct dementia, a disease of similar symptoms caused by multiple small strokes. I was standing outside her office, listening through the door, when she explained to my mother what she had found. She paused when she first said "Alzheimer's disease."

"Oh," said my mother, real fear in her voice. "I hope I don't have that."

CHAPTER FIFTEEN

Forgetfulness is what I'm fighting as I write this. I want to remember everything because I know it all counts, it's all important, it all composes the constellation I need to see. But I don't remember everything. It hasn't been two years since my mother died, and already my memory of our life with her is softening, going vague and filmy. I have a few intensely clear images, a few notes of things she said, a few of her personal things and items of clothing, a few photographs, and I work from those into the weeks and months of her nearly four years with us that are only a blur, a fogged-in landscape, an absence. From what I know I write my way into what I don't know, or don't think I know. I'm a restorer, rubbing at the weathered surfaces, looking for the shine of life.

But it isn't restoration. There was, there is, no finished work to be restored. No artist, no art. There is only my experience—*experience*, that oddly unruffled term that tries to subsume the prodigious flux and welter of a human life. I'm not restoring my experience, I'm forming it. I'm constructing it. Actually, I'm creating it. I just looked again at something John Burroughs wrote in *Riverby:* "It was not till I got home that I really went to Maine, or the Adirondacks, or to Canada. Out of the chaotic and nebulous impressions which these expeditions gave me, I evolved the real experience."

Evolved it, that is, by writing it. The real experience of the birch forest in Maine occurs not when he is walking through it but back home at Slabsides in his study, where he "compels that vague unconscious being within me, who absorbs so much and says so little, to unbosom himself at the point of a pen." If he means that last phrase as a joke, it's a serious joke. There *is* compulsion in it. My own vague unconscious being—and who could it be but Bob Bourgeois?—would rather poke around the hardware store or hike in the Cascades, he'd rather blow the afternoon watching the Forty-Niners on TV, he'd rather clean the lint filter on the dryer than unbosom himself at the point of anything. But I, whoever I am, need to evolve the real experience out of what I remember and what I don't. I need to make memory into something whole, a monument, a place where meaning can live. And where I can live, too. A home I can live in and leave behind, returning when I need to for the rest of my life.

But the Inspector has a concern. He has a question to ask. Am I telling the truth, or only a truth I can live with? There are parts of the story I would prefer to leave to my vague unconscious being, because they don't please me. They don't show me as I like to think of myself, as I like others to think of me. The point of the pen has to demand those too. To evolve the real experience, it has to demand the fullest truth memory can provide—memory the unreliable, memory the self-serving, memory the liar. It isn't just a matter of giving birth, of bodying forth the mystery. It's an examination, an interrogation. It's an act of will. I'm the one pointing the weapon—the necessary weapon—and I'm the one filing the report. It's got to be a full report. It's got to be a report I believe.

My mother had been a strong and vibrant woman. It grieved me to see her reduced to a stooped crone who dithered over vegetables at the store, who couldn't remember what she'd read half an hour before, who forgot to take the pills I placed directly in front of her at breakfast. It more than grieved me—it enraged me, and there was no one to be enraged at but her. The psychologist's diagnosis confirmed that she couldn't help the way she was. I knew she was blameless, and yet I blamed her. I hurried her when she couldn't hurry, I was short with her, I cut off conversations as often as she did—because she said something she'd said before, because I was in a rush, because I wanted to get away and do something else, because I was stuck with caring for a feeble old mother and didn't want to be. Because she was what I got for a child. A wizened old child growing the wrong way, growing into senile dementia, growing into death.

There were moments when I wanted her dead. It's hard to write that, but it's true. There were moments when I hated the house, hated Portland, hated my writing and myself and blamed her for all of it. Moments when I felt racked between mother and wife and imagined no relief for years and years. Moments when I felt so trapped I wanted just to keep walking, ankle weights and all, when I wanted to stride back to the sixties and stick out my thumb on I-5, slip down to Swan Island and hide myself on a rusty tanker and sail wherever it took me. There were many evenings I wanted to sling dinner in the sink and sit out back with George Dickel or Jack Daniel or whoever I could find in the liquor cupboard and just not care. Once I left the dinner table to fetch more wine and lay down on the kitchen floor, crying silently to the cutlery clicks and scrapes of my wife and mother eating silently in the next room. And once I burst into my study slamming the door behind me and screamed, "Just die then, *die*," and sat down sobbing at my desk.

You'd think I'd remember what set me off that time, but I don't. Usually it happened when she said something snappishly ungrateful about the caregiving things I had to do—take her blood pressure, make sure she took her medicines, remind her to use her cane and later her walker. I knew she wasn't ungrateful, and of course she hated all that. Why wouldn't she? Why wouldn't she chafe under the enforcing eye of her all too fatherly son—her son with more than a passing resemblance to her own reverend father? Why wouldn't she hate to take a diuretic when she was already partially incontinent? Why wouldn't she be jealous of the wife I wanted to spend time with? Why wouldn't she be going half crazy from the tedium of her changeless days? She felt as trapped as I did. Once, when she was going through the tests with the psychologist and had recently endured an exhaustive medical assessment—not her idea, of course— she and I had a small fracas over something and she told me, "Just leave me alone and let me *die.*" She only said it once, but there must have been many moments when she felt it.

She *was* dying, of course. She was declining toward death the whole time she lived with us. If I could have seen that more clearly and accepted it, I could have been a better help to her than the dutiful blood pressure taker and moody cook and conversant I was. You don't get a second chance to live your mother's last years. She dies and it all freezes in place, everything you did and didn't do. I wish I could have been more patient with her, more supple, more willing to follow her lead instead of so often imposing my own will. And I wish I could have provided her with a ritual, a ceremony, some form or path for approaching death by which the troubles and longings of her spirit could have expressed themselves. I wish I could have found a way to talk with her about Franz, about little George. I wish she could have cried and laughed and worked it all through and come to something, to a final *Yes, this is what my life has been, and it's all right.*

She couldn't do that, because she didn't have the memory for it. But why do I think she had the need or the desire? Her memory loss, though it vexed and grieved me, didn't seem to disturb her all that much. She knew at least the gist of what was happening to her—she had come from Maine with homeopathic salts to improve her memory—and though sometimes she was impatient with her forgetfulness, by and large she took it with humor and her uniquely eloquent grace. "My memory is so *slippery*," I remember her exclaiming once. And another time she volunteered, "I'm forgetting everything these days. The only thing I don't forget is the fact that I'm alive!" It was harder for Marilyn and me to take a laughing view, of course, because it was harder for us to live with her and care for her if she didn't remember to use her hearing aid and take her pills, and her lapses could be dangerous. Once, shortly after she moved in with us, we came home from a movie to find the empty steel tea kettle rocking on a red-hot burner, my mother sunk into a book in the living room.

But what do I know of what she finally came to, or didn't come to? What do I know of what she experienced most deeply within, what she couldn't or wouldn't speak? She had that photo of her husband smiling at the oars of a boat—the man she had loved in his handsome prime, his brightest mood—and maybe that was enough. There had been much between them that surely she wouldn't have wanted to remember even if she could have, and why did she need to? Why wasn't a difference over dandelions, real or imagined, a sufficient summary of their troubles? And how do I know she didn't come to some similar resting point about the son who had died in her arms, about the other pains of her long life? And if the only resolution was forgetfulness, what's wrong with that? I keep thinking of her Alzheimer's or whatever it was as a robbery, an awful diminishment, but maybe it was a kindness too. Maybe it did for her the necessary work of winnowing the harvest of her life, leaving her a small but ample nourishment as her soul started from the world. Maybe memory loss among the aged is only an overflowing into life of the river Lethe, the water of forgetfulness, the good balm of oblivion in which they and all of us bathe at last.

And that's what scares me, isn't it. That, underneath it all, is what grieved and enraged me about my mother's condition. Forgetfulness is what I'm fighting, all right, because forgetfulness is exactly what

I most fear. The oblivion of Lethe holds no balm for me. In that childhood nightmare of floating dead among icy stars, what terrified me
most was not the vision itself but waking and knowing that even the
vision was a lie, that when I died there would be no me among the
stars or anywhere, not ever again, not *ever*. I could stand to lose my
family, my friends, the places I know, even my body, but to lose this
awareness, this precious light, this way of looking at the world—to
lose what I *am*, to know that I will not remember . . . I'm the one un-
reconciled. I'm the one without a ritual or a path.

CHAPTER SIXTEEN

The diagnosis of Alzheimer's or multi-infarct dementia changed little in our relationship with my mother. She didn't mention it—it wasn't clear at all that she remembered it—and we didn't speak of it to her. Who wants to say those words aloud? *Alzheimer's* has a deadly, terrifying ring, and dementia—the broader term—is, if anything, worse. To be demented is to be de-minded, drained of one's inner life. I hate the word. In the last week of my mother's life, as she lay in the intensive care unit of Emanuel Hospital with a respirator pumping her lungs, a cardiologist I liked very much asked us to think about what further life-prolonging measures we wished them to take, given her age, her frailty, and her demented condition. It was a good question, a timely question, but I felt a jolt of rage when he said "demented." He knew my mother's body. What did he know of her mind, beyond the clinical language he had read in her medical history? What did he know of her life?

There really aren't any comfortable names for what happened to my mother and happens to many older persons—at present about four million, according to the National Institute on Aging. More than 10 percent of men and women over sixty-five have probable Alzheimer's or a related condition. Among those eighty-five and older, the figure approaches 50 percent. "Senility," the old generic term for deterioration with age, is used less these days as more specific conditions are identified and diagnosed. I'm glad, because I dislike it too. The very sound of the word is ugly, its connotations grotesque. "Second childishness and mere oblivion," wrote Shakespeare, "Sans teeth, sans eyes, sans taste, sans everything." Yet senility may after all be the fairest and most meaningful term. *Senex*, the Latin root of the word, means simply "old" or "old man." My brother Jim, who came up from California to care for our mother when Marilyn and I went on vacation, was unconvinced that the psychologist's arcane testing and analysis meant very much. "Don't you think maybe she's just *old?*" he asked.

In geology, I've learned, "senile" refers to a landform or landscape that has been worn away nearly to base level at the end of an erosion cycle. It helps me to look at aging that way. Time wears all of us down, and how well we last depends on what we are made of and what our weather has been. Some persist like fresh granite; some dissolve like limestone in the rain. My mother stood like a crag as she advanced into age, but eroded suddenly toward the end. There are many who slump and slide far more rapidly and drastically than she did, falling utterly from their own lives while still alive, beyond the reach of family and friends. In our boundless scientific optimism we like to think we will find a preventative or cure for senile dementia, but it may turn out to be as incurable as mortality. Death is not a point in time but a process of time. There are as many ways to die as there are ways to live, and all of them involve the psyche as well as the physical being.

My mother knew in her years with us that her death was near, and, as I'll relate, I have reason to believe she didn't fear it as much as

I fear mine. What she did fear, palpably, was something else—not the end of life but any major *change* in life. I became aware of this in the spring of 1990, shortly after the diagnosis, when Marilyn and I bought a house in a different Portland neighborhood and prepared to move. We hadn't owned a house before, and we were excited. The new place had a ground-floor bedroom and bathroom for my mother, a spacious upstairs for the two of us with a weaving room for Marilyn, and a detached garage I could convert into a writing study. There were birches, pines, and dogwood trees, rhododendrons front and back, and the house was in a quieter part of town than our neighborhood at the time.

Though my mother seemed agreeable enough when we talked about the move, she did wonder aloud why we needed to change homes. What was wrong with the house we lived in? The issue of owning versus renting didn't seem important to her, and—of course—she pooh-poohed the notion that she needed a ground-floor bedroom. But those doubts she voiced formed only the apparent surface of a deeper fear, a fear that became evident one night in the upstairs hallway. I looked up from the book I was reading in the den to see my mother in her white nightgown hovering in the doorway. I don't know how long she had been there. She was deeply agitated, almost in tears. "Remember," she said, her voice breaking, "I need something to hold on to."

I felt a flash of annoyance that she could say something so irrational—we were moving only a few miles, not around the world. But for once I restrained my irritation. I went to her and held her, my arms around her humped back, her thin bony shoulders against my chest. I tried to comfort her as I might have comforted a child. I told her that she was part of the household, that we were moving together, that I would be there to help her. All the while, I struggled to understand what she had said.

"Mother," I asked her, "what do you need to hold on to?"

"Oh, nothing," she said. "I was only being silly."

"But you weren't being silly. How can I help you if you don't tell me what you're feeling?"

"It's nothing," said my mother, her grayish-green eyes turning away from mine. "*Questo non far niente.*"

My mother spoke her fears only rarely, and to voice one with such open feeling was unprecedented. She may have forgotten, in the solitude of her bedroom, what she had understood in conversation with Marilyn and me a few hours before—that the three of us were moving together. She may have felt abandoned. But I think it's more likely that in her disoriented condition the prospect of another move was simply distressing. It had been only a year and a half since she had left her home and friends in Maine, a little over a year since she had moved from her apartment to live with Marilyn and me, and now it was out the door again to still another place.

Her room in the new house was small, big enough for her bed and not much more. We couldn't enlarge the room but we did open up her view, replacing a window that would have shown her only the patio roof with a sliding glass door that looked out into the trees and flower beds of the backyard. Marilyn arranged all the furniture that would fit as closely as possible to the way it had been in my mother's old bedroom: two beat-up bookcases; a small oak chest of drawers that held her clothing and jewelry; and her nightstand with its familiar lamp, pictures of Sai Baba and my father, and several bowls and boxes containing shells, crystals, and other treasures that had come to her along the way. When Marilyn drove her to the house and helped her into the room, my mother said nothing but sat down on the bed and wept—for joy.

It was to be her last room, her last house. I think she knew that, and I knew it too. It wasn't the perfect place. I'd like for her to have lived out her days in sight and sound of the ocean, the salt breeze on her face, or at least in the country rather than a city. But if it wasn't perfect, it was at least a good place. She had Marilyn's flowers and the birds that came to the feeders to look at, the changing weather and the changing light, the dogwood tree in the window by the kitchen table. She had the tall Douglas firs in the park just north of us she could watch from the living room. She had, when we walked, the alleyway out back with its profusion of dandelions and a redbud tree that reminded her of the South. She had our friendly neighbor Tom, she had Marilyn and me, she had Jim when they spoke on the phone or he visited. She had something to hold on to.

What she didn't have, of course, was a way to hold on to herself. That was what she had cried for the best way she could in the hallway of the old house. That was the fearful need that erupted into words through all the strata of her stoicism and self-reliance, the same need that spoke itself in a less emotional way when she talked about returning to Maine. She was referring to a real place, a real landscape and community of friends, but I believe it was also her way of wishing aloud that she could be herself again. People with Alzheimer's and the similar dementias characteristically want to go "home"—to a place where things made sense, where the compass of reality reliably guided them, where they were capable and useful and secure. The wandering that some of them are prone to may be an attempt to return to this place that is no place. They seek outwardly what they are losing within, trapped in a metaphor of their own unconscious making. The mind, though failing in cognitive function, does not give up its habit of trying to understand the world by connecting likenesses. Memory may become entirely unreliable, telling gaping lies of omission and misconstruing the facts and images it does recall, but the deep tendency to give *form* to memory doesn't die. It still finds analogues, still makes stories and imagines places, still cobbles together a raft of meaning to keep identity afloat in its own chaotic waters.

My mother was too frail to wander, and she probably wouldn't have even if she'd been able. Though it ravaged her memory and caused her much confusion, her condition never progressed to the extreme stage. She never permanently forgot why she couldn't go

home again in either sense. She spoke of Maine only occasionally after the move to our new house. But once in a while she did mention
a certain clock, a ship's clock, that she had left behind somewhere. It
seemed very important to her. I can't say for certain that there wasn't
such a clock, but I know her possessions fairly well and don't recall a
ship's clock among them. I thought it wasn't a good idea to encourage
delusions, and so at first I wasn't responsive when she mentioned the
clock. But eventually, one evening as we had a drink before dinner, I
engaged her about it instead of dismissing it.

"Did you leave the clock in Maine?" I asked.

"I don't remember their name," she said, frowning intently. "But
you take the road *toward* the coast, not all the way there, and then
you turn . . ." She put fingers to her forehead, trying to see the lay of
the land, trying to find the forgotten way. "And then, well . . ."

"What was the clock like?"

"It was brass . . . not heavy but very substantial, you know."

"Was it used on a ship?"

"Oh yes, it's the real McCoy. A real ship's clock."

She sipped her whiskey, looked out the window at the trees in the
park, and was silent for a while. She glanced quickly at me and out the
window again. Then she went on.

"Sometime we might drive over there and maybe we could find it.
You know, *toward* the coast. Not all the way there. It was a good clock,
it rang the bells and kept good time."

CHAPTER SEVENTEEN

I like to see my life as a
seeking, a moving toward, but if I squint my eyes a little it looks like
one long running away. As a boy in Maryland I spent a lot of time
outdoors, like most kids in semirural places. I poked around the little
creek that ran between two sections of our suburb, catching frogs and
water striders, failing to catch minnows, turning over stones to check
for crayfish. Sometimes, alone or with a friend or two, I made an ex-
pedition down to the C & O Canal with its old wooden locks, and beyond the canal to the sloughs and muddy channels of the Potomac
River. Occasionally I went to fish, but more frequently to explore—
to wander the sycamore forests along the polluted river as if I were
the first white person ever to walk there. I dreamed of discovery. After my parents bought an old cabin in northern Virginia when I was
twelve, I spent much time fishing nearby farm ponds for bass and

bluegills or hiking the Blue Ridge. I'd walk for hours or all day, taking in the woods, spying on animals, dreaming westward from that promontory on the Appalachian Trail.

It's no strange thing for a boy to be drawn to nature. We're born wild and with a love for the wild. But if I was attracted to the outdoors by affinity, I now see that I also ran to it for refuge. Trees don't stagger or erupt into argument. The creek runs evenly, always its mild self. The stones expect nothing from you and don't disappoint you. Nature is good company in part because it's no company at all: it's reliably unhuman. Its dangers are limited and comprehensible, or so they were in my natural worlds. If you scraped your knee or got stung by a hornet, at least you knew where you hurt and why. The pain was localized, it was treatable, and it went away.

None of this, of course, was in my awareness at the time. I don't know what was in the mind of that solitary hiker. It's amazing—all those thousands of hours being me as a kid, and I have only the vaguest idea of what I thought or felt. I know what I did but not who I was. But whatever I thought about, it certainly wasn't the troubles between my parents. What was there to think? They hadn't divorced over my mother's affair, in part perhaps because I had begged my father to stay. But if I'd succeeded in keeping them together, I failed at getting them to be happy together. The drinking and fighting went on, worsened if anything, and eventually I went to my father and told him they should separate if they were so unhappy. I think he took my statement as a rejection of him. They didn't separate, not for another four years. I failed at that too.

How much of my passion to go west, I wonder, was an unconscious desire to get as far away from my broken family as I could? I hardly considered Cornell or Wesleyan; it was Reed all the way. And even after I dropped out of Reed—which must have been partly a shot at my parents, who took great pride in my academic success—I never lived in the East again except as a temporary convenience. I didn't see myself as running away. I was being a hippie, transforming the world, in love with the western land—but now, thirty years later, the boy I was sure looks like a boy on the run.

I took up rock climbing and mountaineering with a fierce hunger that far exceeded my skill, continually pressing myself into danger-ous situations. Crags and clouds and glacial brilliance seemed a secret language I was always on the verge of understanding, and I sensed obscurely that the riddle of the mountains somehow was the riddle of myself, that in the wild hills if anywhere I might discover the sure and undivided human being I wanted to be. I climbed in an ecstasy of fearful exhilaration that simplified my confusions and uncertainties into snow and stone, a hand here and a foot there, rising toward the possibility of a clear-cut success that no one, not even I, could dis-pute. And the ease of an exhausted peace.

I've climbed little since injuring my ankle, but recently I went with a friend to Mount Washington in the central Oregon Cascades. The West Ridge, a route I first climbed in 1969, rises steeply at some points and at others narrows to a thin edge, a drop of hundreds of feet on either side. The volcanic rock is frequently loose. My friend led the hard sections, which I followed on the safe end of the rope, but still I struggled awkwardly, overgripping the holds, my knees trem-oring beneath me. As a twenty-one-year-old I climbed that ridge without a rope and without a partner, exulting in my own sufficiency and the blue brilliance of a summer afternoon—and so driven by a demon it scares me now to watch. He had a lot to prove, that young man. And he was lucky.

Back in the city—I shuttled back and forth between Portland and San Francisco—I sought my wholeness in other ways. I took LSD and mescaline and psilocybin, hoping to break through to a compel-ling spiritual enlightenment that would settle my life and give me peace. And I took hard drugs, which seemed safer in a way because they were so much more predictable—and the peace they gave me, though not very spiritual, was thorough while it lasted. I don't like to recall that part of my life, but like it or not there I am: alone in a room or with a using friend, tightening my belt around my upper left arm with the same kind of fearful ecstasy I found in climbing. When the vein stands out I slide in the needle, a little blood rises in the glass syringe, and I squeeze the solution into the vein, into my mind, easing back in the chair as the good stuff waves me away from all uncertainty and sadness.

I shot morphine and heroin for the dull oblivion they brought, but my drug of choice was methamphetamine, good father speed. Its tingling rush delivered me not to oblivion but to a vibrantly intense awareness that was itself a perfect sufficiency—an alertness such as the gods might know, I enthused with fellow users. An alertness, I suspect, closely akin to the seductive mania of the manic-depressive. An alertness requiring neither food nor sleep, clouded only by the progressively troubling question of how to get more speed. And when there is no more, body and mind crash-land together, plunging as deep as they had soared high. All that had glowed with self-meaning now falls inert and meaningless. Color has leached from the world. People are ugly, mechanical, and against you. It's an effort to move. I remember one night in my room in a Portland student house, exhausted and unable to sleep at the end of a three-day run, staring at the glow of a streetlight on the floor and thinking that happiness was there, was just that close, if only I could go to it and touch it. If only it could live in me again.

I wondered, in those deep depressions, if I was crazy. "I'm hopelessly divided from myself," I remember saying again and again one afternoon in a mountain meadow, where—strung out on speed—I had hyperventilated and collapsed on the way with friends to climb a Cascade peak. *Hopelessly divided from myself.* I saw my self-destruction clearly, and it frightened me. At home I spent hours drawing hierarchical diagrams of my broken mind, struggling to understand what was missing, what was wrong. I didn't know what I wanted except to be whole and happy, as whole and happy as I assumed other people were. But how? You either were or you weren't. I was too ashamed to see a psychiatrist. I sealed myself off from my friends behind an air of self-sufficiency, successfully practicing the Daniel Way. How could anyone help me with my troubles, I reasoned, when I didn't understand them myself? I knew only two remedies for my depression. One was to buy more drugs. The other was to venture into the mountains again, where I was lonely but enlivened by cliffs and glaciers, where I could prove myself once more and maybe scare some happiness into my head.

In the early 1970s I lived with friends in San Francisco, dabbled in Zen meditation, hiked and climbed in the Sierra, took drugs and sporadic college courses. I felt pulled in a thousand directions. Posters on storefronts and telephone poles announced encounter groups, political rallies, environmental causes, religious sects. Each one seemed a door behind which people were engaged in something authentic, and I was walking the hallway unable or unwilling to knock. I studied classical guitar, then dropped it when I realized it would take years to develop the skill I wanted right away. It had been in my mind since childhood that maybe I could write, but the few lines I forced out seemed merely contemptible. They confirmed what I'd known all along—I had nothing to write about. I had dropped out of college in order to live, but without my student identity I didn't know *how* to live except by drifting aimlessly from one job or interest to another.

There was no further west I could go. I had fled to land's end, to the very brink of the abyss I had imagined as a little boy. It came close to swallowing me. And even at the far edge of America, it turned out, I couldn't shake off the family pain that had set me in motion in the first place. My parents had both done well since their separation. My father had stopped drinking and launched a successful civic life in Springfield, Missouri. My mother had set out on her travels and her quest. They corresponded and had patched together a relationship at a distance. In the summer of 1971 they each came to Berkeley to see their granddaughter Heather, who had been born to my brother and his wife the fall before. The visit went fine for a couple of days, but then—of course—it went to hell. In the parking lot at Candlestick Park, after a Giants game, my mother wanted us to go to a party a friend of mine was throwing, my father didn't want to, and in a flash they were wrangling—he with his feelings hurt because no one respected his wishes, she alternately soothing and berating him, and me in the middle where I'd always been. I wanted them to be happy, I wanted to please them, I felt somehow to blame for the terrible discord when all had been fine just a minute ago.

I think it was the next evening, in the shabby duplex I was renting in Berkeley, that I blew up at my mother. I don't remember exactly what I said, but I know it erupted out of me. *Why do you have to come here from thousands of miles away and start this shit all over? Don't you think I had enough of it as a kid? Why do you and Franz do this? Why?*

My mother, taken aback and defensive, said something like "I didn't know you felt so strongly." And I suppose she didn't, since all my life I had been so successful in burying my feelings. But she did know, of course she knew. She knew very well how hard our family life had been on all of us, she wanted to make it right somehow, she thought this get-together would be a step in that direction, and she too was frustrated and regretful. My outburst must have raised up all of that, a load of thwarted love drenched in guilt.

They left the Bay Area soon, and I never saw them together again. My father died in 1976, and though we were on good terms in his last years, we visited infrequently and never found a way to talk about our feelings. I don't think either of us looked for one. My resentments toward him were buried so deeply beneath my love and admiration that I scarcely knew they existed. And even if I had been able to express them, I would have been afraid of hurting him and unsettling his hard-won sobriety. My father—the stirring orator, the tough strike leader—was emotionally a very vulnerable man. He carried some enormous painfulness within him, some ruined cathedral that no one, not even he, could enter. He could only shore it up with sad eyes and silences, and the many who were drawn to him, me included, helped him keep it safe. Talking baseball and Beethoven was as close to intimacy as we got.

I did get closer to my mother, but we never entered the dialogue that my explosion in Berkeley might have made possible. We communicated by letter mostly, and in hers she tended to write of our family troubles in terms of her religious ideas. She wrote that all of us were worthy souls struggling under the necessary burden of our personalities, the particular burdens each of us had entered the world to bear. That we loved one another deeply, purely, despite the deformations of personhood. That our strife and griefs all served to help us know ourselves, which is the soul's work in the world. It all seemed apt enough, right enough, but now when I look at those letters I'm struck by how general those terms *love* and *burden* and *personality* seem. I can't help thinking that my mother needed vessels, large and sturdy vessels, to hold harmless the many hot pains of her marriage, and in her spiritual beliefs she found those vessels.

Few of my letters to her survive, but I'm sure I wrote less about family matters than she did, and in terms no less general. I wish I could have—wish I *would* have—told my mother in a controlled way the strong feelings she both knew and didn't know I had. I wish I would have said, *You hurt me. You and Franz hurt me. You fought the whole time I was growing up, and it wasn't all his fault. It was your fault too.* I wish I could have found a way to say that. Not to revile her. Not to punish her. More than anything, to forgive her.

For many years she was probably capable of hearing that and responding to it. But by the time I became capable of saying it, she was losing her memory and clarity of thought. It would only have troubled her, unfairly clouded her mind with things she could not fully understand or deal with. And of course it's only now, a year and a half past her death, two decades past my father's, that I'm really capable of saying it, and saying it only to a sheet of paper. After running for all those years I double back now when everyone's gone, late as usual, late to my parents' lives and late to my own, I poke and worry through what I can find and make this vessel to hold it.

CHAPTER EIGHTEEN

I don't know why I should be tired," I can hear my mother saying. "I haven't *done* anything."

It runs through my mind like a tune that won't stop playing. She's lying on her bed as she says it, her head propped on pillows, or maybe sitting in the living room with a book or magazine in her hands. There's a certain laugh in her voice as she says *do* or *done*—a guilty, self-mocking laugh, as if she were derelict for not being busy, for spending her days eating meals, drinking tea, and reading. She doesn't need a bath, she says, she hasn't *done* anything. She really oughtn't to be hungry. What has she done all day to work up an appetite? It seemed almost as though she felt she didn't deserve to exist because she didn't do anything with her life.

When I had time and she was willing, we took short walks together. The exercise was good for her, I wanted her to keep in contact with the air and odors of the outdoors, and a walk was a break in her oppressively restful day. Sometimes we drove to a nearby park, where forsythias might be blooming in spring or maples turning in the fall, but usually we didn't drive. In the old house, when she was stronger, we walked around our home block—and sometimes an extra block or two if she was up to it—pausing to admire flower beds, shapely Victorian houses, the majestic copper beech on Hancock Street that was my mother's favorite tree. She leaned heavily on my arm, her wooden cane in her other hand, and every half block or so she stopped and had me change sides. She shuffled along in her sure-footed way, breathing rapidly, her white head bowed. Her circulation was poor—poorer than I knew—due to age and to heart valve damage from a childhood bout with rheumatic fever. Her lungs, like her feet, tended to collect fluid.

In our new neighborhood we would sometimes drive a few blocks to the University of Portland campus and walk there, usually to a bench that looks off the bluff to the Willamette River, which was likely to be busy with tugs and pleasure boats. The Swan Island shipyard would have a freighter or tanker in for repairs, maybe two or three. My mother loved ships and boats of all kinds, but I always sensed something uncertain, something unresolved in her attention, when we watched from the bench. I don't think she ever grasped the linkage of waterways, Willamette to Columbia to Pacific, so she may not have understood what big ships were doing in front of her. When I glanced at her face it looked as though she didn't quite know what she was seeing—as if she didn't truly believe that the ships were ships, as if she were playing along with the imposture only for me.

Walking was labor for my mother, harder and harder the longer she lived. When we returned she would be ready to lie down for a while or sit for a long time with a mug of tea. But though it taxed her physically, walking didn't make her feel useful. It wasn't *doing* something. We tried to involve her in the chores of the household, but because of her frailty there was little she could effectively do. For a while she was able to set the table for dinner, but before long it became too much effort for her, too many trips between table and kitchen with plates and silver and glasses, her balance precarious without her cane. Folding laundry was the only job she could consistently do. Marilyn or I would set a full basket by her chair in the living room, and by and by she sorted napkins and washcloths and dish towels into neat stacks on the footstool in front of her. Some days she would put off the folding for a while—mostly, I suspected, because it raised her spirits to have the prospect of work ahead of her. "I'll be back," she would say, shuffling into her bedroom. "I've got that basket of laundry to do." For me, the laundry became a rough barometer of my mother's health. If a load sat unfolded for more than a few hours, it probably meant that she was feeling poorly and I should try to find out what was going on.

When I had produce that needed preparation for cooking, I always asked my mother if she would like to help with it, and I can't remember that she ever declined. She would sit leaning forward at the oak kitchen table, a dish towel in her lap and concentration on her face, shelling peas or snapping beans or hulling strawberries or shucking corn. "Oh," she would say, "what fine red berries." Or "This corn looks *terribly* good." James Hillman has said that the fingers are the soul's means of involving itself in matter, of enacting its desires among the things of the world. And the connection, once opened, works both ways: the soul takes nourishment through the fingers even as it uses them to express itself. As she bent to her work, my mother was connected to old rhythms, irreducible truths. In those intervals of shucking and hulling she felt herself a contributing member of the household, redeemed from marginality. She belonged.

Back in my LSD days I was fond of saying that the purpose of existence is simply to be. What we do, I believed, doesn't matter much; that we are is everything. I thought scornfully of jobs and careers as nothing but servitude exchanged for money, blinders that obscured the shining truth of being. The world was perfect, if only we would pause from our busyness long enough to see it. Real fulfillment could occur only outside of what one did for a living. I had no idea what work actually was and how badly I needed it, as I drifted from place to place and job to job, looking for enlightenment beyond the horizon, my hands, except while climbing, almost as empty as my mother's in her last years. I revered freedom and a simplistic idea of love. What I wanted, and took years to find, was a necessary task to which I could bend myself.

My mother's life had been replete with meaningful work: her mission in the labor movement, the raising of children, the explorations of her quest for the Self, and lesser tasks along the way—learning Serbo-Croatian, making tile art from pieces of sea-smoothed glass, editing a friend's manuscript on Iran under the Shah, studying Haitian culture. But in her last years that energetic directedness melted away, along with her memory. Now and again as I straightened the books and papers on her bed I would find a note she had penned in a margin or on a scrap of wastepaper, a self-exhortation: *Get paper clips etc. Laurens van der Post book on Jung. Write Jim* . . . She missed that sense of engaged activity that had defined her, she wanted it back, but she never did retrieve it.

Like many with Alzheimer's or other dementias, my mother had trouble executing simple sequences that the rest of us take for granted. When she was done snapping beans, for instance, there would be bean ends among the beans and beans among the bean ends. She got fouled up stringing popcorn and cranberries at Christmas. She had to concentrate while dressing to put her clothes on in the right order. When she wrote checks at the beginning of the month—for her Medicare supplement insurance, her VISA account, her share of household expenses, and so on—I had to cue her at each step of the process: the date, the payee, the numerical amount, the written amount, her signature. Sometimes before writing the check she recorded it in the register, so she wouldn't forget.

Then she would pause, staring at the checkbook and the pen in her hand, and I would have to remind her to write the check itself, telling her the date that she had just written in the register. It was a long and tedious process for both of us. I could have made out the checks my-self—we had a joint account—but I wanted her to retain as much control of her own affairs as she could. I thought it was good for her. Now I wonder if I wasn't inflicting a form of torture.

That trouble with sequences, along with her memory loss, made it impossible for my mother to pursue any kind of sustained research, any activity much more complicated than folding laundry. But something else was missing, too. My mother had a great many friends and relatives and received letters from most of them, but af-ter her first year with us she almost never answered the letters. This puzzled and grieved me for a long time. An active correspondence was work she *could do,* I thought, work that could ease her isolation and help sustain her. She had been a letter writer her entire life, and she was still capable of writing. The lettering was labored, the lines of her clear cursive sometimes inked over two or three times, as if she didn't trust that the pen was making an impression on the page. But she could write, and in a voice recognizably hers. Her sister Adelaide received this postal card, a rarity, in 1991:

If this beat-up card reaches you
let me know. I am mostly very well.
I go nowhere, hardly; to the
Farmers' Market, across the
Willamette River, with John.
Marilyn is exhausted tonight,
from her full-time job. John is
working on his book of essays.
I just live, but glad to be alive.
    Love always
    Zilla

She wrote a few others, but the letters and cards mostly piled up on her nightstand. Gradually they mixed with her books and magazines, were rediscovered and read anew a month or six months later, and set aside once again. She wanted and intended to answer—"I *must* write the Gorskis," she would say as she read their letter. Her little card file of addresses was by her bed, and we made sure she had pads and envelopes and even stamps handy. I gave her a clipboard for writing in bed. She had time—God knows she had time. But she didn't write. Something in her had washed out, some canyon had formed between desire and action. I know that in the simplifying lens of her dementia, most things not physically present were essentially unreal to her. She saw the last leaf on the dogwood tree, but after it fell she could scarcely remember it. It may be that when she set herself to write she simply could not bring into focus the individual she was addressing, though that person's letter was before her. It amazes me—and frightens me now—how far the mind leaps and how broadly it casts its net in faithfully performing, for most of us, the simplest tasks of day-to-day doing.

Had my mother's will weathered away? Not the bulldog will that got her through her arduous walks with me but some less physical, more subtle form of it? She wanted to write, intended to write; maybe she simply could not will her desire and purpose into fulfillment. Maybe volition was not there. And what *is* volition? What spurs us into the actions of a lifetime, and then, at some point in some of us, quits? I know that something as quickly desired and accomplished as getting up from a chair often took my mother many minutes, and not only because of her physical weakness. Many times I watched her secure her purse strap across her shoulder, lean forward in her chair, look around, look at her lap, sit back a little, look around, start forward, scratch her shoulder, look at her lap, look out the window, sit back, sit forward . . . It may have been simple distraction that delayed her, but I got the distinct impression that distraction was invading in the absence of will.

But probably it was something even deeper and more essential than will that failed. Alzheimer's dissolves the very core of an individual: the self, the identity. Maybe my mother's difficulty was not in bringing to mind her correspondent but in bringing to mind her own self. It's possible that "I go nowhere" and "I just live," along with a very few particulars, were the fullest accounts of herself that she was able to give. Writing a letter, like writing this book, is an act of mythologizing, an attempt to make from life lived a meaning that another might understand. But if the life makes little meaningful sense to the one who is living it, if life is essentially changeless, eventless, a vagueness unavailable to words . . . Was my mother's silence an inability to reflect? Or was there in her own inward view no substance, no firm matter of experience, no landscape of being to receive reflection and return it?

CHAPTER NINETEEN

Today I told my psychologist about a dream in which a dark-haired woman led me down a winding staircase—or I tried to tell her, but my psychologist was interested in something else. The dream began with two men arguing nearby while I dozed on a park bench. Then the woman came along and led me down the stairs, which seemed to me the important part. She had some work for me, and I wanted to find out what it was.

"But who are those two men?" my psychologist asked. "What are they arguing about?"

I thought about it—a bit irritably—and couldn't come up with anything. Just two guys arguing. Bit players, I told her. Bums probably. But they've been in my head all day and half the night, and I just realized I know them both. And I know what they were arguing about.

Bob Bourgeois will sometimes wake with a thought to prune the birches or split firewood or fix the leak in the washing machine, and he'll follow that thought right into the heart of the new day. It's easy to like Bob. He ruffs the fur of friendly dogs, he makes small talk with salesclerks. He greets shuffling geezers he passes on the sidewalk, causing them to light a smile and nod and mumble good day. Bob is pleasant. He's decent, he's cheerful, and the work he does he does pretty well.

The trouble is, there isn't a lot of depth to him. He hasn't earned his happy glow; he was born with it. He's a smiling cipher. He's comfortable being like everyone else, just another citizen in the grocery line, uncomplaining even when the checker yaks too long with customers ahead of him. He glides along on his even keel, soaking up sunshine, soaking up rain, soaking up anything that comes his way. He'll never be anything more than what he is, and he doesn't care. "I just live" could be his motto. "Hi, I'm Bob. I'm not going anywhere." Bob doesn't think very much. The truth is, he isn't very smart.

At least that's how the Inspector would have it. And it's the Inspector, as usual, who has my ear at 2:16 in the morning as I sit in my bathrobe at the kitchen table unable to sleep, as usual, the left side of my back hurting, as usual, a bowl of shredded wheat in front of me to ease the gnawing in my gut and settle my nervous mind. The Inspector may think *too* much, he acknowledges that, but he points out that a man in his position inevitably *will* think, and if he thinks excessively it is only a sign of his caring. *Someone* has to examine life lived. *Someone* must exert the discipline to stay awake and watchful, alert to the nuances. *Someone* must be willing to make the necessary judgments: *You should have behaved differently. Don't be so satisfied. How poor of you. Your work is flawed. You'll have to do better.*

And someone has to say, *You were selfish. You did not attend to her as she deserved. She gave birth to you, she raised you, and when she herself was a child in the last years of her life, you failed her.*

No one failed her, Bob says back. (Or is it me saying it back?) Nothing failed her except her body, her broken-down body of eighty-four years. Bob misses her. He mourns her. But when he thinks about her now, he's as likely to smile as to cry. She lived a good long life, after all. She lived most of it on her own terms. She did more than most people do. And she died pretty easily in the end, not in great pain.

Easily? snaps the Inspector. *What about the nightmare she had to endure in intensive care? And why were you out of the house when she fell? Why did you leave her alone so often? Why didn't you spend more time with her? Why did you make her feel unwanted in your home?*

She *didn't* feel unwanted, Bob insists. She said herself this house had been a real haven for her. She said she was lucky . . .

The Inspector only scowls at such evasion. He might as well be arguing with a child. *He* knows where responsibility resides, and he knows it is his duty to point it out. Responsibility must not be glossed over, and neither should pain. Pain must be felt. It must be contained and endured with dignity. With discipline and vigilance. The Inspector regrets that he has lost his digestion, but duty will exact its costs. He would like to get over his insomnia, but he suspects that ordinary sleep will always be an elusive thing for someone of his acuity and caring. Ordinary sleep is for the Bob Bourgeoises of the world. And depression? Of course the Inspector is depressed. Life is nothing trivial and nothing easy. To live is to be injured. Joy is possible in moments, perhaps, but happiness? Any fool can be happy, because any fool can fool himself.

Privilege inevitably has a price. And it *is* a privilege, the Inspector insists, to be night magistrate of the province. To be the only one awake in the house, likely the only one on the block, just him and the occasional teenager cruising slowly on Princeton Street with muffled bass beats thudding from his car. Of course it's a privilege. The province may be small, a limited territory, but who knows it as intimately as the Inspector? Who else has spent such time with it? Who else can nod and smile and bite his lip and shake his head so knowledgeably? Who else is capable of such caring? And who else, the Inspector points out with some pride, can look upon this province in the middle of the night and know it to be his, all his, as long as he shall live?

Bob and the Inspector hardly recognize that the other exists. They share nothing of temperament or inclination. Bob is a man of action and an optimist; the Inspector is a thinker, a brooder. Bob's a morning person. The Inspector begins to wake at dusk, with the owls. Bob spends little time in the past, the Inspector little in the present. They both drink, but differently. Bob quaffs a pint or two with friends, shares a bottle of wine with his wife. The Inspector drinks with himself. He likes the bite of whiskey, its measured burn, the confirmation of its glow. He lets the liquor cast his province in an amber afterlight, an aura that softens his criticisms—he knows that sometimes he's too harsh—and lightens his heart without impairing his watchfulness. He drinks not exactly to ease his pain, but because his pain, his position, entitles him to drink.

When they do encounter each other, Bob is noticeably less relaxed than he is in other company. He doesn't understand the Inspector and admits that he doesn't care for him. The Inspector, for his part, is abrupt and out of sorts. He's embarrassed to be seen with Bob. The boy is the only reason they meet at all. The boy is all they have in common now, and they disagree sharply about him. That's what they were arguing about, the boy asleep on the bench. The Inspector, you see, is terribly protective. He's a solitary man, an aging, childless man, and the boy means everything to him. It's for the boy, at heart, that he keeps his careful vigil, enduring the sleeplessness and knotted stomach that come with it like wounds of war. He wants the boy to live exactly as he's always lived, safely home in the province, undisturbed. The boy has had a painful childhood, and the Inspector feels he needs time to heal. He is delicate, unformed. To change his circumstances might only hurt him more.

Bob thinks those ideas are weird. He loves the boy but doesn't think he needs protection, at least not the way the Inspector does.

How can you protect him from life? And why would you want to? Is the Inspector looking out for the boy, Bob wonders, or for himself? If he cares so much about the boy, why does he keep him so far away, all the way back in what he calls his province? It isn't natural. It's not where the boy belongs anymore. Everyone's had some pain in his life—all the more reason the boy should get away. He ought to pack his knapsack, Bob believes. He ought to strap it to his skinny shoulders and come on out to Oregon.

CHAPTER TWENTY

I still argue with myself about my mother. Why should it have been so hard to care for her? She didn't have an advanced dementia, after all. In a bedrock way she knew who I was, who Marilyn was, who she was. She recognized the faces, though often she couldn't recall the names, of our friends. She didn't wander, didn't become belligerent, didn't fritter her money (which in any case amounted only to the six hundred and something a month she received from Social Security). She wasn't forthcoming in conversation but spoke well—so well it was hard for many who met her to believe she had a mental deficit at all. She could read. She was not confined to bed or a wheelchair. She couldn't cook but could feed herself. She did not require constant supervision or care. And when we lucked into the treatment half of a government study called the Medicare Alzheimer's Project, some of the care she did need—help with bathing and grooming, straightening her room, and so on—was provided by a nurse, Patty, who came for a few hours two or three times a week and became my mother's good friend.

So what was it? What made me mutter to myself, what made me yell or cry in the other room, what made me hide in irritable silence behind the morning paper? It was no one thing, no one task—not making meals or checking her blood pressure or driving her back and forth to doctor or dentist or Sai Baba group. More than what I did, it was what I didn't do. It was feeling that I should take her out to lunch, for an ice cream cone, for a drive in the country, feeling I owed her those things more often than I gave them. It was feeling that I should spend more time with her, time not directed to matters of her health or feeding—that I should sit in her bedroom and let her talk to me, if she would, and talk to her with no purpose in mind, to see if between us we might break out of the well-worn ruts of our daily exchanges about the quality of the breakfast fruit, the names of the birds, whether she had taken her morning medicines, and did she feel like a walk that day.

For Marilyn the chief daily irritant was my mother's bad hearing, the continual need to repeat herself in slow, loud, carefully enunciated syllables. For me it was my mother's eyes. The eyes whose gaze I felt on my back whenever I stood cooking at the stove or washing the pots and pans. The eyes that glanced away quickly, back to her plate or her reading, when I looked up from my newspaper. The eyes raised just enough to observe when I took a bite of French toast, when I took a sip of coffee, when I raised the blue cloth napkin to my face. When my mother and I were in the same room, I never felt free of those eyes. If I looked out the window she looked out. When I took another bite of breakfast she did too. At times I felt the rageful frustration of a kid in the copycat game, his every action mimed relentlessly by a friend.

It wasn't that my mother didn't know how to eat without having me or someone present, but the blankness inside her was extensive enough that she used a model when a model was there. The simple

daily acts that most of us accomplish automatically weren't so auto-
matic for my mother. She was lucky, and we were lucky, that her
breakdown didn't progress further than it did. People with advanced
Alzheimer's often lose the ability to feed themselves altogether.
Plaques and nerve tangles in the brain scramble the intended movement—lifting fork to mouth, say—into a different one: scratching
an ear, reaching for a purse. Eventually, if the individual lives long
enough, there may be no outward motor activity at all, only the re-
flexive ability to swallow when food is placed in the mouth. And
eventually not even that.

My mother lived out her life in an in-between state, partly enfee-
bled and partly quite capable. She was well enough to miss and desire
the active life of her past, but not well enough to resume it. She
wanted to go to poetry readings, but afterward she complained that
she hadn't heard a thing and the seat had been uncomfortable. Mov-
ies were a little more successful—especially the seats—but it was a
laborious trek for Marilyn and me to shepherd her through the
crowded lobby and along the sloping dark aisles of the theater. Sometimes she leaned so heavily on my arm I was half carrying her. The
best excursions I made with her were to the farmers' market on Sauvies Island in the Columbia, where my mother would sit in a chair
apparently enjoying the quiet hubbub, watching with a smile as I
drifted among the produce stalls filling a basket. Marilyn sometimes
took her to Holladay Market in northeast Portland, where they
would have *caffè lattes* and some pieces of bittersweet chocolate, for
which they shared a passion. (My mother earned many credits in
Marilyn's heart when she announced one day that eating chocolate
was essential because it "grounded" her.)

Our trips to the coast were generally successful, too. A few times
a year the three of us would drive to Oceanside and take a room
where my mom could gaze at the gray or shining Pacific, the moonlit
Pacific, the breakers rolling in from chartless reaches, the veering
and crying gulls. I think she enjoyed that—surely she enjoyed it—

but those trips exhausted her, too. Walking down to the water to wet her feet required both Marilyn and me, one on each arm. As at home, my mother spent most of those weekends sleeping and reading. And when she looked at the sea—this other sea, this sea of final distances where the sun doesn't rise but only goes down—I sometimes thought I saw in her face the same disconnection, the same perceptual disbelief, that showed when she stared at the Swan Island tugs and freighters.

One of our hottest altercations occurred at the coast. The three of us, in my mother's Dodge—which Marilyn and I had bought from her by taking over the payments—pulled in to a state park and stopped by a curb where my mother would have a sea view while Marilyn and I walked a few minutes. When we came back she was livid.

"*John Daniel,*" she exploded. "Do not ever again leave me stranded in my own car without the keys."

"Mother," I said, "what happened?"

"Someone . . . a vehicle needed to get by . . ."

"Well, they must have *got* by. What was it, a motor home?"

"He got by with great difficulty. You were extremely inconsiderate. Don't ever again—"

"Jesus, Mother, you don't *drive* anymore."

"This is *my car.*"

I was so mad I clammed up, sulking like a reprimanded child as I drove us on to the motel. Silently I was writing her out of my life and welcoming her to drive her goddamn car off a cliff. My mother sulked in the passenger seat. Marilyn, in back, wove a peace between us once we both had cooled off a little, and the rest of the weekend went fine.

I don't know what happened in that parking lot, but I do know that my mother from time to time was prone to delusions. Her poor hearing contributed to these, along with the bitter fact that she was no longer in control of her life. When Marilyn and I tried to talk to each other at dinner, not speaking up for my mother's benefit, she was sure at times that we were talking about her, making some decision without consulting her. We weren't—though of course we were struggling with decisions all the time outside her presence, decisions about how to deal with her incontinence, how to relieve her boredom, how to find a good and affordable caregiver so that we could get away on our own for a while. My mother was wrong in the particular instance but right in the general fact.

Other delusions were more severe. One morning as I passed her door at the foot of the stairs, I saw her sitting in her nightgown on the edge of her bed, arms folded across her belly, rocking back and forth. She clearly was in some pain.

"What's wrong?" I asked.

"It's you," she said after a while.

"What do you mean? What's me?"

I sat down in the wicker chair in the corner of the room. She rocked on the bed, almost in tears.

Finally she said, "You're the one who gives them to me. You make me take them."

She meant, of course, her pills—the diuretic, the blood pressure pill, the antibiotic against urinary infections, the children's aspirin to thin her blood against clots—the pills whose sizes and colors she clearly saw but whose purposes she could never remember for more than a few seconds at a time and probably didn't believe in. The routine we went through every morning, the forced ritual that had come to symbolize for both of us the deterioration of her body and the failure of her freedom. I was the one who made her take them, who tracked her down if she left them on the breakfast table, and the cramps of constipation or indigestion that were hurting her this morning she believed to be the work of the pills. My mother thought I was poisoning her. I came near tears myself as I explained and explained to her, wondering all the while how long she'd been awake in the thrall of that idea, how many other mornings she might have thought it but held it unvoiced.

Another time she asked me, at lunch I think, "How is it back there? Your little house."

"My house?"

"You know, where you live back there."

"Mother, that's just where I *write*."

"Oh, I know that," she said quickly, but the moment before she hadn't known it. I took her out to see my garage-turned-study with its cluttered walnut desk, its puke-green carpet, its workbench layered with books and papers. No bed, I wanted her to see, and she did. But for how long did she understand? Staircases had become too much for her, and so she never saw the upper floor where Marilyn and I slept, where Marilyn did her weaving, where we read and watched TV. We described it to her, reminded her of what she could not see, but we never knew for sure just what she did see, we never knew how the house and its occupants mapped themselves in her mind.

Once in our first few months in the new house, Marilyn was unpacking extra linens into a closet in the hall outside my mom's bedroom. After a while, through the open door, she heard these words: "I know you and John are having trouble, and I'm sorry you have to leave. I wish you well." My mother's demeanor was grave. Marilyn, smiling, explained that we weren't having trouble, that she was unpacking, not packing, and that it was only a box of spare linens. My mother nodded, smiled without conviction, maybe convinced and maybe not.

Afterward Marilyn wondered if my mother's delusion expressed an unconscious wish. They had always gotten on well, often beautifully and deeply well, since the moment they first met in Marilyn's living room in 1982, when my mother, visiting from Maine, walked in and gave her a great hug before saying a word. But a household of husband and wife and mother is bound to know some tension, even in the best of circumstances. How could ours not? With or without delusions, a triangle is a triangle.

It was hardest when Marilyn and I went out for the evening. My mother was at times up to being a good sport about it, at others only capable of a grim acceptance. I remember all too clearly the way her eyes would frown when I told her we were going out for dinner and a movie, the way she wouldn't look at me as I reminded her that her dinner would be on the kitchen table, her tea in the steel thermos. I learned never to tell her until very late in the afternoon—if I told her earlier she might forget, and we'd have to go through the same little crisis all over again, or if she remembered she was likely to dwell for hours in a gloomy funk. I put off entering her room until I absolutely had to, dithering outside the door, finally forcing the breach. I hated it. And coming home was sometimes worse, because my mother— a night owl, like me—would rarely be asleep for the night. She'd be reading in bed, maybe dozing with her mouth open, and depending on what had passed through her mind in the time we were gone she might welcome us cheerily when we stopped by her room, or she might acknowledge us soberly, or she might snap, "I've been waiting here for *hours.*" And she had been.

CHAPTER TWENTY-ONE

I drew a picture when my mother died. Six strokes in red watercolor, a child waving good-bye. He is waving toward the right, one arm outstretched, upraised, the other at his side. The finality is what I was feeling. It made a child of me, a small child filled with sadness. *Good-bye.* I knew I would never hold again her veined and purpled hand, never touch her white hair, never feel the weight of her on my arm as we walked. All that is ashes now, and what isn't ashes rose into air and sky, into the ready emptiness of wind. And yet she lives. She is here as I write, interfused with what I am, strangely in me and around me. She is more present in this moment than anything I know. It's she who stirred my memory, and she whom memory bears forth.

But the other one. The other one who died, the one who never lived—how can I say good-bye to the one I never knew? A parent is supposed to die; a child is supposed to live. I knew only the earliest light my child sent before itself, the first wan light that comes to snowy fields before the break of day. *I feel as though I'm carrying a little ball of light*—and how the world slowed, how *I* slowed when Marilyn said that, how her face shone and the moment shone. The light of entrance to the world. A light all new to me. The light of yes.

I wanted what everyone must want. I wanted to see her face, I wanted to see his face—me and Marilyn stirred loose from ourselves, everything we are somehow swirled together like birds in a wind and formed again. To see that face, to welcome its cheeks and red scrunched brow, to welcome the gift that had been borne so far, to honor it from the tips of its tiny toes to the hairs of its head . . . To hold it to me, light and squalling—nothing to search for, nothing to be found, nothing like this unsure scratching at the page, this nearsighted groping, but *here*, achieved, alive. And knowing it good, knowing *this that has come of us is good.*

I wanted him to crawl and climb. I wanted her to shout, to run, to laugh in the rain so that I would laugh, cry so that I would cry. I wanted him to dash and tumble, to roll on the ground, I wanted his thin limbs to grow. I wanted to hear the syllables she would croon, the words she would speak, the words I would speak back to her. I wanted some best part of me to bound forth smiling, press footprints into frosted grass, saunter beneath arching trees and know the company of every rock and soul it met. I wanted a part of me to unfold that only she or he could have touched, I wanted to bloom this once like a century plant, to shower forth in a bright new body. I wanted to look into the clear eyes of my child. Not to seek my reflection there but to enter those eyes and discover my place to die.

How do I say good-bye? I knew the earliest light and only the light. Memory has nothing with which to conduct its ceremony—no image, no touch of hands, no slightest cry. Of my gone brother George I have photographs, accounts in my parents' letters, the living memories of my aunt and cousin. But of the one who was not

born there is only a slow pale shape rising from the depths, rising toward me, almost resolving into a form I recognize but not yet
formed, a face but not a face. It rises, wavering, the face of nothing
and of everything. It shimmers suspended on the verge of being and
wavers into formless light again, a sheen of motion, a stirring in the
clear dark sea that conceived it.

CHAPTER TWENTY-TWO

T he cat showed up our first summer in the new house. Suddenly she was hanging around in back, rubbing up against the picnic table, curled in the beds between rhododendrons. She gave insistent chirpish cries like a bird. She didn't mind that we didn't feed her or invite her in—she stayed anyway. For a while we fancied that she liked us, but what she really cared for was the place, a fact we learned when a girl knocked one evening looking for her cat. The girl had grown up in our house; we had bought it from her parents. The cat had lived all seven of its years in and around the house, and now was with the girl elsewhere in the neighborhood—or had been. The cat kept returning to her old and only home, and after a few days we and the girl agreed that she was ours.

She was, and is, a black-and-tan tabby with a nervous disposition. The three of us never came up with a better name for her than Cat or

Kitty; when the vet had to have a name for his files, I called her Spook, short for Spookus Maximus or Spooky Spookissima. She is wary of strangers, starts at small noises, and does neurotic things like dash up the stairs as you walk down or down as you walk up. Turns up her nose at fish. Won't allow her front paws to be touched. And will not settle down when stroked but presses her face to your fingers in a purring agitation, demanding more and more, chirping birdlike all the while.

Puss, my mother called her. "Where's Puss?" she'd want to know, several times a day. She loved to watch the cat grooming herself— licking a paw and rubbing it across her ear, or licking her chest while propped indecorously in the easy chair, her buff-and-white under- region on general display. And she liked the way the Spooky One stretched after sleeping, reaching far forward with her front paws, her rear end high and the rest of her tapering low to the rug, as if she were performing some act of wild obeisance. And she delighted to see the cat smacking her chops as she sauntered through the kitchen af- ter breakfast.

But most of all it was the cat's tail that entranced my mother, her gray and black and brown-shaded tail that she almost never, while awake, held entirely still. Even when the cat and most of its tail lay flat on the floor, the tip, the last two inches, would be upraised and stirring, gently turning and flicking like a self-willed creature of its own. My mother would point it out to anyone who might be around, smiling her most delighted smile.

"It's a *semaphore,*" she exclaimed one afternoon. We were out back, enjoying an easy wind that stirred the hanging branchlets of the birches. The cat was sprawled on the concrete between Marilyn and my mother, the drifting tail-tip its only sign of life.

"What does it say?" I asked her.

She smiled steadily, captivated. "My dear," she said after a while, "it says what words cannot."

This time, I thought, it wasn't the blankness inside her covering for itself by cutting off conversation. This was one of those occasions when she spoke not from absence but from intense presence, an untranslatable richness, a seeing not diminished by her age but empowered by it. I suddenly remembered a morning twenty-five years in the past at Reed College when I had glanced down at wet yellow leaves on a concrete walkway, glowing in the rainy light, and suddenly knew them to be *signs.* Not symbols or types but signs, tokens of the tao, the spirit, the unspeakable meaning within and behind all things. I didn't know their meaning but felt it, understood it with my body. I almost rose off the walkway in my joy.

With that in mind I smiled at my mother and nodded, holding her eyes for a moment in mine.

The cat gave other signs, some of them annoying and some enchanting. Some evenings after dinner I would read aloud to my mother in the living room. Marilyn would join us if she felt like it; more often she would go to her weaving or a hot bath. We began with *Huckleberry Finn,* and from there took a vagrant path through *Moby Dick* and Joseph Conrad, P. G. Wodehouse, many weeks with the *Norton Anthology of Poetry,* J. R. R. Tolkien and Isak Dinesen, back to Twain for *Life on the Mississippi,* and on like that. My mother seemed to enjoy it all. She had always loved literature—she had been an English major at Vassar, and her father had wanted her to be a professor. It must have been a pleasure to relax and let the language come to her instead of having to pick it off the silent page, line after line, with her dogged, overworked eyes. She drank coffee as she listened, watching me like an attentive child, now and then asking to hear a sentence or short passage again.

The cat, it turned out, enjoyed the readings too. We couldn't predict when she would show up—she seemed to like e. e. cummings as well as Tennyson, Melville no more than Wodehouse—but when the mood struck her she would pad into the living room from upstairs or downstairs, hop into my lap, and proceed to rub herself all over me, turning in circles and purring loudly between me and the book I was trying to read, fairly intoxicated with pleasure. This delighted my mother greatly and me a little less, since managing cat and *Moby Dick* simultaneously could be a little tricky, but I hated to shoo her off. My readings rarely elicit such adoration. All we could figure was that my voice, a reasonably sonorous baritone, must have tickled the cat's nerves at precisely the right frequency.

On other evenings the cat attended the reading with a less passionate interest. She might lie on her side in the middle of the room, queen of the carpet, licking a paw and languidly taking in the verse or prose of the hour. Or if we were lucky, she might decide that the evening outdoors was of more interest than anything in the living room. She would hop to a chest beneath the window, slip between the closed, cream-colored drapes, and stare out from the sill, invisible to us except for her tail with its roving semaphore tip. When she treated us to this show, I stopped reading and we gave ourselves to the silly wonder of it.

My mom never said it and would have denied it, but I think she must have identified with the cat. They lived much alike in some ways. Each of them napped in the day and spent many hours alone, day and night. Each had to rely on others to let her in and out of the house. Each had her meals prepared by others and placed before her. Each was dependent and inveterately independent too. Each was a creature of the moment. Each seemed to gaze through door or window toward things beyond my sight or knowing. And neither could tell me in any thorough way about what she saw or what she wanted. "She's picketing," my mom used to say sometimes when the cat paced neurotically back and forth through the kitchen. I don't know what the cat wanted—not food, because often she did this right after eating—but after a while I discovered what my mother wanted and could express only through comments on the cat. If I made her a sandwich at such moments, she devoured it hungrily.

But if my mother identified with the cat, the cat did not identify with my mother. She wasn't particularly affectionate to any of us, but I could occasionally entice her into my lap and force her to submit to petting, gradually subduing her to a warm purring bundle—for about three minutes. She would accept the same from Marilyn, but usually she strode by with the merest glance or no glance at all when my mother patted a leg and urged her to hop up. I can see my mom now, leaning as far forward in her chair as her back would let her, extending her hand to the uninterested cat, or bending precariously from a standing position, balancing with her cane—and the cat would walk away or sit like a statue just out of reach, withholding her soft thick fur.

"She *simply* does not like me," my mom would say with a scowl. I reminded her that cats are wilder than dogs, domesticated a shorter time, aloof by genetic disposition. It's part of their charm, I told her, and to myself I wished the damned spookish thing would just once jump into her lap and warm her with rubs and purrs. I couldn't help thinking that the cat, with one of her keen senses, could sniff the chill of death on my mother and so carefully cut her a wide berth.

CHAPTER TWENTY-THREE

So when was I happy? It seems that all I'm remembering are the hard moments, the painful ones. I know I need to remember those, I need to dredge them up and see what they become in the light of consciousness. Anything can grow, even seeds trapped in caves for thousands of years. Anything, if you bring it to light, becomes something else.

But there's more to remember, and it's my infertile sadness that gets in the way. I've been reading about depression and memory, and I've learned two things that should have been obvious. The first is that depression dulls remembering, just as it dulls everything. Remembering is an active state, a dynamo of firing neurons—it's a fire in the mind (a fire of renewal, maybe), and depression is the damper in the stovepipe. It shuts the fire down to a smolder, clouding the mind with smoke. That's the Inspector's problem. Memory is his province, but his memory is depressed. His memory doesn't go anywhere. He patrols in the same ruts he's worn for years, sees the same views over and over, smiles and grimaces and goes on with his rounds.

The second thing is that it's not only the self trying to remember who's depressed—the self being remembered was probably depressed too. It didn't begin yesterday. Not with my mother, not with the miscarriage. It goes back at least to my drug days, and my psychologist keeps hinting that it goes back farther than that. I think she's right. It goes back to that boy with his feelings clamped inside his ribs. The boy who wanted to make things better and couldn't. The boy I can see but can't quite be. The boy still waiting.

He was vigilant, he was wary of the household weather, but vigilance and wariness don't necessarily make for sharp recall. They convert the mind to a defense system, a radar that wants to see nothing because the things it might see are threatening. Memory comes from attention, and attention is not a defense system, not a passive absorption, but an active reaching of the soul. Attention is the reason I remember the snowy parapet by the Potomac as well as I do. Depression cages the soul, ties it to a rock so it can't reach. Depression says, *There's nothing here I want to touch, nothing to keep.* And so I didn't, and so there are stretches of my life I recall poorly. I know where I was living, some of the people I was with and some of the things I was doing, but I recall few particular images, few certain feelings.

A friend asked once if I'd had a happy childhood. "I guess so," I answered. It seems strange to have to guess about your own past, your own youth, but I don't know that I have enough evidence in my memory to say anything more definitive. There was plenty of unhappiness, but there was happiness too. There was an afternoon when I dropped my bike and myself on a grassy bank and lay there writing a poem, the first I wrote outside. I don't have it, and I don't remember what it was about, but I remember being happy writing it. And other moments. When I caught a three-pound bass in a farm pond, when I tackled one of my brother's friends in a football game, when I tore around the yard full of steak and strawberry shortcake on my birthday.

And more, I'm sure, but where is happiness if you don't remember it? If you have to guess?

There's a certain form of happiness, a certain form of pleasure, that I remember best. It started early—a glow of satisfaction when my father showed off my baseball knowledge to his friends, when I danced with a tambourine to calypso music as my tipsy and delighted parents applauded on the sofa. After that it was mostly about my life in school. Being praised in class by my eighth-grade geography teacher, Mr. Fries. Opening a telegram from Lyndon Johnson telling me I was a Presidential Scholar for 1966. Being class president and valedictorian. As a kid I specialized in that kind of happiness, the happiness that comes from the approval of others. The pleasure of being a good boy in the eyes of parents and teachers and the world. That's not what I'm looking for now.

When was I happy for myself, happy in my own eyes? When, without drugs, was I happy to be alive? Driving west in the Jeep, singing to Route 66 and my unknown future. Seeing the glowing leaves, and *knowing* them, on the Reed College walkway. After making love with my girlfriend in my shabby Fillmore district room in San Francisco, having a vision in which she and I were perfect beings and everyone everywhere was a perfect being. Climbing straight into the noonday sun up the West Ridge of Mount Washington, alone and untethered, a gulf of space off either shoulder, my hands and feet in jubilant concert with the spirit surging within me.

But those were joyous moments, ecstatic moments, and what I want to find now isn't exactly joy or ecstasy. When I soar that high I always feel a devastation near, as if I've soared *too* high and can't accept that gift without also accepting a corresponding plunge. In Emerson's phrase, I am glad to the brink of fear. What I'm after now isn't that intensity of feeling but something more like garden-variety happiness—the "happiness" that's related in its roots to "happen," which comes from the Middle English "hap," meaning chance, fortune, that which occurs. Haps are what happen to you, and happiness means that you have it in you to be content, or at least reconciled, with the haps of your life.

Where can I find that? I can't, of course. By definition, it can't be sought. At any given moment it's either in you or it isn't. It's not seeking or striving. It's being.

Once at Reed I had an especially harrowing acid trip. I spent the night alone in a swampy wooded vale called the Canyon, trying to hold together not just myself but the world—the very firmament of reality was cracking open, actually splitting into jagged sections with a bright light shining through. The light was salvation or insanity; either way I didn't want it. Many hours of that night are lost to me. When I came back to myself, I was holding the trunk of a small tree. Birds were singing their liquid songs in the cool of the morning. All the waking green world was one, and I was both part of the one and outside it, the most privileged of beings. I walked around campus kicking pools of pink blossoms fallen from the trees, not ecstatic, not enlightened, but happy. Just happy. I kept saying, inside me, a four-word sentence that had come with me out of the Canyon: *I am this moment.*

It's been many years since I've said that sentence or even thought of it. I used to carry it with me and speak it sometimes as I might touch a lucky stone in my pocket, as I might feel the smooth touch of an amulet under my shirt. In the early 1970s, I remember now, when I was at loose ends in San Francisco, I would sometimes sit in a park, say the sentence, and try to let the doubts and confusions that burdened me fall away. I'd feel the ground beneath me, smell the eucalyptus, the sea tang in the air, and try to focus on my breathing in what I thought was Zen meditation. I didn't have to try to breathe, I told myself. It happened on its own, reliably, by some agency that had nothing to do with the loud cluttered rooms of my mind. The stillness of the trees was what I was after, the way their leaves stirred in the wind, or didn't stir.

I have a hunch that those moments of doing nothing might mean as much to my life as moments of decisive action or intense realization. There's something hard to define but very important they allow to happen, a way of remembering who you are. Not of knowing who you are, since consciously you may learn nothing, but of sensing your hidden dimensions—as a man alone in a small boat senses the depths of the sea and the great lives that move there, though he knows them not at all. LSD had shown me an extraordinary world dwelling in the ordinary one, and in those quiet sitting spells, without the tumultuous storms the drug was liable to set off, I could feel the presence of that world like the afterglow of sundown in the desert, when warmth still lingers in the stones. I could feel a larger Self within me, smiling.

It was LSD that taught me the value of such moments, but the moments didn't originate with drugs. I remember something that happened in the late summer of one of my high school years, when I was living with my mother in Washington, D.C. For a few weeks I'd been working graveyard shift in a Little Tavern hamburger shop on Connecticut Avenue, not far from the Twenty-eighth Street apartment we shared. One morning at first light I walked home with a piece of French apple pie in a white sack and climbed the iron fire escape to the roof of the little apartment building. I sat on a vent housing and ate the pie, which I had never tasted or even liked the looks of before that morning, when the night boss had offered it to me. It tasted wonderful. I scooped up bites with a plastic fork, taking great pleasure in the soft white icing, the few plump raisins mixed among sweet and spicy pieces of apple.

As I ate the pie the sun was rising, lighting an orange glow above the treetops, above the slopes and flats of various rooflines with their clutter of antennas and pipes. A few clouds were lit and shining. I was eating the sunrise along with the pie, happily taking in everything before me, swallowing the world, and then I stopped. How strange it all seemed. How familiar. How unlikely yet inevitable that I should be sitting on a graveled roof in Washington, D.C., eating French apple pie for the first time as the sun rose behind these particular trees and cluttered building tops and filled the sky with an orange glow. Why should the sunrise be orange? Why should I be here to see it? How unlikely, *impossible,* that I should be me. That I should exist at all. That anything should. A little sun rose inside me.

It sounds crazy to say it, but before that morning I don't think I believed that the world is real. Or I believed it, but I didn't *know* it. I'd forgotten it—because even as a young boy, it occurs to me now, I had a similar moment of knowing. (Memory amazes me. I walk its wilds and stumble upon place after place where I once camped.) I think I was eight. My shirt was a faded blue plaid, short-sleeved, a shirt I liked. I had just put it on, not tucking it into my jeans, and now I walked out my bedroom door and saw a broad shaft of sunlight slanting between the picture-window curtains and falling on the dark walnut table that had been my grandfather's legal desk. Flecks of dust drifted in the light. As I walked by the table I reached my left hand into the light and stopped to look at it, slowly closing then opening my fingers, extending them in the clear radiance. *This is my hand,* I thought. *This is a dream, and the dream is true.* I felt I'd been withdrawn from time. Then I walked on into the kitchen, the summer day, the rest of my life. That's all there was. That was everything.

CHAPTER TWENTY-FOUR

My mother kept a clock on her nightstand, a battery-powered portable that had accompanied her on many of her travels. She paid attention to it—when it stopped she asked me to replace the battery—but I don't know for sure that she could read the time on the clock, or if she could read it, I don't know if it meant to her what it meant to me or Marilyn. If I told her that she needed to be ready to leave the house at 11:00 A.M. for a doctor appointment or whatever, I'd be likely to find her sitting on the side of her bed, fully dressed with her purse strapped across her shoulder and cane at the ready, by 10:30. Maybe she knew how long it took her to dress and prepare herself, and she was overcompensating. Or maybe memory could give her no guidance on how long her preparations would take, and so she began right away to be safe. Maybe she didn't trust the clock to tell her, or herself to understand, when "11:00 A.M." would arrive. On a few occasions she wasn't ready when the departure time came and had to finish hurriedly as I stood holding her coat like an impatient husband.

Aside from her infrequent appointments, of which I always reminded her several times, clock time had little bearing on my mother's life. We had meals at no set hour; when the food was ready I came by her room, or else clanged the brass yacht bell she had ordered from a nautical catalog and I had mounted on the dining room wall. She didn't watch TV or listen to the radio, so she had no need to check program times. She didn't divide her day into various activities with budgeted time for each. She had, for the most part, drifted out of time's main channel and was turning slowly in the eddies.

She lived in an older kind of time. She saw the light changing in the shrubs and trees of the backyard, their shadows shifting, reconfiguring. I'm sure she saw the dawn of many mornings. She saw blocks of sunlight move across her room as the day progressed, she saw color in the western sky at sundown. She watched the beginning of rain and the end of rain, the gray sky brightening and darkening. She watched wind stir the birches and pines. She saw leaves drop away in the fall and watched closely, intently, for their reappearance in the spring. "We'll see the leaves soon, won't we?" I remember her asking as early as January, with two to three months of leaflessness still ahead. "You can tell by the twigs," she observed one late March morning, studying the dogwood tree at breakfast. "They're getting fatter. Don't you think they are?"

As the days and seasons turned around her, my mother gazed and drifted. She had no need to know what time it was. Her personal river of more than eighty years had borne her close to its mouth, to that great mingling of waters where the current slows, where the channel widens and deepens, where time itself is drowned in timelessness. One afternoon when I stopped by her room, she had just wakened from a nap, and she said, "I hope it's the same season. I feel as though I've lived a whole *life*." There was a tone of wonder in her voice.

"Since when?" I asked.

"Since I fell asleep."

Physicists from Einstein on have insisted that our sense of time as separable into past, present, and future is an illusion. A peculiarly tenacious illusion, but illusory all the same. Time does not happen incrementally, second by second. Like space, with which it came into being and from which it is inseparable, time is all here all the time. Past, present, and future are one. No one knows why we don't perceive them as one, but writer-physicists Paul Davies and John Gribbin have speculated that it may be something in the working of human memory that creates our certain sense of immersion in a moving present flowing out of the past into the future. We think of memory as a function of time. It may be truer to say that time, or our illusory sense of time, is a function of memory.

And if that's the case, it may well be that when memory fails, as it did in my mother, a physically more accurate sense of time may come to awareness. Who was experiencing the greater illusion? I as I worked at my desk with one eye on my digital clock, or my mother as she drifted, unmoored to the clock by her bed? It was as though eternity was opening to her, showing glimpses of itself as the ocean sometimes will, appearing and disappearing in fog. In medical and psychological terms, my mother was a cognitively impaired octogenarian suffering the confusions of senile dementia. But in terms of her own sense of being, in spiritual terms, I believe she lived parts of her last years in the presence of the eternal and in the eternal present.

I also believe she *saw* differently than I and most people do. At times at least I think she experienced a visionary kind of seeing, a seeing perhaps like the psychedelic awareness that many of us sought in the 1960s, a seeing-into-things that reveals a deeper level of identity than name or category. A seeing in which all things glow with the fullness of their being. Like me on LSD, my mother didn't always know who she was in a personal sense and couldn't always name the city she was in or the day of the week, but in her visionary moments she always knew *where* she was—deep in the world's unspeakable being.

On one of our walks in the rainy season she couldn't stop looking at the brilliant green moss that lined each crack in the sidewalk and lay in velvety waves here and there along its borders. "So green, so *green*," she said. She seemed transported, ravished, as if the beauty of it hurt her eyes. She reached a hand down, wanting to touch the moss, to feel its greenness with her fingers, but even with me to steady her she couldn't stoop that far. At the corner of the block, the sidewalk makers had stamped into concrete the date—1911, I think—and the name of their company: a partnership, Miller & Bauer. The lettering was filled with emerald moss. "If only they knew," my mother said. "Their names magnified in moss."

And then there was the morning I set a large nectarine on a saucer at her place at the breakfast table. It was an especially colorful fruit, its rich yellow shading into orange and a large splotch of deep purple. My mother shuffled in, got herself dropped into her chair and her cane hung on its hook, and when I scooted her chair into place she saw the nectarine. She stared disbelievingly, her mouth agape. She seemed horrified.

"Is it . . . *corrupt?*" she said.

"It's just a nectarine, Mom," I said in my let's-get-through-breakfast voice.

She ate her soft-boiled egg and toast but wouldn't touch the fruit. She stared at it, silently, for long intervals. It was not "just a nectarine" to her. I don't know what it was—vision fruit, ember of the other world, portent of her own consummation and decay—but it was no mere docile object. My mother may have been seeing in that moment as Van Gogh or William Blake must have seen. She was not looking at a thing. She was in a presence.

Very little was just a nectarine to my mother, and in a way this was the triumph of her late life. The diminishment that her dementia brought, though a very real impairment, allowed at the same time an enlargement of her spirit. It may have allowed, in a way she didn't foresee and wouldn't have chosen, a culmination of her spiritual quest. Her forgetfulness had an aspect of remembering—a religious remembering, a cleansing of the doors of perception. The conventional certainties we carry in common in our ordinary lives are themselves a forgetting of the primary world, the world we knew best as children and are in danger of never knowing again. The world, in the words of painter Harlan Hubbard, whose "radiant beauty should be an unending source of wonder and joy, yet most people live and die without noticing it." What could be more fitting, as one draws near death, than to slough off by one means or another the tired definitions we have imposed on the world and remember it in its unfathomable mystery? "The invariable mark of wisdom," wrote Emerson, "is to see the miraculous in the common." By that standard, my mother at the end of her life was a very wise woman indeed.

One evening in the fall of 1990, when my mother had just read an essay of mine about the limits of our visual perception of nature, she and I were having a drink in the living room. I argue in the essay that nature's chief beauty and value lie not in what we see of it but in what remains hidden and mysterious. It ends with an image of a desert canyon opening itself to a hiker but always withholding its further reaches in mystery.

My mother rarely commented on my work, but this time she had been moved. We had a conversation I think of often, a conversation I'm grateful for. She asked if I knew ahead of time where I was going in my writing, if I had a destination.

"Not usually," I told her. "Or if I do, I only see it in a nearsighted way."

"It's like the canyon?"

"It's like the canyon."

She seemed happy to hear that, and she seemed to have taken some kind of important inner step on her own journey. There was exaltation in her voice.

"I think we know too much now. And if we don't know everything, we *think* we do. We need more mysteries."

I asked her if she was afraid of dying.

"Not so much," she answered. "Not so much. I worry more about things I haven't done."

"But you've done so many things . . ."

"Oh, I think of what it would have been like to explore unknown terrain. I think of the explorers . . ."

"I think of them too," I told her. I wish I had told her that she was an explorer. I wish I had told her that I was proud of her. I hope she knew it.

We were silent for a time. We looked out the window at our neighbor's house across the street, glowing softly yellow in the failing October light. A man walked by, limping. Crows were flying among the tall trees of the park. After a while my mother raised her glass of whiskey.

"Here's to the Unknown!" she said.

CHAPTER TWENTY-FIVE

I'm thinking that maybe I've always had a faith in the unknown. As I was living my desultory life in the Bay Area in the early seventies, I was unsure about most everything. I had dropped out of college and landed only in more self-doubt and confusion. I didn't know what I wanted to do or what I could do. I was waiting for my life to find me, and wasting it as I waited. Looking back now, I can see that two unknowns sustained me in that time. One was the larger Self, the sure and undivided Self, whose smile I could sometimes sense. And the other was the greater West Coast itself, where I was certain, despite my uncertainties, that I somehow belonged. The mountains had told me this from my first year in Oregon, and so did the breezy streets and bright housefronts of San Francisco, the soaring exclamation of the Golden Gate Bridge —they raised a yearning for I wasn't sure what, a sense of tantalizing destiny never quite swimming into shape.

Eventually I got a job as mail clerk for a railroad inspection bureau with offices on Market Street. The bureau had field positions up and down the coast, and when an Oregon job came open I put in my bid. I was twenty-four and hoping for simplification, for a new beginning. And so one gray winter morning in 1973, my girlfriend and I awoke in our Volkswagen bug in a highway rest area on the outskirts of Klamath Falls, just east of the Cascade Range in the southern part of the state. The landscape puzzled us. No Douglas firs, no tumbling streams or emerald fields, no green at all . . . just sagebrush flats and barren hills studded with a few disconsolate junipers. In the nearly seven years since my first arrival in Oregon, I had missed the fact that two-thirds of it is desert and steppe. My girlfriend and I decided we wouldn't stay long in that bleak country.

Things didn't go well between us. We quarreled and stormed, as we had in California, and before too long she left for law school and we broke up. She told me what others had: I was too aloof, too self-enclosed, I didn't give enough of the me she loved. I knew it was true, and I knew my helplessness. What did I have to give? If I was holding out, I was holding out on myself as well.

I took refuge in my new job, which was criminally easy. For a handsome monthly salary I spent three or four hours a day in the Southern Pacific and Burlington Northern freight yards, opening boxcars of lumber to see if shippers were cheating for a lower rate by misdeclaring their loads. My nearest supervisor was four hundred miles away in San Francisco. I called in each morning to announce that I was working, drank coffee with the clerks in the freight office, cracked open a few boxcar doors, and passed time with the hoboes—who greatly admired my job—under the highway overpass. I could usually complete my paperwork and call it a day by noon. It amounted to an extended fellowship in fooling around.

The forested mountains I'd thought I was going to be living in weren't far away. I hiked and fished and skied the southern Cascades and, after meeting a few other climbers in town, made expeditions with them to Mount Shasta and other peaks. North of Klamath Falls we found a clean basalt rimrock, a perfect rock-climbing playground where we'd divert ourselves for an afternoon putting up new routes and then hit the taverns for pool, pinball, and many cold pitchers of beer. I loved the cool and cavelike beer halls with their lights and ready laughter, their swirling flow of life that I could join and drift with any time.

I also began to explore the drier country east and south of town. The openness of the land, though strange to me, was somehow inviting. I found I liked the way junipers apportioned themselves on the rocky slopes, how each shaggy tree stood solitary and whole. Even clumps of sage and crusty scab rocks came to seem not bleak but friendly as I walked among them. I'd sit and watch big cloud shadows traveling the hills, a light breeze stirring the bronco grass and the hair of my arms. There was something settling in all that spacious stillness. I didn't feel tugged in all directions, as I had in the city, and despite the turmoil with my girlfriend and the pain of our parting, I began to feel a kind of wholeness that was new. The great dry land seemed an open secret, a secret with room for me.

It was there in the Klamath Basin that I began to write. I built myself a stand-up desk (I'd read somewhere that Hemingway had used one), bought a Webster's Third International and a used Royal manual typewriter, enrolled in a correspondence course in story writing, started keeping a notebook, and put my fooling-around fellowship to use. My father, in a frank moment, had asked if I intended to be a railroad dick my entire life. That had goaded me, and so did the face I sometimes saw in the bathroom mirror after a long night in the taverns with my climbing friends. My twenties were waning, and I figured if I was ever going to try to be a writer it had better be now.

I was hoping for publication, fame, and money, none of which I found. What I did find, to my surprise, was a kind of difficult and pleasurable journeying that was a lot like rock climbing. Move by move, each one making possible the next, you pursue a route you couldn't have planned in advance. You find your way only by stepping up, persisting, staying alert to the possibilities. Sometimes you advance easily, sometimes you need the climber's almost tearfully desperate grit. Sometimes you can get ahead only by changing course. Sometimes you have to give up the attempt. And sometimes you succeed—you achieve a height from which a landscape is revealed to you as you hadn't seen it before, a landscape limited but whole. Along the way you're sustained to some extent by faith in yourself but more by faith in the unknown, faith that there will be a way for you in what at the moment lies beyond your vision.

I had resisted writing all those years because I felt I had nothing to say. I felt I had to know something in order to write, had to have achieved a clarity of thought and feeling that I could then present in words. What I stumbled upon when I finally got myself to pick up a pencil and keep it in my hand was not clarity but a way of stumbling *into* clarity, if I worked at it and if I was lucky. And, as each sentence made the next sentence possible, I gradually came to see that each story, each poem, each notebook entry, each letter to the editor, undistinguished and shortfallen as it might be, makes possible the next piece and the next. I was impatient with my progress, tossed between scornful self-doubt and giddy inflation. Sometimes I ignored the typewriter for a week or two at a time, but I left it on the desk or the living room table (I wasn't always as good a man as Hemingway), manuscript pages piled beside it. Drunk or sober, happy or sad, I couldn't go through a day without seeing it, and eventually I had to stand at the desk or sit at the table and have at it again. For years I refused to call myself a writer, but a writer I was. I had found an engagement. I had found a necessary work.

As with climbing, I've picked up writing craft as I've gone along. My work ways have become more efficient, my route finding sharper. I bring to any passage the experience of past efforts; I bring an informal ongoing study of how others have made their passages. I think of it more like gardening now. I have some pretty good compost built up through the years, some seeds and cuttings that are likely to grow, and always some volunteers. But through it all, now as I write these pages just as twenty years ago in Klamath Falls, the essential predicament is the same: I make my way by not knowing what I'm doing, by scratching these lines on a green legal pad, sniffing my way in pursuit of the story I need to tell. I've been doing it long enough that I know to remind myself, when the writing goes poorly, to be patient. Something worthy may come of it yet. It's valid and necessary to write this way.

And I also remind myself, from time to time when my life isn't going so well, that it's valid and necessary to live life the same way—in the same uncertainty, the same faith that one thing leads to another, that confusion will settle into clarity, that incompletion will somehow give birth to wholeness. When I was teaching freshman English at Stanford I frequently counseled eighteen-year-olds who had their entire lives mapped out. It was hard not to advise them to take some acid and melt off the map. I've never set goals in life. My young dream of going to Oregon is about the only long-range plan I've ever made, certainly the only one I've ever carried out. I didn't plan to be a writer, didn't plan to get married, didn't plan to have my mother with us, didn't plan to write this book. Life can't be marshaled. You have to honor fortune or chance or providence. Or, as my mother used to say when I was managing her life a little too intensively, you have to "let go and let *God*."

On the other hand, maybe all I'm doing is spiffing up my drifting, desultory nature and presenting it as a Way of Life. And maybe I don't even believe in it. I've taken some losses for living the way I write. If I had planned to have children, I might have them. If I had planned to be a writer, I might have gotten a quicker start. If I had planned to make more than twenty thousand a year, I might be making it. If I had planned to live in the country, I might not be lying awake these nights listening to sirens, car alarms, and the college kids' bad taste in music from across the street.

And of course there's the final loss, the one I always come round to writing about. The trouble with honoring the unwritten future is that the end is already written. I know how the story of my life concludes. Or I think I do—I know how the ending looks from here—and I don't like it. That starry void off Oregon will swallow any wholeness, any knowing, any clarity I might achieve. Death surrounds the revealed landscape. Death *is* the landscape, finally. And though I don't seem to be as frightened as I used to be, not so submersed in terror, I'm still the kid who stood on the porch roof watching snow come down on Christmas Eve, knowing that the warm and festive room beneath him couldn't comprehend the universe of cold icy light. I want this faith of mine to comprehend the final mystery, but it sags and falters. I don't want to die. I want to seize the story, write a different ending. And what I really want is the grace and courage of the woman who was my mother, the old crone on her life's last shore who raised her whiskey glass and toasted her own extinction.

CHAPTER TWENTY-SIX

There's not a lot of night sky to see from our backyard, what with the tall birches and the impinging rooflines of our house and our neighbors'. The stars we do see are only a few wan specks, dulled by the diffused electric radiance of greater Portland. But the moon, riding high on clear nights or shining through thin overcast, sometimes with a coppery ring around it, the moon is something better. At some point in the fall of 1990 I started walking my mother out at night to see it, especially when it was full or near full. It seemed a small thing I could do to get her off her bed for a while, to keep her in touch with the life of nature beyond the walls and roof of her circumscribed world.

We stayed out only a minute or two. It was hard for her to stand for longer than that, hard for her to straighten her crooked neck and raise her eyes to the moon for long. She liked seeing it—it always made her smile. "Oh, yes," she'd say, "there it is." And I know she liked it that I took the time, that I thought of it and troubled to do it.

It made me feel quite virtuous, of course. It quieted, at least temporarily, my nagging sense of guilt that I didn't spend enough time with
her. That Marilyn and I were just boarding and feeding her until she
died. It was a nice way of sharing something we didn't have to talk
about, a nice way of saying good night.

What I didn't know at the time, and wasn't even close to knowing,
was that Marilyn was upstairs sobbing into her journal as I walked
my mother out and walked her back.

"*I* want that," she finally told me one night. "I want that to be you
and me."

I heard it not as a plea but as an unjust criticism. I was stung.
"What do you mean you and me? We do things together. She's an old
woman, she hardly gets out . . ."

"I know that. It's wonderful how devoted you are. But John,
you're just consumed with caring for her."

"I'm not consumed. I'm just doing it the best I can, and I'm not
even doing very much. What the hell is wrong with taking my
mother out to see the moon?"

"There's nothing wrong with it. It moves me to hear you out
there. But what about *us?*"

I couldn't understand why my wife, who was whole and healthy,
couldn't make allowances for what I saw as my minimal attentions to
my mother, who was old and declining. I couldn't see what Marilyn
saw clearly: that the accumulation of those attentions had enveloped
me and taken me over, so that between caring for my mother and trying to get my writing and teaching done I had little time or temper for
anything else, including my wife of seven years. She tried in various
ways, subtle and blunt, to make me see what was happening. "You
have all the symptoms of a stressed housewife," she smilingly told
me once. She knew the syndrome personally from her first marriage,
when as a lawyer's wife she had been busy to bursting with two
young children, entertaining, and various service boards. And she
was right—I was rushed, crabby, defensive, and depressed.

But as I saw it, what were my options? My mother was with us.

She had certain unalterable needs and the right to such companion-ship as I was able to give her. My writing needed all the time I could give it and more. And so when Marilyn confronted me about the moon watching, I took it as a gratuitous extra pressure. When she complained that she couldn't take a bath in her own house—the only tub was in the downstairs bathroom, the one my mother used fre-quently—I told her with some impatience to make do with showers. When she said that the two of us needed to get away together, I said sure we do, but we'll have to find a decent caregiver, the caregiver will be expensive, she won't know my mother's needs and habits as I do, it'll be confusing for my mother, we'll just worry about her, it's too much. I appealed to Marilyn to be flexible. I told her I needed her sup-port, it wouldn't last forever. Now when I listen to myself in memory I hear my father telling my mother, all those years ago in the thirties and forties and fifties, that he really needed her support just now in this bad time, he had a lot of pressure on him, she simply had to buck up and help with the cause.

Marilyn and I did take trips, but not very many, and each one had to be planned in stifling detail. We couldn't decide on the spur of the moment to go to the coast for the weekend or stay a third night when we had planned only two. We made time for ourselves, some time, but forfeited our spontaneity. And always we returned to a house filled with tensions that no one desired but that seemed beyond our control, tensions that brittled the feelings of all three of us and turned us inward and dried up the generosity we were capable of.

Marilyn, to put it simply, felt crowded out of her house and her marriage. She worked long days in her downtown office, came home to an irritable husband and a difficult dinner with a hard-of-hearing and sometimes sharp-tongued mother-in-law, then retired upstairs to a usually solitary evening while I took time to read aloud to my mother or show her the full moon and spent the rest of the evening holed up in the sanctuary of my study. Guiltily holed up. There were nights when I shuttled from the garage to one woman for a few minutes and then to the other, just to make contact and keep both appeased, Bob Bourgeois being cheery to both as the Inspector made it perfectly clear that I wasn't attentive enough to either.

A crisis reared when I was offered a one-semester writer-in-residence job at a Tennessee university in the spring of 1991. The job paid what to us was a small fortune. We talked it through and decided that the extra money would be worth four months of separation, four months in which Marilyn would have to care for my mother on her own, with some additional help from Patty, my mother's regular home-care nurse. We talked it through, but we didn't feel it through. Marilyn felt underappreciated for the burden she would have to bear. I—advanced practitioner of the Daniel Way that I am—didn't acknowledge the burden as fully as I might have and then felt our agreement betrayed when she acted out her resentment. We had the roughest passage of our marriage in the month before I left for Tennessee. Soon after my departure Marilyn dreamed that I had cut down a huge deciduous tree. She knelt by the stump, caressing its cut top, moving her hands along the gap where the trunk had split. I looked on, shaken. Neighbors said we could plant another. Marilyn cried and cried, stroking the moist stump.

She got through the four months with her strength and sanity intact by half-seriously imagining her task as an assignment to attend to the Great Goddess as manifested in Zilla. "Some days she will get great care," she wrote in her journal. And she also wrote, "Caring for Zilla will make up for all the spiders I have ever killed." In one important way it turned out happier than she had expected: as a twosome they got on much better than they did as members of our usual tense triad. They had words at times—Marilyn learned firsthand that managing my mom was sometimes like dragging a mule by the ears—but by and large their natural liking for each other was able to sprout and bloom in my absence. They huddled under quilts when the furnace went out, enjoyed a sixty-dollar lunch now and then, and kept the house well supplied with dark chocolate. The finest mo-

ment came when Marilyn, acting on many months of disgruntle-
ment with the dark vinyl living room wallpaper, sprang from her
chair one evening and started stripping it off in great noisy sheets as
my delighted mother cheered her on.

At the end of my teaching stint Marilyn joined me in Tennessee
for a slow and winding journey home. My brother Jim took leave
from his work in southern California and saw to our mother's care,
along with her friend Sarah Holmes, a fellow devotee of Sai Baba. It
was a joy for Marilyn to be free of the "dear old bird," and it must
have been a great joy for the bird herself to have her older son in the
house for an extended period. She asked about him all the time and
always relished his calls and visits. Jim had been little over a year old
when Georgie had died, and he grew up with the impossible task of
filling the golden shoes of perfection. He had a hard go of it through
his teenage years, clashing often with our father, while I secluded
myself in schoolish achievement and an air of self-sufficiency. Our
mother gave Jim key support when he needed it and developed a
closer relationship with him than with me—or so it sometimes
seemed and felt. There were moments as a boy when I felt a twinge
of jealousy and a spark of anger over that.

Our first days home, before Jim left, were very satisfying. It was a
pleasure to walk into a restaurant, two tall and graying sons with our
white-headed mother between us in her "Give thanks and be joyful"
dress, a bright red-and-green printed smock with an embroidered
collar. People looked at us, and I was proud. The core of the family
was arrayed as it ought to have been. I felt a simple happiness, a happiness I guess I didn't get enough of as a child. Healing means whol-
ing, and despite the pain and tensions of my mother's years with us,
she did bring the gift of healing. In her living and in her dying, she
made the family whole.

Marilyn and I felt the old pressures closing in as the household resumed its normal pattern, and I suppose my mother did too. There
was one element in the pattern that she particularly resisted. For

about a year she had been going two days a week to the Interlink Center of the Volunteers of America, a day-care program for frail older adults. We had started her there because we felt, and were advised by counselors, that she needed to be around other people, people her own age. When I picked her up at the end of a day at the center, she was worn out but usually in good spirits. She couldn't tell me much about the day. There was singing sometimes, which she liked, and she didn't mind the exercise routines. I know that she took part in recall and reminiscence sessions, but she remembered almost nothing of those. I'd like to have been an eavesdropper. The lunches and the occasional Bible talk were very much *not* to her liking.

For a while my mother went gamely, sometimes referring to her days at the center as her "work." I encouraged that notion, choosing to believe that she meant by it her concern for helping the other attendees, some of whom were wheelchair bound and variously infirm. She always wanted to help, never to be helped. But she also could have meant that going to the center felt like a job—a job she hadn't chosen, a not very pleasant or meaningful job that exhausted her. She took to saying, when I reminded her at bedtime that the next day was a center day, that she wasn't feeling strong and might not be up to it. "Let's see in the morning," she would say. And then some mornings, if I pressed her to go, she would emerge from her bedroom in her old burgundy jersey-knit nightshirt, maybe with a belt drawn around it, sandals or rubber boots on her feet, depending on the weather. I laugh now when I recall it, but at the time it gave me a spasm of intense annoyance.

"Mother," I'd say, "that's a nightshirt. You can't go to the center in that."

"It is also a *dress*," she'd come back at me, her eyes flat with anger.

"It's not a dress. It's what you wear around the house with your slippers. You can't go in that."

"All right, then," she'd say very slowly, "what *should* I wear? If you don't find this suitable."

And so we'd parade into her bedroom, and I would pull a dress or skirt and sweater from her closet, and she would dress and eat her breakfast, and we would troop to the car and drive in silence to the center. I always won that power struggle, and winning always felt crummy. It was a violation somehow. It wasn't right to be lecturing my mother as if she were a wayward girl who didn't want to go to school. It wasn't right to make her spend the day with people she didn't particularly care for, doing things she didn't find meaningful. It *was* good for her to get out of the house, to sing, to interact with others, but it wasn't my place to engineer good into her life. She mutinied over the center while Jim and Sarah were caring for her, and when I came back, I decided she would go only if she said she wanted to. She never did.

The other reason we had started her there, of course, was for *my* good. It got her out of my hair for a few hours two days a week. She knew that, and I don't like to think about how it made her feel. She knew many things, including the difference between a nightshirt and a dress. Sometimes I think she knew much more than I knew, and in the end she may have been braver in acting on it.

CHAPTER TWENTY-SEVEN

I see the bedroom clearly, my little bed facing the window, the window I used to watch with one eye open in the morning wondering what I was hungry for. (It wasn't pancakes or bacon or strawberry shortcake, it wasn't any kind of food I could think of but something outside, something in the songs the morning birds were singing, something still hidden in the world or maybe nowhere in the world at all.) I see the three-drawered dresser, the closet in the corner with its door open, the smooth scarred length of hardwood floor, my wooden top with a steel tip that I used to spin ferociously. It's the same room where I lay staring through the doorway at the ceiling light the night my parents told my brother and me they were going to divorce. And out the other doorway (like a woodchuck's burrow the room has an entrance and an exit) is the hall and the door to the basement where I had seen my parents as a windup toy, or would see them soon. This may have come before, maybe after.

This is my mother, standing in slacks and leather shoes—I think they're brown and white—just inside my bedroom, the door open behind her, the hallway lit with a kind of half-able glow from the ceiling light. It's dark outside my window. I think we're alone in the house. It's fall, October or November, sometime when night comes early and there's a chill in the air. My mother may have a hand on the doorknob, she may have both hands at her sides. She is turned part toward me, part away, looking down at me, her dark hair cut short, her lips dark with lipstick, the light burning behind her with the vague forms of dead moths in the bowl. I see everything, the entire tableau. I see even the mussed and rumpled bedspread made of ridgy cotton fabric, yellow *National Geographics* on the bed and the floor, my idle wooden top with the string that spins it—from time and again of going there, I know everything about this scene except the words my mother speaks.

I know they hurt me. Whatever she said was said to hurt, I feel sure of that. I know it from the look on her face. I know it because I felt it, I can feel it now, a kind of crumpling inside, a stiffening pain that contracts and arches my whole being and shrinks my eyes to the floor. She might have told me that she was moving out of the house—she did, for a time—but it couldn't have been only that, because whatever she said was personally wounding. So wounding, apparently, that my psyche has dissolved or obscured the language and won't let me hear it again—protecting me, maybe, the way some accident victims are protected by amnesia. In the absence of her words my imagination goes to the scene again and again, touching and probing the way the tongue tip moves to a missing tooth.

What did she say? I've tried and tried to remember, with my psychologist and by myself. I've even thought of undergoing hypnosis, but a little research convinced me not to. The hypnotized subject remembers with great confidence and in great detail, but many of the details are likely to be invented. Hypnosis heightens the confabulating power of memory, and it does so by inducing a condition of ex-

treme suggestibility to intended or unintended cues from the ques-
tioner. It's for this reason that hypnotically "refreshed" testimony,
common in the 1970s, is now disallowed in many courtrooms. Some
of the adults who are now remembering being sexually abused as
children are doing so under the influence of hypnosis, and in some
cases their "recovered memories" are turning out to be wholly or
partly false.

As I write this book I'm filling in details I can't be sure of. I'm add-
ing to remembered events people and things that might not have
been part of them. I'm filling out scenes with crickets and barking
dogs. I'm even putting into mouths—Marilyn's, my mother's, my
own—words that probably were never said. All this, yet I insist I'm
telling the truth. I'm writing from what I remember into what I don't
remember, not away from the truth but toward a fuller realization of
it—or at least that is what I'm trying to do. Truth means conformity
to fact, but it also means fidelity, faithfulness. I owe fidelity to events
as they happened. I gather all I can; I wouldn't want to misrepresent
them. But I also owe fidelity to the wholeness of the story of which
those remembered events form only a part. I owe fidelity to what
memory can't provide. I owe fidelity to imagination, and what can
imagination be but memory entered with faith and encouraged in its
form-seeking ways?

And yet there are certain liberties imagination must not take.
When I was eight or nine my mother said something very hurtful to
me. I know she did. Actually, I don't know she did. Memory may
have conjured the entire scene, complete with a sense of something
hurtful having been said, out of some childhood resentment, or out
of nothing. But I have a sure belief that she did say something cruel,
and to know what she said would help me understand who she was
and who I am. It would be highly relevant to this story. But I simply
don't remember, and in this instance it would be unfair to imagine
words into her mouth. I don't recall, and I will have to be satisfied
with that. The vague unconscious being I hold at the point of a pen

will not relinquish what I want. What shall I do, threaten him? Run him through? If he's protecting me by withholding her words—or if, as it occurs to me, he's protecting *her*—well, maybe we need his protection. Maybe his recalcitrance is an act of discretion, an act of generosity. Maybe he too has judgments to make, and maybe he's making them.

And what would it really matter? Would I love my mother less if I remembered? Would I find it so hard to forgive her? She was far from a perfect mother. My father was far from a perfect father. They both hurt me. They both could have done better. And yet here I am almost half a century old, grown of body and still growing in spirit, carrying the hurt of my mother's words along with other hurts as a tree takes inside it by its own expansion a strand of barbed wire that once chafed its bark. My mother's words aren't lost. I can't recite them but they are remembered within me, part of what I am, part of what William Wordsworth called the dark inscrutable workmanship of the human spirit. Maybe Wordsworth was the best psychologist, the psychologist of wholeness, when he wrote this passage of *The Prelude:*

> How strange that all
> The terrors, pains, and early miseries,
> Regrets, vexations, lassitudes interfused
> Within my mind, should e'er have borne a part,
> And that a needful part, in making up
> The calm existence that is mine when I
> Am worthy of myself!

My passion to remember is coming to seem a bit excessive to me, a little overardent and compulsive. That's the way it feels these nights when I lie awake wishing I was asleep, the endless neuronal circuits of memory lit like a pinball machine I can't stop playing. The damn thing keeps giving me replays—how can I resist free games?—taking me back through looping passageways that eventually lead only to themselves again. I wish I could will myself away from the game, but you can't will yourself to sleep. You get there only by giving up. Who's playing the machine? Why can't he just close his eyes, let his fingers slip from the buttons? Because he—not me, but that wired, compulsive part of me—is afraid of losing control, afraid of letting go, so afraid of dying that he won't even give himself to the little death of sleep. For a while I thought he was another self I need to get to know, but now I realize I'm looking at the Inspector, hypnotically hitting the buttons, his eyes wide and glazed. The game's playing him as much as he's playing the game.

Maybe I should give Bob Bourgeois a little more credit. He forgets what he doesn't need to know. He forgets, he lives, he does what he does. And he would probably sleep a good sound sleep if the pinball wizard would let him.

What's so wrong with forgetfulness? Maybe my anger and repulsion at my mother's memory loss only reveal my own overvaluation of memory, my own inordinate desire to fix my every experience as I tried to fix the snow on that Potomac parapet—to batten down my life as lived in order to cling to it always, to make it keep me afloat in the sea that made me and would have me back. The sea that scares me, the sea of no land in sight. The sea where I will drown—or maybe, just maybe, find myself swimming from the wreck of my life in a way I didn't know possible.

Marilyn thinks there might be consciousness after death but no memory. The Greeks thought so too. Mortals crossing over drink from the fountain Lethe and remember no more. Only a very few, such as Tiresias, retain memory intact in Hades. A rare privilege, but what kind of privilege would it be? Tonight—this morning—it sounds like damnation, insomnia with no hope of ease. Oblivion would be better—sleep, perchance to dream. Or if indeed there's consciousness, why wouldn't it be best to drink as deeply of the fountain as you can, to wash this life entirely away and embrace what's there?

I've felt inklings, but I've never really believed in a soul that survives death, with memory or without. I've read about near-death experiences, I've read some of the spiritual teachers, I've wanted to believe, but I haven't been able to surmount the suspicion that it's all just wishful thinking, wishful imaginings projected onto that cold black void. But now I don't know. My mother threw the whole thing open for me. My mother with her hints and clues, my mother with her smiles and seeings, my mother whose forgetting looked a lot like remembering. My mother who came to Oregon bearing her death like one last gift, the gift that I most needed.

When my mother commented on a topic in the news, when she stated a preference of any kind, she almost always added, "But that's only *my* opinion," as if her view shouldn't count for much. The habit irked me because I *wanted* her opinions. I wanted her to pull out of her drift and assert herself in words. I wanted her to be engaged, to struggle against the dissolution of self wrought by the changes in her brain. But it wasn't only her dementia. In her last years she was purposefully curbing her ego, intentionally diminishing and separating from the person she had been.

Passages she marked in her books of Sai Baba's sayings repeatedly exhort the spiritual aspirant to "break the bonds of 'I' and 'Mine'" through concentrated meditation on the God within. In *Dharma Vahini* Sai Baba says this: "Whoever subdues his egoism, conquers his selfish desires, destroys his bestial feelings and impulses and gives up the natural tendency to regard the body as the self, he is surely on the path of Dharma; he knows that the goal of Dharma is the merging of the self in the over-self." My mother underlined in pencil almost every word in the long introductory clause.

This concern hadn't been new to her with Sai Baba; she had tried for decades to subdue or transform what she didn't like about herself. She had attempted—bridling all the way—to make herself the supportive and unquestioning helpmate her husband had wanted her to be. In the 1970s, when many women were striving to develop more assertiveness, my mother was trying to become less judgmental and outspoken. (Qualities she had sorely needed, she said in *Refuse to Stand Silently By*, as a woman always outnumbered by assertive male colleagues in the labor movement.) Even in 1988, when she was eighty years old, I know from a tape recording of a spiritual exploration guided by a friend in Maine that she wanted to round her edges, to make a more fluid and loving person of herself. This ongoing effort may have borne fruit in the childlike warmth—the warmth of her deepest, most irresistible smile—to which she was frequently given in her final years. But she never came close to shedding her old self completely. The frank and opinionated Zilla of old coexisted, within the same hour or even the same minute, with the Zilla who wished to be egoless, attentive only to the views and concerns of others.

If detachment from the ego was hard for her, detachment from the body was harder. It's clear enough why she would seek it. Who wants to identify with a vessel of hurt and incapacity? Her gut pained her, her neck scarcely supported her head, her ears heard indistinct risings and fallings of voice that resolved into human speech only through sly lip reading. To rise from a chair she had to thrust herself up by her straining arms in a several-second siege of uncertain outcome, like a weight lifter at her limit. Her urethra left little splash trails behind her as she shuffled her way to the toilet, lecturing herself under her breath. And it was her body with all its infirmities, the ones she understood and the ones she didn't, that caused her to be shuttled time and again to the doctor, to be examined and asked to give specimens and sometimes stood up by her son against a cold white panel as the x-ray technician aimed the crosshairs at her naked back and commanded, "*Holllld*" and "*Breeeathe.*"

So of course she put her pen to the page where Sai Baba writes, "But remember, you are not this body; this body cannot be you. Tat Tvam Asi. *Thou art that. . .* You are the indestructible *Atman. . .*" Of course she underlined in double pencil strokes, penciling an arrow where the passage breaks between pages, his commentary on the *Bhagavad Gita:* "But what is clear, what is clean, what is indestructible and what is effulgent and shining, is only one and that is the soul . . ." And of course, as her porous and slippery mind let her down as surely as her body did, she would find solace in a definition of atman that seems written for a senile dementia sufferer: "The *atman* is the unseen basis, the real self, one's divinity. . . . It is inherently devoid of attachment. It has no awareness of agency or of its own needs or nature or of its possessions. It has no 'I' or 'mine.' The *atman* does not die. Memory is a function of the intellect, not the *atman*. The *atman* is imperishable."

Try as she might to transcend them, though, my mother's pains and corruptions pressed continually on her awareness—kept her wincing at her bad knee, admonishing her bladder, and panting from the short walk between house and car. The body may not be the real self, but it knows real hurts and limits. Still, my mother was not easy at the prospect of leaving it. She became agitated when her blood pressure was up, asking nervously if it was time yet to take it again. She was concerned when Tom Harvey, her physician and mine, explained to her the danger of congestive heart failure—though after lunch and a nap she seemed to forget her worry, one of the many instances when her failing memory proved a blessing. Two or three times in her years with us she was convinced she'd just been visited by a small stroke or heart attack and wanted to go immediately to the doctor or the hospital. There must have been many stretches of her timeless time when fears for herself were stewing in her mind, fears she couldn't or wouldn't express.

There was one experience of my mother's body, though, that kept her pleasurably attached to it right up to the last week of her life. She loved to eat. She slurped her soup voluptuously and scraped the last film of it from the bowl. She sucked every slick fiber of goodness from the pits of plums and nectarines. She chomped her false teeth into corn on the cob, ate asparagus spears from her fingers. On nights of cracked crab she lingered at the table long after others were done, carefully licking her fingers as she picked through the mound of wreckage in front of her. My mother was gratifying to cook for because she wasn't picky; she just liked good food. (Once she exclaimed about Marilyn's cream of broccoli: "This is the best soup I ever stuck in my mouth!") Though mostly a vegetarian since first going to Sai Baba's ashram, she wasn't doctrinaire in the least. She ate chicken and fish and occasionally relished a plate of sautéed chicken livers. If very hungry she was quite capable of wolfing her meals, but more typically she ate at a stately pace, clearing her plate by small forkfuls and eventually leaving bones and other detritus in one neat pile on its polished empty surface. As Marilyn's mother once commented, "Zilla doesn't eat. She dines."

Another detachment my mother sought was from current events of the nation and the world, and in this, as in her other efforts, she was only moderately successful. The humanitarian and social activist in her was still alive and keenly interested. She read the *Oregonian* at breakfast, the *Christian Science Monitor* when it arrived in the midday mail. She read determinedly, often with a set mouth and a steady slight frown. By and large she seemed weary, more than weary, of the numbingly repetitive accounts of human meanness and misery that make up the great bulk of what we call, without a trace of irony, the news. She chuckled at lighter stories, the odd photo of traffic stopped for a goose and goslings, and she lit up at anything affirmative. She followed Nelson Mandela's release and triumph, the Earth Summit in Brazil, features on poets and artists and musicians. She clipped articles about cooperation, self-sacrifice, peaceableness between enemies. My mother was after the real news. She was gleaning hope.

One morning when she had arrived in the kitchen ahead of me, I found her in tears over the front page of the *Oregonian*. Her eyes and cheeks were red; she had been crying a long while. An intruder in a Portland home—a glue sniffer, as I remember—had taken a little boy hostage and held him with a knife to his throat. Police marksmen couldn't accurately fire through the house windows, and so three cops entered the house and confronted the intruder in a hallway. He was crazed, unpredictable, the edge of his knife on the boy's throat. Fearing he might cut any second, they opened fire. The knife man was killed, and one bullet killed the little boy.

I think my mother could comprehend, much as she hated it and despaired at it, the news of rape and torture and murder in Bosnia. She had had some experience in her own life with the ferocity of human passion. And she could accept, with sadness, the toll in human lives taken by hurricanes and earthquakes. Nature was vast and blameless in its power, human beings weak and small. But the death of an innocent boy at the hands of three innocent men doing exactly what they had to do to save him . . . What consolation is possible? How does one detach herself from that? How can it be reconciled with any notion of God or justice?

In the view of Hinduism, which in a general way became my mother's religion, God does not reward or punish. He only reflects. We humans create our own destinies, our deathless spirits born into bodies again and again in order to learn what they need to know, acting out the infinitely complex drama of karmic evolution. Seen in that way, the fates of boy and knife man and policemen were determined by the acts of their previous lives, as their acts in this life would contribute to the shaping of their lives to come.

My mother may have believed in karma, but if she did it gave her no solace as she cried her eyes red over the awful news that morning. Bound as we are in the joys and horrors of the flesh, the idea of karmic justice is just as abstract and ultimately as hapless as the Christian idea of a personally attentive God. It can explain, if held with faith, but it cannot justify. The pains and evils of this world may all be maya, illusion, but if so it is hard to imagine a crueler ruse. To the boy's parents and the policemen who killed him, and in a more distant but still painful way to my mother at the breakfast table, his death was an illusion as real as agony. Maybe it needs to be so. But the human soul must be an awfully poor learner to require such schooling.

The death of that boy made my mother readier to quit the world. I got the sure sense that morning, and at other times too, that she was saturated with the ills of humankind and wanted no more. But was her movement toward death only a fleeing, then? Were her religious ideas only an apparatus she borrowed and adapted to help her escape her fear of dying, the pains of her body, and the sufferings of humanity at large? I think she was fleeing those things, but I also think she was reaching toward something, toward a truth she experienced within and knew to be good. I believe she felt intimations at least of the clean fire of the soul, the light in which the contrarieties of mortal consciousness interblend as one. Deeper than her fears and ditherings and delusions, deeper than her smile and her tears of anguish, I believe my mother glimpsed her wholest and truest identity, that which her religion calls the atman, the Self that understands its own infinite nature and approaches with a smile the body's death.

In January of 1992 she told me she might not have much longer to live.

"How does that make you feel?" I asked.

"Thankful for everything I've had," she answered after a pause. "It's been a privilege."

Not long after that, a month or two maybe, she tried to show me something. She would try in the same way several times before she died. We were in the living room after dinner. I was about to read the next chapter of Tolkien's *Lord of the Rings.*

"Over there," my mother said with a smile, pointing out the window toward the park. "Do you see a bird in the top of the tree?"

I got up and stood next to her chair. "Which tree?"

"The tallest one," she said. She spoke very surely, very deliberately. "Do you see the bird?"

I didn't. The tallest Douglas fir stood like the others, clearly silhouetted against the twilit sky. There was no crow or hawk, and no smaller bird, perched on its point.

"I don't know," I said. "There could be a bird, I guess."

"Oh, yes," my mother said, smiling, watching with her sharp eyes. "It's a great bird, isn't it."

CHAPTER TWENTY-NINE

I think of branchings, forks in
the trail, points of opportunity where I might have taken a different
way. When my mother said she might not have much longer to live,
that was such a point. I keep feeling that I missed my cue, or heard
the cue but didn't step forward, didn't understand the part that was
required of me. I keep feeling that having heard her say that, I should
have set about building her a bower for her dying. I should have honored with more attention her sense of death's imminence, should
have helped her prepare herself for the great departure, the great
embarkation. It's not that I denied what she said. I took her at her
word, asked how it made her feel, and was gratified, and moved, to
hear her answer. But mostly, in the weeks and months that followed
our conversation, I went about cooking and caring for her as I had always done, and our uneasy triadic household creaked along with its
accustomed and increasing tensions.

A man from India I've corresponded with, a former Jain monk, tells a remarkable story about his own mother. When she was eighty or so she said to her family, "I'm now too old. I can't cook, I can't see, I can't do anything for you. What point is there in carrying on? From tomorrow, I'm going to start dying." She made the rounds of the village, stopping in to visit relatives, friends, everyone she knew. "I have come to say good-bye, because I am going to die," she told them. Then she began to fast. As she lay peacefully, bearing herself into death, villagers chanted, sang hymns, prayed and meditated around her. They did their part to launch her on the voyage she had chosen.

My mother made no such forthright decision—no decision, at least, that she communicated. I think she was much more ambivalent about dying than my correspondent's mother was. But she did sense, she did know, that death was near, and she did communicate that. And why didn't I respond, beyond asking how she felt? Why didn't I ask, at the very least, "What can I do? How can I help you?" I didn't know that she was right, of course. She was weak, but she was also tough. She might well have lived another five years. I suppose, too, that I didn't want still another duty, whatever it might be—caring for her failing life was a regimen quite full enough. And I had other things going on. My book of essays came out that spring, my first prose book and first with a New York publisher. I was giddy and fretting, fussing with one or another detail of the book's release. I was teaching part-time. I had minor surgery in late winter. I was occupied. I was busy.

And I was denying the prospect of my mother's death. I didn't want her to die (except in those private furies when I did). I loved my mother and didn't want her to go from the world, and I didn't want myself to feel what I would have to feel if she did. I didn't want my mother or Marilyn or myself or anyone to die. I didn't want to deal with death—and in that stonewalling, of course, I was acting out the deep denial of my culture.

Who dies in America? Certainly not us. Our birthdays conspire to

prove that we age, but we defeat their perversity by devotedly making ourselves younger and younger. We dye our hair, plump out
wrinkles, sweat off fat, tone muscles, condition heart and lungs, improve our diets, curb our vices, have great sex longer, and stay ac-
tively engaged in our jobs and hobbies and recreations. We can't
possibly die! Only others do, those poor unfortunates who didn't
care for themselves correctly, who didn't improve their lot if poor,
who didn't see the doctor when they should have, whose self-esteem
was too low or anger too high, who didn't laugh or meditate or play
enough golf, who didn't see to their personal growth as they should
have, who drove cars too fast or themselves too hard, who took too
much whiskey or not enough garlic capsules, who should have drunk
twelve glasses of water a day whether or not they were thirsty and
attuned themselves to the universe through psychotherapy or deep
massage.

And so, since it clearly doesn't involve us, there's no need to talk
about death. Why would we? Where we live, the sun is shining with
no end in sight. Death is elsewhere, in the backcountry maybe, in the
deep wilderness, somewhere far outside our lives. Death is a back-
ward thing, a primitive, apelike thing, a violence we may have lived
with once but long ago, before progress delivered us to the modern
world. It is only a quirk, due to a temporary imperfection in our tech-
nology, that death still lives anywhere. But that it survives at all is a
sign that we must try still harder, we must rededicate ourselves to
progress, we must fulfill our quest to eradicate death even from the
margins of our human realm. It is outrageous that it still victimizes
anyone, outrageous that dark uncivilized shadows should be able to
breach our security every day and seize fellow humans, even people
we know, who were innocently enjoying their lives.

In any case, we do not go gentle into that good night. When we
cannot ignore death, we fight it, we stave it off, we hold out nobly
against it. But how much nobler was my correspondent's mother in
India. There came a point in her life, a point of sudden clarity, when

she realized that to die was the next thing to do. To *do*, not to avoid or even to wait for. She recognized death and reached out her hand. She knew when and how to die in the same way that a hunter knows when to move or stand still, when to shoot or hold fire, in the same way that a farmer knows when to plant corn, that a wave knows when to curl and give itself to the shore. She exercised a natural intelligence that our technological world tends to stifle under thick wrappings of comfort, convenience, and relentless distraction.

My mother felt the promptings of that intelligence well before the day in January of 1992 that she told me she might not live much longer. In 1989 I started writing down some of the more striking things, all kinds of things, that she said. In February 1990, she told me with a sigh, "Sometimes I feel as ancient as the ancientest days." Later that year, in October, she said one afternoon, "It feels as though I were swimming, and it's hard to keep up." In 1991 I read to her from *Passwords*, William Stafford's latest book of poems. Like me, she loved Stafford's work. She kept the little hardback by her bed, and after she died I opened it to certain pages she had marked with torn strips of Kleenex. She had circled in pencil the title of a poem called "Four A.M.," which is about waking at night in the forest with a sense of ghostly figures floating among the trees. The poem ends:

> Some night I will breathe out and become
> part of the silent forest, floating as they do
> toward the thin lids of dawn,
> and like them, unknown.

The title of the poem on the facing page, "Security," also was circled. The poem compares each tomorrow of our lives to an island we always find, day after day, until there comes a tomorrow without an island:

> So to you, Friend, I confide my secret:
> to be a discoverer you hold close whatever

you find, and after a while you decide
what it is. Then, secure in where you have been,
you turn to the open sea and let go.

My mother had bracketed that final stanza in wavery pencil lines. Within a year she would be dead. And one year later, in August of 1993, William Stafford died suddenly of heart failure.

"Fear can arise only when there is another," my mother wrote on a yellow Post-it note within six months of her death. The full sentence, which she read in a book of quotations from Sai Baba's discourses, reads, "Get over fear by establishing your mind in the One, for fear can rise only when there is another." The idea goes back at least three thousand years to the *Brihadaranyaka,* the earliest of the Hindu spiritual treatises known as the Upanishads. According to Joseph Campbell's translation of the story, in the beginning there was only a Great Self that perceived nothing else. "This am I!" it said, and immediately it fell afraid, as anyone alone can be afraid. But then it thought, "If there is nothing but myself, of what, then, am I afraid?" And its fear vanished, because there was nothing, no other thing, to fear. That Great Self, as I understand the story, is the immortal Brahman, soul of the cosmos. When the spiritual aspirant recognizes that through the atman, or deepest human soul, she is part and parcel of the Brahman, all fear melts away. She sheds her body, which she thought she was, as a snake slides out of its skin.

I know this story now. If I had the privilege of turning back the tape of time, I would know it sooner. I would enter the world of my mother's religion at least far enough to help her, if she wished for help, to express her fear and locate herself in the One. I would offer to read Sai Baba's words to her. I would copy out his sayings in large letters and post them on her walls if that's what she wanted. I would find her tapes of sacred music in her boxes of possessions and play them for her. I would ask what she needed to help her pray. I would ask if there were friends, fellow devotees, she wanted to call.

She may have wanted none of this. She didn't like fusses made over her, and if I had been too forward with my attention to her dying she might have disavowed it—I might only have pushed her into denial. But still, if I could live those last months again, I would find time to make myself available to my mother and her dying. I would find room for death in the household, so that it wouldn't have to sneak in like a thief while I was away. I would do this for my mother, and I would do it for myself. What can I gain by locking the door? What can I learn at a distance? I would admit death to my company. I would eat and sleep with death, I would walk with death through all the rooms of the house, and maybe after a while I would recognize its face. Maybe I'd become easy enough in its presence to look into its eyes. Maybe I would ask to hear what death had come to tell me.

CHAPTER THIRTY

The waitress stands, waiting and waiting as my mother struggles with the menu, trying to choose, trying to know what she wants, her eyes shifting here and quickly there across the welter of print, the salads and sandwiches and hot entrées each with its brief description, the specials of the house set off in boxes. She clears her throat, she straightens in her chair as if to force concentration into her mind. Her eyes flit, she clears her throat. The waitress stands, pen in one hand, pad in the other, as I pick up the salt shaker and set it down, as I shift in my chair and tap the floor with my foot, as I stare out the window at the rush of traffic on rainy Burnside Street, as I wait and wait and wait in my flushed prickling impatience until I just can't bear it, and "*Mother,*" I say, "will you please *pick* something."

And she does. I don't remember what. I remember her helpless gray-green eyes, large in the lenses of her reading glasses, sad and earnest like the eyes of a child who has failed a parent, as she says, "I'm sorry, John," her voice breaking.

The remorse that stabbed me then is more painful now. My mother needed my patience, and in the end I just couldn't summon it. I couldn't take a deep breath, I couldn't smile, I couldn't make small talk with the waitress. I couldn't let my mother dither as she needed to dither. Or I could have, but I didn't. And I didn't smile and take a deep breath one evening later in the spring when she just couldn't get herself into her chair at the table on the back patio. One hand on the chair back and one on her walker, she couldn't see or get her limbs to see how to make the transfer. She stepped slightly forward, stepped back, regripped the walker, looked down, looked to the side, scraped the walker ahead an inch, reached into her purse, reset her feet . . . Finally I took her under the arms from behind, swung her forcibly into position, and lowered her into the padded chair.

Marilyn too lost her patience that spring—her patience with me. She loved and admired my mother, but she also had to live with her, and she absolutely resented that my mother had taken over our household and our lives. She saw me eaten up by caregiving and hated it. She didn't look forward to coming home in the evening, rarely enjoyed dinner, and could hardly bear to hear me reading to my mother or singing with her, as we had begun to do that year. And of course she felt guilty about her feelings, and of course when she tried to express them I didn't want to hear them. I was mired in my own guilt, my own sense of helplessness. I told her not to push me. One morning after I'd snapped short another conversation, she smashed her favorite tea mug on a rock in the garden, then threw the bed pillows hard and furious against the wall. She almost fled the house for the coast, Seattle, anywhere. "It took a lot of control and suddenly a huge burst of tears to keep me at home," she wrote in her journal.

Something had to change. Marilyn had known it for a year or longer, and finally, in the early summer of 1992, I recognized it too. I

saw that my mother would have to live somewhere else. For Marilyn, for our marriage, and—the hardest by far to acknowledge—for
me. I think it must have been my own behavior that persuaded me,
my impatient outburst at the restaurant, my roughness on the patio.
It was my behavior that finally tipped the scale against all the *shoulds*
that had piled up in my mind, all the evidence that we *should* have
been able to care for my mother and live our own lives too. We had
help from a good home-care nurse, we received a modest monthly
support check from Aging Services, she didn't require continuous
care, she was able to get herself to the bathroom and the dinner table,
I worked at home anyway, my brother spelled us several weeks a
year, she wouldn't live forever and she should have the right to live
out her days with family and the family should be willing to have
her, able to have her, happy to have her . . .

But no one was happy. I wasn't happy, my wife wasn't happy, my
mother didn't seem happy herself. Maybe, a wild hope tried to convince me, maybe she would bloom in a different home. Maybe she
would feel restored to some of her former independence, maybe it
would do her spirit good to be freed from the daily watchfulness of
her domineering father of a son, the daily presence of a daughter-in-
law who claimed more of her son than she could. We would visit her,
bring her food and flowers, take her for walks and drives, talk with
her like lively friends again instead of housemates stale and tense. I
even remembered something she had said two years before, when
we were thinking about moving from the old house—"I don't have
to live with you and Marilyn, you know." She had said it in a helpful
spirit, as if all options should be open. As if she might have been stat-
ing a preference, even, as openly as she could.

I knew the lie of it, though, even as I imagined it. We weren't moving her out for her sake. We were doing it for us, and I despised myself for it. We were doing it, the Inspector harangued me, because we
didn't have the generosity to make it work. We didn't have the simple
grit and decency to see out of the world the woman who had seen me

into it. I hate that America is a society of foster homes and nursing homes and retirement towers. I hate that we farm out our elders when they aren't useful anymore and can no longer do for themselves and begin to intrude on our precious convenience. I wanted us to be different. I wanted us to be able to say, "Such as we are, we are a family. We live here in this house, all together." Now I had to admit to myself that I was just another self-absorbed and self-regardful member of my generation and my culture. "We tried it," Marilyn and I rationalized to each other. "We tried it for three and a half years." And, we didn't say, *we failed.* Once again my family was falling apart. Once again I had tried to hold it together, once again I had come up wanting, and this time I was the reason for its failure.

I called Aging Services and got a list of adult foster homes in our part of town. It was a depressing document. Most of the homes had only shared rooms available, most of them were not interested in Alzheimer's clients, all of them had strict specifications as to mealtimes, bedtime, visiting hours, and the like. I imagined dormitory food, TVs blaring. Otha Cunningham and Helga Falconer and Dottie Lou Labenske probably were fine people, but what did they cook? What did they talk about? What would they think of a woman who dangled a pendulum to make decisions and came with pictures of an Indian holy man with a spreading Afro? No doubt they were fine people, but theirs were the foster homes that had contracted to accept Medicaid as payment—the homes at the lower end of the scale, the homes that my mother and we could afford. I drove by two or three of the ones closest by, drab Portland houses on streets where Marilyn and I wouldn't have wanted to live. I couldn't get myself to call and visit a single one. The list sat on my desk.

My mother, of course, knew nothing of this, unless she sensed it in the air. I could imagine, barely, finding a place we could afford where she might be comfortable and reasonably well attended. I could even imagine her eventually liking such an arrangement, but I couldn't begin to imagine telling her that she had to go. I could hardly bear to tell her when Marilyn and I were going out to dinner. I had to screw up my courage to face her inevitable disappointment when I was too busy to read to her after dinner. How could I possibly break the news to her that she had to move to a foster home? Marilyn felt the same way. We knew what we needed to do, and we felt perfectly incapable of doing it.

Then we made a discovery that seemed to answer everything. We heard of an outfit called ElderPlace, a program of Providence Medical Center for the frail elderly. It offered day care, comprehensive medical attention—and when the time came, social workers helped the family find a foster home or nursing home. The program was aimed precisely at clients with limited financial means. Alzheimer's people were welcome. Marilyn and I visited the center, met with the staff, and couldn't believe our luck. The initial commitment they asked of those joining the program was attendance twice a week at the day-care center. I took my mother to see it and appealed to her, very earnestly, to try it out. I framed it not as something that would be good for her—I had learned never to do that—but as something she could do to help *me*. I didn't go into specifics. I appealed to her generosity, her wanting to be helpful, and she agreed. The staff took to her immediately, as people usually did. She liked them and the ElderPlace setting better than the center she had gone to—and not gone to—before, or at least she seemed happier about the new arrangement.

Marilyn and I felt relieved to have entered a process that would make the necessary change much easier to handle. Nothing would happen right away, which privately comforted me. My mother would attend the center for a while, and eventually we would talk with the staff about locating a foster home. With their help we were certain to find the best place that could be had through Medicaid. There would still come the moment of truth when I would have to talk with her about leaving our home, but maybe by then her involvement with ElderPlace would have prepared her for it—and, I hoped, prepared me.

In the meantime I was still too busy, still too tense. I felt run into the ground by our repetitive routines. My mother's incontinence was worse. She forgot or refused to wear her protective pads, and I found myself sponging up her splash trails and cleaning seat cushions almost every day. I was irritable, short tempered, prone to cold silences and peremptory remarks. When I apologized she usually responded graciously, sometimes quizzically, as if she wasn't quite sure what I was apologizing for.

One evening I tried to go further than apology. I walked into my mother's room and sat down in the wicker chair in the corner, the visitor's chair, my elbows on my knees. "Mother," I said, "I know I'm often impatient and out of sorts with you, and I'm sorry. It's not your fault. I know that being old isn't a picnic. I appreciate the way you bear up under it. I admire your spirit."

"Oh, my dear," she said. "Thank you." She took off her reading glasses. She was choked up, and I was too. We shared a smile. Not an easy smile, not a relaxed smile, but a real one.

"What can I do to help you?" she asked me.

"Help me? Oh, I don't know . . . Just know that it's hard sometimes, you know, doing everything."

"You do a great deal, child."

"I don't do so much. But it really is hard sometimes . . ." I wanted to tell her more. I wanted to tell her why and how it was hard. I imagined us talking about where she should live, speaking easily, kindly and candidly, reasoning out the best thing to do, all the usual shunts and angers swept away. I heard us talking as easily as a river talks, the two of us resting beside it in no hurry and no need. I saw it and heard it, right there in the room, but I couldn't make it be. I was afraid to say more, afraid she wouldn't understand, afraid I would hurt her, afraid I would seem unworthy.

"What can I do?" my mother asked. "Are you sure there isn't something?"

I will forever remember her saying those words.

"Just be yourself, Mama."

I went to her and kissed her, her bony hands hugging my shoulders with all the tremulous power of her old body.

That conversation took place in late June, maybe early July. On July 14 my mother and I signed an agreement with ElderPlace confirming her participation in the program.

On July 23, early in the afternoon, I came home from coffee with a writer friend in downtown Portland. The cat shot out the front door as soon as I opened it. On my way to the kitchen I heard a voice from the bathroom—not words but a voice, a beseeching, close-mouthed call. My mother was on the floor, in her nightgown, her head propped against the base of the wall. She couldn't tell me anything. Her eyes were present, but she couldn't form words. I tried to lift her but quickly saw she couldn't sit or stand. I called 911 on the kitchen phone, looking down at the uneaten lunch I had left for her. I gave her a sip of water, and within five minutes the paramedics pulled up in front of the house. From the moment they came in, with their questions and instruments and friendly efficiency, the life I had looked after for nearly four years was no longer in my care. As they carried my mother out the front door on a stretcher, I was not leading but following. It had been no more than twenty minutes since I had come home.

CHAPTER THIRTY-ONE

I remember my father calling from the hospital, or maybe it was before he went to the hospital. He didn't know then how shot through with cancer he was. He may not have known he had cancer at all, but he knew something was wrong, something was badly wrong. He said, "I'm awful scared, Johnny," and there was a fear in his voice I had never heard. It was the most emotionally open thing he ever said to me. I don't recall exactly what I said in return, but it was something positive, something banal, something that returned us to our accustomed depth. "I bet you'll be fine," or something like that.

Now when I hear his voice in memory, I know that he knew he had come to his end—that the four packs a day of Chesterfields and the decades of hard drinking had caught up with him. But I didn't know it then. I was twenty-eight, he was seventy-two. I heard fear in his voice, but he was a tough and vigorous man, hale despite the long-time insults to his body. He was a veteran of countless picket-line fracases, severe beatings at the hands of company goons. And he had a rich vein of luck, too. Once in LaFollette, Tennessee, he had been shot point-blank in the chest by thugs from the United Mine Workers; when they left him for dead, he pulled his wallet from the inside coat pocket of his jacket, and the flattened slug fell to the floor. Surely, I told myself as we spoke on the phone, surely they would fix him up in the hospital and he would resume his reading and coin collecting, his AA meetings and his work on the public utilities board. He would go on growing his tomatoes and smoking his turkeys and living his retired warrior's life in the pastures of age.

Two days after we spoke he was dead. I would like our last conversation to have been something more than it was. I wish I had understood what he understood, at least in the depths of his being: that he was dying. I don't blame myself much, because there was no precedent between us for the kind of conversation I wish we had had. He was a reserved man, a patriarch of the Daniel Way, and I grew up his son. But he opened a little at the end, he confessed his fear to me, and I wish I could have opened myself just a little in answer. I wish I could have given him more than hackneyed cheerfulness in my last words to him in this world.

Death comes when it comes, of course. Who knows which words, which acts, will be the last? I think the dying person knows, with a glimmer of consciousness at least, that death is drawing near. The dying person must see in a kind of light of lastnesses, though he may not recognize the light. But even he won't know which words or acts will be his last—unless, like my correspondent's mother in India, he makes his death a voluntary act—and those around him won't know either. Death comes when it comes.

I have no clear recollection of my mother's last morning in our house. It must have been a morning like many others. I would have made coffee, scrambled or soft-boiled an egg for her, made oatmeal for myself or maybe French toast for both of us. We would have read the *Oregonian*, we would have talked a little. Later in the morning I made her lunch, I remember that—a sandwich with a sheet of plastic wrap laid over it, a bit of leftover something in a bowl, soup in the steel thermos—and I laid it at her place at the table. I stopped by her bedroom to tell her I'd be visiting a friend for a couple of hours and her lunch was ready when she wanted it. This was easy enough to tell her; she didn't resent me leaving during the day. She looked up from her book, smiling, thanked me for the lunch, and wished me a good visit. I don't *know* she did this on the morning of July 23, but it was her way to do it. I probably didn't kiss her; I usually kissed her only when saying good night. If she raised her left hand, I took it for a second, then left the house.

Death comes when it comes, the next thing that happens. We do not stop for it, most of us; it kindly stops for us. It calls at the door—not Jehovah's Witnesses this time, not a salesperson, not the Greenpeace canvasser, but the long-expected, half-forgotten guest. Or maybe the guest has already arrived and has been waiting, sitting in the chair in the corner, the visitor's chair, sitting still in meditation until one moment of one morning when its eyes open and it says, "Yes, it's time." And she slides one leg off the bed and then the other, straightens herself in her nightgown and sits a moment, looking around as if someone has called her, then leans far forward and pushes herself up from the edge of the quilt-covered mattress and stands on her two bare feet. She shuffles ahead, stiffly for the first two steps, steadying herself with her left hand on the nightstand, reaching with her right for the bedroom door frame. She doesn't take her walker because the bathroom is just around the corner, and the walker is hard to maneuver in the tight space by the toilet. She doesn't take her walker because she doesn't need it.

She knows and she doesn't know. She wants and she fears. Right hand on the bathroom doorway, left hand lifting her gown a little, it is only the familiar shuffle to relieve herself, the frequent trip her diuretic sends her on each morning. The same white walls, the worn hardwood of the hall giving way to dark linoleum, the green basin, tub, and toilet, gray light streaming through the one high window— all of it familiar but strange now too, a strangeness that will not resolve but opens inside her. Her feet scarcely feel the cold floor, the light streams through the window, her hand presses the bathroom wall, slides down, stops. Maybe something says, *It's time now.* Maybe something tells her, *Choose, choose,* or she tells herself. Maybe something asks, *How can I help? What can I do?* Or not those words, not any words, not a thought or a choice but a sense as sure as the streaming light that a choice has been made, that whatever she is is sliding past thought, past words and memory, that she herself has been the guest and visitor, that the endless, ending instant of her sojourn here was all to reach this moment, *this,* breaking in a flash of pain or dizziness, a buckling like a timber sheared, a slipping underneath and she is falling now, falling toward the heap of what she was and whatever she will be.

The emergency room x-ray showed what I assumed it would: my mother's right hip was broken. The angled neck of bone that connects the femur shaft to its head had been snapped when she hit the floor or else had fractured first, causing her to fall. In old people with osteoporosis, I learned later from Tom Harvey, the calcium-starved bones can become so thin and brittle that they sometimes break spontaneously. The neck of the femur, because it bears considerable weight and slants away from the vertical, is a prime candidate. My mother was surefooted in her unsteady way, unlikely to fall in a place where she could use her hands to steady herself, and the position I found her in suggested she may have slid down the wall in a semicontrolled fall rather than a sudden one. If it wasn't a sheared femur neck that sent her down, it may have been a stroke. She never spoke more than a syllable or two from the moment I found her, something at the time I attributed to shock. As I remember, one doctor who examined her thought she might have had a stroke; another thought she hadn't.

As I waited by my mother's gurney, first for her to be x-rayed and then for the x-ray to be processed and reviewed, her eyes trained on mine with a look of concentration as I talked to her, holding her hand. I think she smiled—slightly, quickly—once or twice. When I wasn't speaking she gazed up at the ice-cube-tray diffusing panels of the fluorescent lights, gazed with her brow gathered, as if trying to see something or to understand. She seemed absent to the sounds and bustle of her surroundings but very present to something in her awareness.

Marilyn was on her way from her office, a long cross-town trip by bus. The shift was changing in the emergency room. At least two doctors, maybe three, examined my mother and spoke briefly to me. Their names and faces and comments are filmy, insubstantial in my memory. Finally an orthopedist showed me the x-ray and recommended immediate surgery to repair the hip, either with a pin or a complete replacement. It was the only way she would have a chance of walking again, and if bedridden she was almost sure to die before long of pneumonia or some other infection. He said there really wasn't much choice. My mother couldn't speak her preference; it seemed unlikely she understood her situation well enough to have a preference. I agreed to the surgery—too readily, I think now. If I had it to do again, I would ask more questions, take more time. I would put off, at least for a while, the immensely authoritative specialists who run the hospital machine. I would try to collect myself, to consult with Marilyn and my brother, perhaps with another doctor. I would try to think of everything I knew and believed about my mother. I would try not to succumb to the helpless passivity of fear, the shocked panic that says to the experts *Yes, do everything, please do it now.*

When I left her side to try again to reach my brother, my mother herself gave a sign, though not in response to doctor or nurse or anything in the emergency room that I could see. She raised her right arm, her good arm, straight above her, her hand mostly open. Her eyes focused intently on whatever she was seeing, whatever she was reaching toward. They moved slowly side to side, tracking it, staying with it, her brow slightly bunched, her hand wavering. She reached and looked for minutes at a time, lowered her arm, and raised it again.

"Mother?" I bent over to ask. "What are you reaching toward? What do you see?"

She turned her head to me with no change in her expression. She tried to speak, I thought, just once. Or maybe not. She shook her head and returned her gaze above. She couldn't say, or didn't know. Or she knew that I couldn't know.

She was reaching and looking when Marilyn arrived. She was reaching and looking until they wheeled her away to surgery.

CHAPTER THIRTY-TWO

We wouldn't hear for several hours how the surgery went, and so Marilyn and I, dazed and hopeful, went out for a bite to eat and then a movie for distraction. When we got home and I called the hospital, the news was good. My mother was not yet out of surgery, but everything seemed to be going well. Soon after I hung up, though, the phone rang. Near the end of surgery my mother's blood pressure had plummeted. A medical team in intensive care had worked desperately to save her. For now, at least, her condition had stabilized. We had better come to the hospital.

As I drove the car, crying, holding Marilyn's hand, the truth held still around me like a shock of cold air. *My mother is going to die.* In that way of seeming outside myself, I felt as I had in that moment long ago when I lay in my child's bed staring at the ceiling light, knowing that my parents were going to divorce. *This is really hap-*

pening. Such moments are like wakings from the sleep of normal life. But why does it take the prospect of death or separation to wake us?

I think there was a delay, maybe an hour, before we could go up to see her. Maybe they had to clean up, make her and the room presentable. A nurse or someone tried to prepare us for what we would see, but it was still a shock. It was worse than finding her fallen on the bathroom floor. A respirator billowed her lungs to a steady gasping beat through a tube inserted through her nose. She had an IV in one arm, she was catheterized for urine, she was wired to an EKG monitor through four patches on her chest, and some delicate high-tech sensor had actually been introduced through a vein in her shoulder into the right side of her heart and through the heart into her pulmonary artery, there to detect fluctuations in pressure and report the information to a monitor above the bed. My mother's eyes were closed, her mouth open, her head tilted to one side, shifting rhythmically with the rising and falling of her ventilated chest. She looked small, puny among the tubes and monitors, her white hair matted. She was there and she was nowhere.

Afterward in the hospital lobby we met with the cardiologist, the one who angered me by using the term "demented." But we both liked him. He told us it had been touch and go during the crisis. They had very nearly lost her, and she might destabilize again any time. He urged us to think about what procedures we might want to rule out if she did. The concentrated pressure of manual CPR sometimes breaks ribs, especially if the patient is old and osteoporotic. "I would not want it done to my mother," the cardiologist said. We told him we didn't want it either.

After I called Jim, there was nothing we could do but go to bed and try to sleep. I lay awake a long time. No one had said anything about my mother getting better—but no one had said she couldn't get better, either. We had a room of hope to wait in, a small but substantial shelter from our worst fears. But the room was no refuge from the second-guessings that plagued me. Maybe I shouldn't have consented to the surgery. I wished—and wish no less now—that someone in the emergency room had taken me aside and talked with me at length. I wish I had *made* someone talk with me. I wish I had at least asked why the operation had to be done immediately, why it couldn't have waited until my wife and brother and I had had a chance to seek further advice. It was a piece of very bad luck that my mother's doctor, Tom Harvey, was on vacation in the East that week. He and I weren't able to talk until after my mother died.

The orthopedist had put it simply: she wouldn't walk again without surgery, and if she couldn't get up and out of bed she would probably soon die. But he didn't assess for me, and I didn't ask about, my mother's chances of walking again *with* the surgery, given her age and frail condition and given the possibility that she had been felled by a stroke. And though of course I understood that any surgery posed a risk to an elderly patient, no one specifically addressed the *degree* of risk to the particular patient in question, a failing eighty-four-year-old woman with at least one damaged heart valve. I know the risk could not have been pinned down in numbers, but it should have been talked about. I let the intense inertia of the emergency room make the decision for me.

To have chosen against surgery would have consigned my mother to bed and death. Choosing for it gave her at least a chance and gave us a room of hope. She was tough and gritty, after all. In stubborn perseverance she outstripped everyone, maybe even me. She had been walking for eighty-some years up to the instant of her fall. Hip surgery works. Why couldn't she rise again to shuffle along behind her scraping walker, joking about the hardware in her hip? We couldn't ask her for her choice, of course. She couldn't speak, and even if she had been able to, what would we have made of her responses? At the very best, even if there had been no stroke, she would have been confused, disoriented, in pain, in shock. How could we have been sure that she fully knew what had happened to her and what could happen, what her choices and chances were?

We had to choose for her, and the hope of surgery may have been the best choice. If we had chosen against it, though, we would have spared her the stress of a major operation and an awful travail in intensive care. We would have spared her the machine existence of respirator and sensors in the heart. To have declined the operation would have consigned her to death, but once she had fallen, once she had broken her hip and very possibly suffered a stroke, wasn't she almost certainly consigned to death in any case? Wasn't death thoroughly written on her situation, there to be read by those with eyes to see? Was the little room of hope really only a room of denial? At the time, of course, the room seems the only place to be. It's a refuge; the weather outside is threatening. The technical prowess and expertise that take over while you wait in the room seem unquestionably right. Everyone wants only the best, everyone wants life. But were we—all of us, doctors and family—were we really serving my mother's life, my mother's whole being, by conspiring to prolong a physical existence that had arrived at its final passage?

I was the one who knew most about that being in her last years. I knew that she had said she wasn't much afraid of dying, that she had raised her glass to the Unknown. I knew she had volunteered, six months earlier, that she might not live much longer and that she felt considerable ease with that. I knew her religion's teaching that the death of the body is no extinction but a liberation of the real being, the soul. I knew she had meditated on her departure, worked at overcoming her fear, sought fortitude in poetry and scripture. I knew that she had recognized her death, had engaged with it, had at least occasionally *wanted* to die, and yet I did not acknowledge her death when it presented itself. I chose to have her forcibly restrained from it. I gave her care and keeping to technicians of the physical and took cover in the little room.

I didn't know, no one did, that her heart would go on strike. All of us did what seemed the right thing, the only thing; but it wasn't the only thing, and I'm not at all sure it was right. Death by pneumonia,

I know now, tends to be relatively comfortable for elderly patients—a slow depression of all systems, a coma, and death. I don't know but feel pretty sure that Marilyn and Jim and I would have stood a better chance of communicating with our mother in her last days if she had never gone into surgery. Even if she hadn't been able to speak, she might have been able to communicate through hand squeezes, certainly through smiles and tears. Maybe, with her good right hand, she would have been able to write. In any event, we might have had more time with her before she slipped into a coma, time for the affirmations and regrets and the simple need to be together that the death of a loved one evokes in us. And her time, *her* time, would have been less troubled.

I don't brood much about this. I don't still kick myself much. But I think about it, and I wish I'd thought about this kind of thing before my mother fell into her dying. My thinking resolves into two images. My mother on the gurney reaching her hand, searching with a concentrated gaze. And my mother wired and tubed and billowing with mechanical wind in the awful clarity of intensive care. The doctors and nurses might not agree—I don't know that they even noticed it—but I am certain my mother was doing something important in the emergency room, something crucial to her being. Something I don't understand, something she didn't understand and needed to. Something was there and she was reaching, seeking to know it. My worst regret is not that I caused her a needless last ordeal. My worst regret is that I interrupted her encounter at the borderland, her sighting of the great Unknown.

CHAPTER THIRTY-THREE

I don't remember how many days my mother was in intensive care—three, I think. She was briefly conscious from time to time, of what I can't say. I think she recognized Marilyn and me. The rest of it—the tubes, the respirator, the strange faces of doctors and nurses, her pain—the rest of it must have been a nightmare, a lighted nightmare she kept waking to. No day or night, nothing to see but the same muted light, the same metal and plastic surfaces, nothing to hear but the gasping respirator opening and closing like some big fist inside her. Any change was hard for her, and now to wake from surgery into this . . . If, as close to death as she was, she still needed something to hold on to, I hope she found it in our faces at visiting hours. I hope we gave her some kind of solace. I hope inside she wasn't pleading, *End this, please end this . . .*

Two messages, one from within and one from without, helped me accept the end. On what I think was my mother's second night in intensive care I paced around the house in my bathrobe, picking up books and magazines for distraction and quickly abandoning each. Finally I dropped to my knees in front of the sofa and prayed. To whom or to what I didn't know, I didn't even know what exactly I was asking. It was a plea for guidance addressed to anything outside the anguished chamber of my mind, anything that might know more than I did. Later I went to bed, and soon after falling asleep I had one of my numinous dreams, the kind I think of as sleep visits or visions. This one was a single image. I saw my mother as I had seen her at noon the day before her fall, leaning back in her chair by the kitchen table, wearing sandals, a faded orange blouse, and a lavender skirt. She had been relaxed and plucky that noon, her mood buoyant, and in my dream vision she seemed made of light—it shone in her clothing, her smiling face, her silvery white hair. Just that, no more. I woke with her image clear in memory, and with the image I knew a twofold truth: my mother couldn't live in her body anymore, but nevertheless she would live. My waking mind accepted neither aspect of the truth, but still it was there, planted in me, mute and certain as a flower that had opened overnight.

The other message came the following day from an internist at the hospital who took Marilyn and me aside to talk about my mother. We liked his manner, which was friendly and forthright. She might stay alive indefinitely on the respirator, he told us, but only alive. If she were going to recover she would have shown signs by now. The surgery had simply overtaxed her heart, which already carried the burden of forcing blood through a calcified aortic valve that had possibly been narrowed to less than the width of a pencil. She had no resilience, no resources in reserve. At this point, the internist told us, we might want to think about easing my mother's decline. We might want to think about taking her off the respirator.

"Will she die then?" I asked him.

"She could die very quickly, but she might not. I'm afraid it's not something I can predict."

"But there's really no chance she'll get better?"

"My opinion is there's really no chance."

It was hard news, but finally it was more reassuring than devastating. It confirmed what we secretly knew, what we could see and sense but hadn't been able to acknowledge to each other or ourselves. And hard as it was, it at least gave us the opportunity, for the first time in my mother's hospitalization, to consider and choose a course of action on our own instead of following and inquiring about and hastily approving the actions of others. To choose a course that would make my mom more comfortable. A course, we believed without hesitation, that she herself would choose if she were able.

Jim agreed with us over the phone that taking her off the respirator was the right thing to do, and he wanted to be there for it. I met his flight at the Portland airport the next day, Sunday, about noon. We drove straight to the hospital and met Marilyn there. While Jim spent some time with our mother, two friends arrived—Sarah Holmes, fellow follower of Sai Baba, and Paulann Petersen, who had known my mother through Marilyn and me for many years.

We each took a few minutes with her, said a few words. I thanked her for being the person she was. I told her it had been a privilege to know her. I told her that I loved her, that I knew she had a voyage to make, that I sent my love with her whenever she decided to set sail. It's funny, I can't remember if her eyes were open or closed.

Sarah sang my mother a devotional song, "Dance, Shiva, Dance in Our Hearts," which the two of them had sung together in the past, and "Don't Have a Worry in the World," a song she had written herself. Both were lively, upbeat celebrations. It was wonderful the way they opened up the antiseptic room. I felt myself smiling. We stood around the bed as the internist shut off the respirator and quickly withdrew the breathing tube. My mother kept on breathing. Her blood pressure, which had been weak, shifted for a while and then stabilized at a stronger level. She even seemed to take on a bit of color in her cheeks. My mother was still my mother—still alive, still dogged, still, in a way, willful. I thought of something she had said a few months before in a chipper mood: "My whole life I've been obstreperous, obnoxious, and oppositional!"

And so, as my mother settled back into life, we settled in to keep vigil with her. Because she was no longer receiving major life support, she was moved from the intensive care ward to a standard hospital room, a narrow single with one window and space for a few chairs beside her bed. I remember the room in a pale greenish light. My mother lay on her back; sometimes, when the nurses turned her, on her left side. Her right leg was propped with pillows to keep it slightly bent, easing the pressure on her hip, which was enclosed in a plastic brace. She had an IV in her arm to maintain her fluid balance and blood sugar and wore a light oxygen cannula on her nose to help her lungs get what they needed. It was nothing like the respirator. What we heard was my mother's own breathing, her lungs inhaling and exhaling as they had for eighty-four years, doing what eons of evolution had designed them to do, what life itself urged and insisted they do.

She drifted between sleep and wakefulness, though not a wakefulness of speech. I know of only one word my mother spoke in her last days. When I leaned over her bed one morning and said, "Hi, Mama," she quickly answered, "Hi." I felt a bolt of happiness, an instant of new hope, but right away I saw the concentrated effort of recognition dissolving from her pale eyes. If she didn't speak, though, she most definitely heard and felt. When Paulann read a poem by Rumi, her eyes opened wide. And when Marilyn, in a private moment, thanked my mother for her strong and inspiring example as a woman, she saw tears flow down my mother's cheeks.

I spoke to her at times and read to her often. Because she couldn't speak herself and because language had been so crucial to her, such a passion and a solace, it seemed important to offer it to her now. I read her poets, mainly—Wordsworth, Tennyson, Gerard Manley Hopkins, Christina Rossetti, D. H. Lawrence, Edna St. Vincent Millay, e. e. cummings, Theodore Roethke, William Stafford. I read from the Psalms, the *Tao Te Ching*, the Upanishads. I read for a while and stopped, looked at her eyes, listened to her breathing, read more when I was ready. Who knows what the poems meant to her? Who knows what *she*, her subjectivity, really was? But they were lines she had loved, lines that had moved her and moved me, lines she had marked in pencil or with Kleenex strips or had noted to me in our sessions of reading aloud. Lines about dying, departure, traveling, the presence of the holy. What can you do when your mother is dying? You give what you can. You give what might strengthen and clarify, you give what might serve. You give the best and most appropriate language you know, and you give it in the same spirit in which Neanderthal people, sixty thousand years ago, gave flints and axes and heaps of medicinal flowers to the graves of their dead. She is leaving now. She will not return. You help her on.

I spent most of the daylight hours at the hospital, joined by Marilyn when she got off work and before long by my mother's niece, Betty Wilson, who flew in from Missouri. My brother took the night shift, catching some fragments of sleep in one of the hospital lounge areas. Technically this wasn't permitted, but Jim struck up a friendly rapport with the night nurses and they looked the other way. Earlier in the year, as he had cared for our mother while Marilyn and I took vacation, he had played her a tape of an ancient mantra, Om Namah Shivaya, sung to a simple musical arrangement. She had liked it, and so he played it now in the hospital room, at low volume on the boom box. Soon we were playing it almost constantly. It soothed all of us, a steady peaceful tide washing through us as it washed through our mother. The phrase means "I bow in reverence before Shiva"— Shiva the Destroyer, the god who decays and dissolves all things, and thereby liberates the human soul from mortal ignorance and delusion.

One morning I walked into the room to a striking change. My

brother, with his sure sense of the appropriate, had turned our mother's bed around to face the window instead of the hallway door, repositioning her IV and other apparatus as necessary. She had the light of morning on her face, the green boughs of a tree moving in a breeze outside. One of the nurses, surprised and a little alarmed, had asked Jim why he'd done it. He told her simply that his mother was alive, and so why shouldn't she have a view? The nurse smiled and let it be.

It buoyed me instantly to see my mother facing the window, and who can say what difference it might have made to her? Clouds, blue sky, the waving boughs—she had known these all her life, and she carried in her genes their unknown influence on ancestors human and nonhuman clear back to the dawn of life. Whatever she recognized, whatever she perceived, whatever she sensed, she faced the good world she had loved and now was becoming again. The world flowed in through her window, flowed into her open eyes whatever they saw, even as she flowed forth to join the world from the personhood of her many days. Even after she fell into a sleep she wouldn't wake from, the sun's light still touched her as it always had, still moved upon her ancient face as it moved upon the face of Earth.

In the afternoon of July 31, her ninth day in the hospital, my mother's breathing changed to a pattern of short inhalations and louder, punctuated breathings out. My brother and I were alone with her. Her breaths grew further apart. At five minutes to eight in the evening there came a stillness of several seconds, and then a long, sighing exhalation—as if, exactly as if, she had finished a long labor and now could rest.

CHAPTER THIRTY-FOUR

Marilyn suggested that we wash my mother. She asked the nurse on duty to free the body of its IV and other paraphernalia while we waited in the hall, then the five of us went in and stood around her—Jim at her head, our cousin Betty at her feet, Marilyn and Paulann on her left, me on her right. We wet towels in a basin of warm water and gently wiped her skin, gently toweled her small breasts, her abdomen with its slanting hernia scar, the sparse silver hairs of her pubic area, her silky upper thighs, her dry and purpled shins and forearms, her feet with their crooked and callused toes, her hands of graceful fingers, her peaceful face. We washed my mother, her accomplished body, the full flowering of her eighty-four years. Somehow she seemed young to me, a girl, but I felt her whole unliving weight when we lifted her to slip on one of her dresses from India, white cotton with raised white embroidery. We placed a string of sandalwood beads around her neck,

and then a small leather pouch containing a few items from her bed-
side at home—a shell, a feather, a photograph of Sai Baba, a packet
of his sacred ash. I read three poems she had asked me, at one time
or another, to read upon her death: Tennyson's "Crossing the Bar,"
Christina Rossetti's "Song," and e. e. cummings's "anyone lived
in a pretty how town." Then I read Robert Louis Stevenson's "Re-
quiem," which she had occasionally recited from memory in her
last years:

> Under the wide and starry sky
>   Dig the grave and let me lie:
> Glad did I live and gladly die,
>   And I laid me down with a will.
>
> This be the verse you 'grave for me:
>   *Here he lies where he long'd to be;*
> *Home is the sailor, home from the sea,*
>   *And the hunter home from the hill.*

Then we kissed her, and we left.

In the restaurant afterward we were spirited, talkative. We cele-
brated the woman we had known. We remembered her. We rejoiced
at the final ease of her passing. We drank wine, ate good food. And
where, I wonder now as I watch us in that restaurant, as I feel again
the warmth and spirit of our little table—where was she? Where was
Zilla Daniel, my mother? Where was the soul I knew and didn't
know? Was she watching somehow, in some way like the way I watch
now in memory? Had she watched us bathe her body, as some who
have entered death and returned to life report having watched the
surgeons struggling to save them? Or was she absorbed into a reality
utterly removed from the hospital room, utterly gone from the restaurant in which we who loved her laughed and drank our wine and
spoke of her? Was she anywhere? In our remembrances she walked
and smiled, she cursed, she climbed the rigging as a Sea Scout girl,

she strode in hat and elegant heels from a Carolina porch, she drove the West in a Land Rover built like a tank, she slurped her soup and shuffled along behind her walker—where was she now, and what? Could she see the landscape of her life? Could she think of us? Or was she anything at all but a stiffening corpse in the hospital morgue, a cold body with blood pooling in its under portions, a parcel of dumb brute flesh already falling to corruption?

Seven weeks after my father died, he came to me in a sleep visit. My memory is mainly of his voice speaking. He told me that instead of vegetables he raised flowers now, and I saw them, masses of radiant flowers in many colors, unlike any I knew. They were flowers of light, a garden of gathered light. He told me he was happy now. He told me he was glad for my good thoughts about him and understood why I had negative thoughts. It was all right to be happy, he told me, even to be happy he was dead. I was shocked that he knew my shameful secret, shocked and afraid, but my fear turned into gratitude. I thanked him and the vision ended.

I hadn't understood, in the weeks since his death, the joy I felt within the tumult of my grief. Did it mean I was glad he had died? That I hated him? I couldn't bear to believe I felt that way. After the sleep visit I was easier; I began to understand my feelings. I saw that I wasn't glad for my father's death but glad for my own life, glad to be walking in the world. I was joyous in my sorrow because I knew it was my world now, my moment to be alive, my time to hit the trail in the clean cold of morning with no one to report to, no one to expect me home. My father had died as he had to die to make room for me, and the joy that thrilled me was not ingratitude but my soul's thanks. It soared in me, I realized, exactly like the strings in the second movement of Beethoven's Seventh Symphony, the violins he had made me hear when I was a boy—the way, as the theme comes to full volume, they soar for a moment high and intensely alone above the orchestra's somber measured march.

My mother, then living in the Findhorn community in Scotland, was overjoyed to hear of the sleep visit from my father. "So many things occur to say," she wrote. "How open you were—and are—to experiencing across the veil. How very concerned Franz was that he found a way to come to you; the love on both sides making it possible. The flowers he is growing!" She went on about a book that had come to her, just after my letter, by a woman who had received messages by thought transference from a close friend who had died, a former Anglican nun. My mother wrote that the nun had been "counseled by guides on the other side to send back the messages to her friend to inform interested persons here what it is like there for a recent arrival. That is where it rings true for me—the eternal part of me says 'yes.' She too had a garden of flowers. She tells how those who wish to get 'through' to someone on this side go about it, and much more that establishes the continuity of life, the carrying on of our dearest pursuits after going over our life history here to learn from it, after understanding why we did this and not that."

I don't remember clearly how I felt when I first read my mother's letter. Glad for the confirmation, I think, but resistant too. Certain about my own experience, the sleep visit, but skeptical of her enthusiasm, her seeming knowledge. How did she know so much? I preferred to think of my vision in its own isolated mystery, not loaded up with metaphysical arcana.

We decided on a direct cremation, and once that was arranged I left Portland almost immediately for Idaho. I'd been assigned by a magazine to write about salmon in the Columbia River Basin. I had delayed the research trip to be with my mother in the hospital and considered delaying it further when she died, but I realized I didn't want to. I was grateful for something to do, grateful to be in motion. Driving east through the great open gorge of the Columbia, the broad river on my left, forested cliffs and white waterfalls to the right, I kept glancing through my tears at the rental car's passenger seat and smiling, as if my mother were riding with me—she who loved journeys, who loved to be moving on land or sea. I didn't see her but sensed her, and something she had said came back to me. As I was leaving the house one afternoon in my shorts and ankle weights, her voice had followed me out the door: "Going for a walk? Put me in your pocket."

Two days later I walked and sat for hours by a stream high in the Sawtooth Range, watching my first chinook salmon. They hovered in the shade of boulders and pine snags, slowly waving their tails, opening and closing their mouths, the biggest of them nearly three feet long in a stream just ten feet across. Their fins were frayed and torn, their dark backs splotched with white infection. They had journeyed thousands of miles in the North Pacific and nine hundred miles up the Columbia and the Snake and the Salmon, thrusting themselves up the ladders of eight dams on the way, to arrive in this stretch of meandering meadow stream where they had been born. Within a few weeks they would spawn, shuddering out the last of their lives to the cold creek gravel, and their bodies would slide downstream with the current they had fought, their ripened red flesh disappearing into bear and raccoon, becoming meadow grass and streamside pines. I couldn't stop watching. I lay on a rock reaching down as slowly as I could, trying to touch their dorsal fins and spotted backs.

That night in a Boise motel I had a dream about my mother. Dead, she was being walked around by friends I didn't recognize as if she were alive. Maybe it was their house we were in; it wasn't mine. She seemed an awkward weight. After they set her in a chair, though, she showed signs of life. She stretched a little and seemed to be trying to open her eyes, which were glued shut with sleep. I went to moisten a white washcloth in warm water, but when I brought it her eyes were already open. She was sitting at the kitchen table, talking and drinking coffee. I was pleased but not overjoyed. I felt a bit out of sorts that she had recovered without my help. She was talking intently with the persons who had walked and wakened her, people I didn't know. When I woke in the morning I wrote down the dream without great feeling.

Two nights later, in the same motel, my mother visited me in sleep. I didn't hear her voice, as I had heard my father's sixteen years before, and I didn't see her. I had just fallen asleep. Someone rang or knocked at the front door of our Portland house. Someone was expected. How can I describe what I saw? I opened the door on a Presence. Down on the sidewalk were bunches of roses arranged in a large loose ring, standing, tilted slightly back, a ring of white and dark red roses glowing softly, deeply, in the dusky light. Roses there and not there, glowing into and out of the dusk, blooms of light and blooms of darkness, a circle of roses somehow arranged, somehow placed there for me to see, wavering in the gathering dusk of Princeton Street on the sidewalk just to one side of the concrete steps that go down from our door.

I woke right away with a longing to keep the roses before me, within me. I took no certain message from the vision except that it *was* a message—that my mother had sent it or been sent in its form, that my mother was the ring of roses, that they expressed her new state of being. I was overcome with awe and happiness and grief. As I tried to get it down in words, I felt I was touching only the husk of it, not the living image. I had been with it, inside it, in its living Presence. Now it was something smaller, something contained within me. Now I was only remembering. And as numinously whole as the vision had been and still remained, I felt that there was yet something in it, something about it, that I didn't quite understand.

CHAPTER THIRTY-FIVE

A month after my mother died we had a small service in our backyard. Her older sister Adelaide, then eighty-nine, flew in from Michigan. She and Marilyn drove to a you-pick flower farm on Sauvies Island and came home with a truckful of blooms, which they placed in pots and vases all around the yard. Ten of us sat in a circle and recalled the mother, sister, and friend we had known. Adelaide told of the many travels she and my mother had shared, beginning in 1910 when the family sailed to Holland for a Unitarian convention. Adelaide, then seven, led her two-year-old sister around the deck on a leash and harness, certainly the last time my mother ever submitted to such restraint. Seventeen years later, as Vassar undergrads, they returned to Europe; they flirted with the one eligible bachelor on the SS *Minikahda*, and Adelaide, who didn't drink, remembered her sister buying and consuming whole bottles of wine alone. Almost half a

century later, on a ferry voyage up the Canadian and Alaskan Inside
Passage—Adelaide's treat—my mother at sixty-five spurned the
comfortable stateroom, spending all the time she could on deck with
her face in the weather, enjoying the company of backpackers,
coastal natives, and the amazing scenery.

Others at the service read poems, sang songs, made their own remembrances. Marilyn read some of my mother's recollections of her
organizing days in *Refuse to Stand Silently By*. When the book had
arrived in the mail, about a year before she died, my mother didn't
recall being interviewed for it several years earlier, and neither did
she remember most of the events she had recounted. She read her
own words with close interest, keeping the book on her bed or
nightstand and returning to it often. She seemed gratified by what
she read, even proud. I seem to remember her saying, at one point,
"I really *was* something, wasn't I."

I read a message from Jim, who wrote of the many places our
mother had lived and loved—Maine and Scotland, India, British Columbia, the Blue Ridge of Virginia, the hill country of Carolina and
Tennessee. "She truly belonged to the world," he wrote. "Feed the
birds, folks. Let the cats come around. She was of all of us." He quoted
from "Ripple," the great spiritual anthem written and sung by the
Grateful Dead:

> Reach out your hand
> if your cup be empty
> If your cup is full
> may it be again
> Let it be known
> there is a fountain
> that was not made
> by the hands of men
>
> There is a road
> no simple highway

between the dawn
and the dark of night
And if you go
no one may follow
That path is for
your steps alone

I read a short piece I had written about my mother's life, a piece that would become, though I didn't know it at the time, one of the seeds of this book. At the end of it, after describing her death, I told about something I had discovered only a few days before the service. I had opened my mother's small deer-hide purse, in which she had squirreled away various items from time to time—money, shells, packets of *vibhuti*, her hearing aid. It's common for those with Alzheimer's to stash money and other objects in hiding places. There were two items in the change purse when I unsnapped it, one in each of its two compartments. One was her pendulum: a small, bullet-shaped, stainless steel plumb bob on a six-inch chain. And the other, which must have come to her in one of the take-out Chinese dinners we occasionally had, was a fortune from a fortune cookie. It read, "Leave your boat and travel on firm ground."

"What can I do?" I remembered her asking. "Are you sure there isn't something?"

I knew she had been preparing herself for death, but had she *decided* to die when she did? She must have been troubled by the tension in the house, the tension in me, and she knew the source of the tension. She knew that ElderPlace meant a change, and she may even have surmised that the change would end with her living among strangers in a strange place. Part of her still feared death, but more of her may have feared the uncertainties of her life. Looking back, it's hard to put limits on what she might have felt, what she might have known, what she might have done. She may have been demented, but she was demented in a canny way. And, of course, she didn't want to be a burden. She wanted to be helpful. Did she choose the time and the way she could help the most? Did she, like my correspondent's mother in India, seize a propitious moment to step out of the failing boat of her body and walk the spirit's firm ground?

It seems unlikely. She fell, after all. There was no sign of an intentional act. But a few days after the service, when I opened the red nylon carrying pouch on her walker, another discovery startled me. Among the contents was a mailing from one of the local hospitals or health care centers, maybe from the AARP, about the dangers of falling—how commonly it occurs, how dire the consequences can be, how to minimize the risk. Such mailings on a host of topics came all the time. Most of them my mother placed in the ash bucket she used for a trash can, but this one she had singled out for her walker pouch. Had it given her an idea, or encouraged an idea? If she did want to end her life, a fall was probably the only means available to her. Could the dithering crone who sometimes couldn't decide whether to get up from a chair have decided to embrace her death by falling to the bathroom floor? Unlikely, I still think, but the answer may be yes. She may have decided through one final act to end the burden of making decisions—and to release herself from decisions made by others.

It seems more plausible that the weakened bone of her hip broke spontaneously or that she had a stroke, neither of which she could have willed, but how can I be sure? Stroke is not the only possible explanation for her wordlessness in the hospital. Her head was near the side of the tub when I found her—she might have hit it as she fell. It's even possible that she deliberately forsook speech as part of her resolve to forsake life, the better to keep her attention focused on what lay before her as the veil between worlds parted. The evidence is ambiguous, the possibilities open. My mother may have accidentally fallen and died as a consequence, or she may have dropped herself to the floor intentionally. Like the speaker of the poem she loved, she may have laid herself down with a will.

I can't find the mailing that came to my mother about the dangers of falling. I have the deer-hide purse, pendulum and fortune still in it, but the mailing isn't here. I have an uncertain memory of keeping it a while, then throwing it out, and I know—not vaguely at all— why I might have done that. Just as I know why, when I've broken down crying in the time since her death, I've found myself saying, "I'm sorry, Mama, I'm so sorry . . ." It's not merely grief at her dying. It's a fear and a guilt, fear and guilt with the force of a conviction, that I pushed her into her death. That I made her feel unwelcome in my house and my life. That snapping at her in the restaurant and treating her roughly on the patio and a hundred other acts of impatience and selfishness built a pressure that said *Go* to her, a pressure that forced her ultimately out of her life. I can't bear to think it, but it is what I have felt.

Two more clues, two more marked poems in William Stafford's *Passwords*. One of them, titled "Young," tells a brief generalized story of a childhood, blessed and vital, giving way to the disappointments of age. "The best of my roads went wrong," says the speaker:

It was far, it was dim,
toward the last. And nobody knew how
heavy it was by the end,
for that same being who lived back then.

Don't you see how it was, for a child?
Don't you understand?

For most of two years I've taken that last stanza, which is lined sides and bottom by my mother's pencil, as a reproach intended for me. And I have cringed to read the first three lines of the poem on the facing page:

Someone you trusted has treated you bad.
Someone has used you to vent their ill temper.
Did you expect anything different?

Stafford goes on to imagine consolation for the injured "you" of the poem, and this section, the final five lines, my mother bracketed in wavery pencil:

> But just when the worst bears down
> you find a pretty bubble in your soup at noon,
> and outside at work a bird says, "Hi!"
> Slowly the sun creeps along the floor;
> it is coming your way. It touches your shoe.

Exactly the kind of solace available to a largely immobile, largely housebound, largely solitary being. And exactly the kind of solace my mother would have been likely to find and appreciate—the consolation of little things, the comfort of the ordinary. I'm glad she put her pencil to that part of the poem and not the first three lines, but it nearly breaks my heart to consider that she *needed* such solace and that I, more than anyone or anything else, must have caused her to need it.

Am I reading too much into a few pencil marks on a few poems? Maybe. I may be reading too much and writing too much into many of the events I'm stitching together. And it may be that I'm too hard on myself, as my psychologist believes. Marilyn believes so too. She tells me that my mother was lucky, that I did well by her, and I don't think she says that just to make me feel better. She believes it, and because she lived it all with me, because she next to me is the one in the best position to know the truth, her view counts. Her view comforts me.

But finally, I'm the one I have to satisfy. I'm the one holding the pen, and I'm the one held at the point of the pen. Bob Bourgeois would like me to put the pen down and be done with this. You can only analyze things so far, he says, after that you're just wallowing in it. Bob loved his mother and mourned her death. He cried because he missed her, because she was his mother, not because he might have done her any wrong. Bob cried a lot, but not so much lately. It's not that he's forgotten her, but somehow he's taken her inside him, her life and her death. Somehow he puts her in the ground with the ferns and flowers he plants; somehow when he whistles as he cleans the rain gutters it's her whistling too.

But there's someone else I have to satisfy, someone who isn't whistling. The Inspector says I failed my mother. He says I drove her from the world. He says it and says it and says it. He's so shrill and insistent that I try to change the channel when he's on, I try to tune him out. When he's got me awake and half-listening deep in the night, I'll turn on a light and stick my face in a book right in the middle of his harangue. Eventually I fall asleep. But it seems the more I ignore him the more persistent he becomes, the more I hear his muffled voice from that observation chamber where he keeps his eyes on the province. Maybe I need to try something different. He's in the chamber by his own choice, but lately he's been sounding like someone in confinement, someone shouting to be heard. He's not going to stop. He's not going to die or go away. And depressed and obsessive as he may be, he isn't any fool. He thinks too much, but he *is* a thinker. My psychologist says I haven't really met him yet. Maybe she's right. Maybe it's time to knock on his door and see if he'll answer.

CHAPTER THIRTY-SIX

A̲t Sai Baba's ashram, Sarah's been telling me, devotees stay in small concrete apartments or set up camp in huge community sheds. They sleep on thin mattresses purchased in Puttaparthi, placed on rented cots or directly on the floor. The ashram charges a nominal fee, little more than pennies, for food and accommodations. Early, around 4:00 A.M., the devotees rise and enter the temple to sing twenty-one *Oms*, the sound of sounds from which the world was born. Then one or two women sing the *Suprabhatum*, the good-morning hymn. "It's like saying, 'Wake up, Lord, we're your devotees!'" Sarah tells me. A fifteen-minute meditation follows. Later in the morning the group walks singing through the ashram grounds. They are from many countries, many religious backgrounds. Sai Baba teaches that all faiths are facets of the truth. "I have not come to start a new religion," he has said, "but to deepen your experience of God in the religion of your choice or heritage." The name of his ashram is Prasanthi Nilayam—Abode of Peace.

After breakfast they wait in the courtyard, monkeys sometimes walking among them. Sarah sees light around Sai Baba when he comes, a halo off to one side or a tall, multicolored pillar. That is what absorbs her attention. "You get the feeling his human body is just a prop," she says. He walks among them, Sai (Divine Mother) Baba (Divine Father), walks in a plain orange robe, his kinky black hair spreading in a large aura around his head. His face, as I've seen it in photos, is broad, fleshy, affectionate. There's a crinkle at the bridge of his nose when he smiles. He might speak, might press a bit of *vibhuti* to someone's forehead as an act of healing. Whatever his actions, Sarah says, his presence is transcendent. She speaks of a long-lasting glow, a sense of peace and restoration—something utterly singular, utterly pure. She says, "The Lord is walking the earth, and you, whatever your age or circumstances, are lucky enough to be alive and know of him."

Sarah believes, as my mother did, that Sai Baba is that rare thing, a true avatar—an incarnation of the formless into human form, here to do service, in humility, to the world. He is not driven about in Rolls Royces, he does not proselytize, he does not launch crusades or jihads. Devotees in the ashram must follow rules—no meat, no smoking, no sex, and others—but are not forced to believe anything. No one summons them, no one makes them stay. "Going to Baba is like walking into a beautiful wilderness," Sarah says. "If you're called in your heart, you go."

Just a week ago I discovered the letter, from 1985, in which my mother first mentions Sai Baba. Findhorn acquaintances had told her "that an avatar has been revitalizing India for a quarter of a century—Sri Satya Sai Baba—setting up colleges for women and young people, schools for children, whose gospel is, simply, love." In the right margin, in red ink, she added an annotation: "*Not a guru.*" She traveled to Prasanthi Nilayam later that year, then again in the winter of 1986–87. I wish she could have spoken more thoroughly of what she experienced there, what it meant to her. She tended to answer my questions with vaguenesses, and she responded to Sarah—who went for the first time a year after my mother's second trip—in the same way.

Yet I do know something of what her pilgrimages meant to her. I think she told it in the rapt, quavery, slightly phlegmy voice with which she sang her Sanskrit food prayer, that unfaltering soft soprano that rose to a transcendent height to leave its *"Shanti, shanti, shanti . . ."* hovering for a long moment before we ate. I've learned what the words of the prayer generally mean: God is the food, the eating of the food, the eater of the food. God through the food becomes the life-fire in the bodies of living things. By God the food is offered into the fire of God.

During her first sojourn at the ashram, my mother and a fellow-pilgrim friend had a personal interview with Sai Baba. She wrote briefly about it, as if there were little of it words could convey, in one of her letter-meditations a month later. Sai Baba would not allow her to kneel and kiss his feet. She sat to his side and held his hand. They exchanged a few words, but she doesn't specify what was said. She writes of the moment as a "sweetness," the sweetness of her brown rice lunch in Maine magnified a billionfold. She writes of feeling his "overwhelming Love."

In my own imagination I go farther. I see tears on my mother's face. I see the woman who had lived and formed herself by words now resting in a garden beyond words. I see the obstreperous woman, the woman of spite and rebellion, submitting herself utterly. I see the advocate of causes shedding all conflict like leaves in a wind. I see the mother whose firstborn died in her arms relieved for a moment of that fifty-year ache. I see the veteran of a tempestuous and painful marriage made whole in a greater marriage, a marriage of peace. And I see my mother the Inspector, she who lectured and drove herself, who could not abide her own failings and weaknesses,

I imagine that woman completely at ease, for one tireless moment, in the sufficiency of being.

I may have it wrong. I may be imagining my own wishfulness into my mother's experience, whatever it was. I may merely want her to have realized her spiritual quest at Sai Baba's ashram so that I can feel easier about her dying. But still—when I remember her toasting the Unknown, when I remember her showing me the great bird I couldn't see, when I remember her reaching and searching with her eyes in the emergency room, and especially when I remember the ring of glowing roses, when I touch their mystery within me, then I feel myself touching an authentic joy, a fulfillment I did not invent. It was in my mother, and it is in these words she wrote in 1987, home in Maine after her second pilgrimage to Sai Baba:

> The sense of joy radiating from me exceeds all bounds. I asked for expanded awareness, now it is here—it comes from within me, where lies the source of all life, all wonder. It has nothing to do with what my mind conceives. It is like gazing into a deep, clear well, where bottom and surface are the same, obliterating limits of physical nature. They do not exist except in my mind that has to define them for its own petty sake. If I cannot hold on to this, it will return—or I will return to it: one and the same, and other openings will occur, as my sense of infinite expandability stays within reach: spiritual reach, which does not turn in upon itself.

I found that meditation only a short time ago, long after my mother's death. Reading it now I imagine a candle burning in the seclusion of her soul in the years she lived with us, a still and solitary flame burning in a place where no dementia or bodily failing or travail with family could extinguish it. I see it burning behind my mother's closed eyes, and I feel it behind my own.

Someday I will make my own pilgrimage to Prasanthi Nilayam. I would like to feel the power that touched my mother there. I'm in no hurry, though, because closer to home I have other places of peace, other beautiful wilds.

What I love about the old-growth forest is not so much the size of the trees, their sheer grandeur of scale, but their complete development, their wholeness, and the wholeness of the forest they compose. Each long-rooted tree began as a stirring in the seed, a tiny remembering spurred by the touch of sun and water, and each as it spired from the ground in the weather of its place took inside itself all that occurred—each urging of moisture and mineral among its roots, each feathery touch of fungus, the rains and slanting sun its boughs received through all its days and seasons, the sudden slashes of lightning, the weight of snow that broke down branches, the awful weight of wind that broke more, the shock of ground fire that charred its bark and killed its smaller fellows but left it living, deepening into earth and air, dripping rainfall from its limbs and channeling it then from the dark of soil back into the sky, turning earth into light and light into earth again. The tree stands until it can stand no longer, until its burdened memory is more than roots and trunk can bear, until the achievement of its peculiar form must forget itself in formlessness, in the darkness of its deepest self, then to echo, rhyme, and remember itself in the forms of future trees.

Remembering, forgetting—mind, I'm starting to believe, is nothing exclusive to human beings and other animals. The neurons we believe to be the source of mind may merely receive the mind imbued in all of nature, the mind that urges from within toward form and wholeness, that opens toward dissolution and decay. Sarah says she senses Sai Baba in the air she breathes, the water she drinks. My mother sensed him in the light of dawn, in the patterned frost on her windowpanes. I don't use that name but I sense it too, I hearken to it, I feel a mindful stirring in the forest quiet. There is mind in the great Douglas firs, in the ferns and mosses that grow on and around them, in the miles and miles of fungal strands in every tablespoon of forest soil, and there is mind as well in the soil itself, that vast unconscious store of memory, and if in the soil, then in the very stones and seeping waters, in the rivers and clear streams where salmon spawn, in ocean storms that freshen the streams and raise the forest, in the ceaseless ocean itself, in the shifting, flowing, spuming volcanic planet formed from the ash of long-spent stars. And the stars. The stars I wonder at, the stars that have scared me so—what can they be, if I see them truly, but fierce and subtle shimmerings in the mind of all that is?

Thou art that, it says in my mother's book, and so she is. She has gone back to that which she always was, in mind as well as body. What was the quest of her last twenty-five years but her attempt to find, to remember, the greater mind she felt intimations of and yearned for? And what was her Alzheimer's, finally, but another nudge in that direction, a further opening of her infinitely expandable spirit? As her accustomed point of subjectivity began to soften, to curl, to droop from firmness of form like a wildflower gone by its time, that personal point of view slowly gave way to a larger subjectivity, a greater Self, not the flower but the field of flowers, the forest bounding the field, the wind touching every tree and every flower. I see her aged face expanding like her spirit—nose and lips and wrinkled skin, the achieved landscape we knew her by slowly extends itself, slowly enlarges, her features forgetting their human forms to remember themselves as mountain ranges, valleys in sun and shadow, forests and fields of wild unknown lives beneath the stars.

CHAPTER THIRTY-SEVEN

The house seemed huge in the months that followed my mother's death. I rattled around in the daytime hours while Marilyn was at work, finding small things to fix or fiddle with, reading, writing my article on salmon and some other magazine pieces. I found myself petting the cat a lot. Marilyn, just a few days after my mother died, had felt a strange intuition that my mother was the cat, the cat was my mother. I didn't feel it so strongly, but they always had seemed joined in many ways. I did feel more tender toward the cat, more tolerant of her quirks and nervousness.

From time to time I sat in my mother's bedroom and looked out the sliding glass door that she had looked out, watching the light change as she must have watched it. The backyard world went on as it always had: the birch leaves yellowed and fell, the dogwood leaves turned red and fell later, the rain came down, the gray sky lightened and darkened, the finches and chickadees came to the feeder. It all continued, unbrokenly alive, but my mother did not. She had breathed for eighty-four years and then one evening at five minutes to eight she didn't breathe again. Her heart had pumped along for however many millions of beats and then stopped. All that she had been in this world, all that could be touched or hugged, all that could sing and shuffle and lift a coffee mug, all of that was a small clay pot of ashes on the closet shelf. In my grief for her I also felt an awe transcending grief, awe that an embodied life could persist so far and then just halt, vanish absolutely, never to return.

We had removed my mother's bed and given a few of her winter clothes to charities (we knew it would have pleased her to make them useful to someone who needed them), but otherwise had left the room unchanged. We weren't ready to turn it into something other than my mother's bedroom. I opened and closed her books, touched her jewelry, sorted through her stacks of magazines and unanswered mail. I suppose I was trying to touch her somehow by laying hands on the things her own hands had touched. And I was looking for more clues, for glimpses of what she had thought and felt in her last weeks and days. I found one, though I didn't know how to interpret it: a small, sealed, unmarked white envelope containing the pit of a single cherry.

When I cried, which was frequently, I knew what I was crying about but not what I was crying for. I missed her, of course, but *what* did I miss? Not the tension, not my irritation, not the pressure of being watched for cues, not anguishing over leaving her alone for an evening, not sponging up her trails of urine. I had been relieved of those burdens and *felt* relief, which I wasn't able to accept. I chided myself for being small, ungenerous. I berated myself for not being strong enough to bear the modest office of caregiving. I blamed myself for my mother's irrevocable absence from the world. Even the numinous roses, which I held inside me, which still seemed—against all reason—an affirmation from my mother herself, couldn't console me when the passion of my remorse was upon me. I worried about what I was still missing in that vision, what I didn't yet understand. I thought in my thinking mind that she probably hadn't left the world resenting me, but that knowledge was tossed about like a little boat in the steep swells of my feelings. As the months passed and I continued to feel racked with guilt, I found myself asking her for another sign, something more than the roses, something more than a cherry pit in an envelope.

I started a new kind of writing during this time. I had never written about myself in any sustained way, had hardly looked inward at all except to find my feelings about something in nature. But now a tiny essay I had written for a magazine, about where I lived and why, turned into a longer piece about coming west and coming of age in the sixties. Even the longer piece, I realized, held potential paragraphs and pages captive within single sentences. I went further into the necessary unfolding, but after a while I floundered. I was turning up the stuff of my life, the stories by which I knew myself, but what was I to do with them? The material had no form. As my life had been, it was scattered, shapeless, a mess of clay. I was frustrated, but now I can see how important that writing was. I had entered upon the paths of memory and begun the work of imagining myself.

At some point I had a lucid dream that both affirmed what I was writing and demanded more from it. I became conscious within a dream and saw what looked like a familiar manuscript, the formless memoir I was working on. A voice—something like mine, my inner voice—was reading the language as it was meant to be, reading surely, steadily, with exact authority and feeling, but I couldn't understand the words. They were English and mine but not quite mine, they were a river moving through but not part of my limited knowing. And then I realized that the manuscript, though it was in my typeface and bore my penciled markings, was not mine either. It was not something I had made but something that was making me. The voice and manuscript were the unknown life inside my life, writing and revising me, unfolding the true and necessary story. I woke knowing that the story was there, that I needed both to find it and to let it find me.

Over a period of about a year I had many dreams about wholeness, work, and lower depths. In one of them, a woman friend called with stunning news that a volcanic island had just risen to the surface of Paradise Lake, a lake I knew. An island being born! I felt blessed beyond measure to know of it. In another dream I watched a miner pulling what he called his Iron Horse, a complex and heavy piece of archaic machinery. It came to me with the force of revelation that he could pull the thing because he and it—and I—were *underwater*, and the water made it lighter. He wouldn't be able to budge it up above, on land. And in the most detailed of these dreams, a woman woke me to ask if I needed a job. "No," I said, "I have work, I've just been sleeping," but I got up and followed her down the winding stairway of what seemed to be a school. I wanted to justify myself, to explain that she had misunderstood me, but I also wanted to ask if there was something she wanted me to build. I thought it might be a system of shelves she wanted, shelves for sorting things out. It seemed too complicated, far beyond my skills, and I was afraid. But maybe she has a plan, I thought. Maybe she knows how I could do it. I kept walking down the stairs, catching glimpses of the woman far below me.

I was being shown, I see now, the necessity of writing this book— the necessity of entering the depths of memory under the guidance of the feminine. But at the time, the dreams simply frustrated me. I woke from each with a glow of wholeness and well-being, but I woke always to my uncertainty about my writing, my grief and guilt about my mother. The dream, as I went about my day, seemed small and merely wistful, utterly separated from my bereaved and confused reality. I continued to cry, continued to speak to my mother, continued to beg her for a sign of her forgiveness, or a sign that no forgiveness was needed.

Maybe she couldn't get through to me at home. I may have been too charged there, the rooms and things of the house too constantly branding me with the reproach of her absence. Maybe she had to wait until enough time had passed. Or maybe she just likes Idaho. In March of 1994 I was spending the night with friends in Lewiston and had just fallen asleep. In what feels like an ordinary dream, my host-friend and I are climbing a rocky height to fly the hobby airplanes he builds. It's *too* high, though. I start to climb down but my friend steps on my hands and I'm falling, fast, hurtling with the full rushing sensation of speed, wondering when I'll hit the ground then realizing I won't hit, I won't die, I'm falling free in space now and there's nothing I *can* hit. I open my arms and turn, still zooming, I feel the hard torquing weight of the turn and I turn again, flying free and rising now in the starry dark, arcing upward toward an intensely joyous light veiled in smoke like a nebula, the bright clouds of creation. But the light is more than I'm ready for, or it's not ready for me, and now I fly toward a more subtle light, a form, a hooded face, a mask of light with shadow interfused, *my mother*—not as she was in life but her face of spirit, her face that is all I can know of her now, her face with the cosmos behind it, nothing and everything behind it, a face of light itself interfused with shadow, smiling the serenity of being.

I want to stay, to hover freely in that presence, but now I'm drifting down from space into the dense unmoving weight of my own body, sleeping on my left side, my hands together between the two pillows beneath my head, and slowly I rise from the immense weight of sleep as if from the core of the Earth because I know I have to, I have to remember, and I'm crying already as I awaken but in gratefulness now for the sign she has given me.

After a while I turned on the light and wrote it down the best I could. I sat thoughtlessly a long time, the image of my mother's light-and-shadow face hovering within me, a stillness around which I trembled. Her smile, which was no smile I had ever seen on her living face, denied no loss, denied no least speck of pain or evil. It was not a smile of joy or happiness. It was a smile of knowledge, and *All is well* is what it said.

The Inspector has his own smile, a quick contraction of his pale cheeks and mustached mouth that looks as much like pain as pleasure. His smiling grimace, his grimacing smile. The thing I never appreciated is how vulnerable he is. I never fully understood his position. He has no child and now no mother, no family or friends at all. He has no life, really. Bob can grow tomatoes and can hammer nails, I can write at least, but the Inspector can only patrol his province and react. He spends all his time in that lonely room, staring carefully and haggardly like some air traffic controller who won't go off his shift. Where can he go? What can he do? I always thought Bob was the one I pitied, but really it's the Inspector. He's no older than me, it turns out, but he looks and acts much older. He's a pale, lonely old man who never was young.

But I don't want to pity him or condescend to him. I want to understand him, I want to give him his due. And so I went to him and told him that I value his observations. I told him I appreciate his commitment and caring. I told him that even though I think he's wrong sometimes, his judgments too severe, I've realized that I'm not a writer without him. It's really for him more than anyone that I'm writing this book—to take his harsh rebukes and make an answer to them. I thanked him for the challenge. I looked into his tired eyes and thanked him for keeping me honest. I touched him on the shoulder, asked if he'd like to take a walk.

We went no place special, just stretched our legs in the Portland rain. We breathed the good wet air with its sour tang of pulp mill. We walked the bluff above Swan Island and looked at the big ships in dry dock. We watched the crows hopping and squawking in the park. We walked the streets among schoolkids getting off their buses, heading home by twos and threes in their bright colors, shouting their clear high laughter. The Inspector walked with a kind of wariness, his hat pulled down on his forehead, but he took it all in.

I told him he was right. I wasn't patient enough with our mother. I wasn't flexible or imaginative or generous enough. I was too self-absorbed. There were moments I'm not proud of, moments I'd revise if I could, moments I'd try hard to make different if she were still here. I'd make myself a bigger person if I could. But I'm in my mid-forties now, I reminded the Inspector, and I've reached limits I'm unlikely to transcend. I am the man I am, lesser than the one I'd like to be—and, like a poem or an essay or this book, lesser than the one that might have been. I'm like the work I do, flawed and good. And that's what I did for our mother, I told him. I took on something hard, something important, and I did a job both flawed and good.

The Inspector held his pale eyes on me as I spoke, and to my surprise, he didn't object. But maybe I shouldn't be surprised. He of all people knows about limits—he's their close observer, their careful noter, and now I know that he very much feels the pain of his own. What he mostly wanted, I see now, was to hear *me* acknowledge my limits, hear from *my* mouth what he's been saying all along. I did that, but I also got him to look at things from my side. I showed him that last poem our mother marked, the one that begins, "Someone you trusted has treated you bad." I told him my fear that she meant those lines for me and why she might have had reason to—nothing new to the Inspector, of course. But then I showed him the title of the poem, and I showed him how she circled it with her pencil. I told him I take that as a message too, for me and for whoever sees it. "It's All Right," the title says. It's all right. It sounds like one of the tunes Bob whistles as he does his work. I can't whistle, I confessed to the Inspector, but I can hum that tune, and I bet him a beer that he could pick it up too. He gave me one of his grimacing smiles. It's our mother's tune, I told him. It's all right. It's something she wanted us to have.

CHAPTER THIRTY-EIGHT

Maybe this is a senile land-
scape, this open tableland. It extends with a slightest roll, a merest
wavering, clear to far blue mountains east in Idaho and south in Ne-
vada, under a sky of dark-bottomed cumulus clouds. Sage and rab-
bitbrush, gray and green going silvery in the wind. Not one tree. A
landscape made of distance, an immense presence made of absence.
Shallow creases lined with scab rock wander the land as if at random,
as if they have lost their way, and that's the way I follow. Long lazy
curvings gather me in, furrow me into the tableland, lower me away
from wind and endless distance. An inevitable winding way guides
me down, slowly down. Little walls of volcanic rock echo the stones
clattering beneath my boots. Bunchgrass, clumps of yellow flowers.
Damp sand, water in pools, then a trickling stream flows next to me.

What gives the solace I feel here? There's no congeniality in sand
or lichen, no warmth in canyon walls except what they hoard from

the sun. Why do I feel so generously welcomed? Because everything is as it should be. Everything is as it needs to be, through no doing of my own. The blind hand of time is scouring this canyon as it must be scoured, slowly, incrementally deepening its way through old flows and spewings of lava. The flat-bottomed clouds slide overhead in a sky exactly as luminously blue as it needs to be. The wind blows, the grasses bow and rise. The stream flows with a thin lilt through the way it has made, the way it was given. I walk deeper, the walls high above me now. Blue sky and shouldering cliffs, a song of water, the winding way as it all must be.

My mother would have loved this place. Desert wasn't her favorite landscape, but she knew the joy of natural quiet anywhere, the silent celebration in all things. She knew the happiness of feeling small in nature's greatness. She thrilled to the Olympic rain forest, its green riot of moss and ferns and colossal trees, when she and I drove there in 1969. She was sixty-one, on the loose at last from her working life in D.C., setting out on the adventure of her old age in her Land Rover, the Green Seal. I was twenty-one, a college dropout, a backpacker and climber in love with the wilderness West. We hiked a long uphill trail to camp for the night—I remember waiting for her, worrying a few minutes until she appeared, smiling, leaning into her pack straps, making her way up the trail at her own measured pace. I never thought about her heart back then, never thought how hard it had to be working to get her up the hills.

We toured around Oregon on that same trip—Mount Hood, down 97 to Crater Lake, and west along the Coquille River to the southern coast, where we ate crab and slept in the Seal pulled off on a logging road. I remember the trip warmly now, but my mother and I couldn't spend much time together without friction. Part of my joy in the West was being away from my parents, and she and I were too much the same—same fingers, same hair, same nose, same moody and cranky disposition. As a child I felt, rightly or wrongly, a kind of restraint, even coldness from her—as if she thought I didn't need her affection, or she didn't have it to give me. My father had wanted another child right away after Georgie had died, my mother told me in one of the conversations I taped, but she refused; she worried that he wanted George reborn right away. When I did come along—I'm pretty sure I wouldn't have if George had lived—I was doted on by Nanny, our maid and helper, to such an extent that my mother had to speak firmly to her, fearing that Jim was being neglected. We grew up calling our parents not Mom and Dad but by their first names, Franz and Zilla—because, my mother explained, she thought that way they would have closer and more personal relationships with us. If anything, I think, it distanced us. It tended to turn Jim and me into autonomous little adults while still children.

Through my twenties and thirties I had a comfortable relationship at a distance with my mother. We wrote letters, we saw each other occasionally. Two or three years might pass between visits. And so I suppose it was inevitable that we would rub sparks from each other when she moved into the house. We were too little accustomed to being together, let alone living together. She was losing her fiercely cherished independence, and I, in having to care for her, was losing some of my own. We loved each other, resented each other, and neither of us had much skill in knowing and expressing our feelings.

And so we did the best we could. We got by, and there were times in those four years when we did much better than get by. If our personalities were hardened and deformed in some of the same ways, our spirits, at our best, were also alike. We shared the same kind of religious imagination. Now and then I wrote down and left by her bed a line or two I had come across in my reading, lines I knew she would appreciate. "All finite things reveal infinitude," from Roethke. "i thank You God for most this amazing day," from cummings. And this from Gerard Manley Hopkins: "All things therefore are charged with love, are charged with God and if we know how to touch them give off sparks and take fire, yield drops and flow, ring and tell of

him." My mother always thanked me happily for these gifts. "Yes,"
I can hear her saying as she read the Hopkins, "oh, *yes.*"

On our walks sometimes, especially early on when she was
stronger, we would delight together in such small wonders as the
neighborhood provided us. We would stop to peer into a small cavern
in the base of a certain maple. "Anyone home?" my mother liked to
inquire, poking gently with her cane. We rejoiced at the fine job the
roots and boles of the older trees were doing upheaving the sidewalk
slabs. We were for the trees, for the spiny horse chestnuts that lit-
tered Hancock Street in the fall, for the moss that filled all cracks and
corners with its emerald wealth, for the dandelions, for the squirrels
that ran across our path—my mother greeted each one—and the
tiny ferns that grew from a mossy crotch of one of the maples. We
were for robins and chickadees, for each and every walker we encountered, for rain and sun, for the wind that shimmered my mother's favorite copper beech. "Think if each leaf were a bell!" she once
exclaimed in jubilation.

We were in league with the good green conspiracy of the world.
We were for and part of much more than we could say, more than we
could know, but in our best moments—when she was feeling spry
and spirited, when I stopped wanting to be somewhere else and gave
myself to the walk—in our best moments we *felt* what we were for
and part of, we felt what we were, without any need to speak it.
We smiled it, laughed it, shared it between us like the roving tip of
our spooky cat's tail. There's something King Lear says to Cordelia
toward the end, when his ravaged mind is both mad and terribly
sane:

> Come, let's away to prison.
> We two alone will sing like birds i' th' cage.
> When thou dost ask me blessing, I'll kneel down,
> And ask of thee forgiveness. So we'll live,
> And pray, and sing, and tell old tales. . . .

And take upon's the mystery of things,
As if we were God's spies. . . .

My mother and I, in those moments when we were most worthy of
ourselves, took upon us the mystery of things. We were God's spies.

And imprisoned as we were in our personalities, caged in our history, we did sing sometimes. I remember an afternoon walk when
my mother suddenly piped up, "I'll give you one ho, Green grow the
rushes ho," thumping the sidewalk with her cane. I piped in to join
her, following her lead, learning the verses that she remembered
better than I did. Arm in arm we sang our way around the sunlit
block in the company of trees and new spring flowers, stopping to
laugh when a neighborhood sheepdog briefly joined our chorus. As
I helped her into the house, my mother said, "They forgot to put it in
the Bible: *Have fun*."

How strange that I should feel uneasy telling this—as if, in re-
counting a moment of blithe happiness with my mother, I were con-
fessing something embarrassing, something shameful. How very
strange that I should have to say to myself, it isn't shameful. It's as
natural as anything in the world, and it's important. It's what I
wanted at the beginning of my life and received at last at the end of
hers: to walk with my hand in my mother's hand, circling toward
home in the light of forsythia and the shading trees, singing the song
my mother sings in her glad voice.

The light of my fire plays up the canyon wall, a few sparks rising. It's
good to be here, good to be weary and resting, listening to the ru-
morous voice of the stream—the voice of a life bound up like ours
in time and consequence, changing and changeless, free and con-
strained, young and ancient and ageless.

My mother didn't get cheated. She lived in her human way as long
and thoroughly as the flooding and trickling waters have worked this
canyon. She wore her body down, played it out, scoured it away with

living. Maybe she did end her life on purpose. And maybe she did it not because she felt unwanted, not because of anything I did or didn't do, but because her boat was failing her, and like the stream singing in darkness, she wanted to go on. The decision might have come from the deep place her food prayer came from, the place of God offering itself to God. The place of her quavery but clear *shanti*.

And if she did feel pushed? Maybe, just maybe, that's all right too. Maybe, a friend wrote, she needed a boost to get over the Great Divide, and maybe it was my part to provide it. And as she probably understood far better than I did, I needed to move on too. The Navajo say that old people have to die in order to make room for the living. I have a life to live, my own boat to steer. I needed a shove into open water, and it would have been typically forthright and generous of my mother to give me one as she brought her own boat in to shore. I keep thinking of her plucky mood the day before she fell, as she sat in the kitchen dressed in orange and lavender. I keep seeing the smile on her face—not her deepest childlike smile, but the smile of someone content in her own mind, a woman capable of doing the necessary task.

I only wish she could have laid her bones down more easily. I wish she could have crossed the divide not in a hospital room but at home, or—if she could have expressed the wish and I could have heard it and honored it—in a place such as this, where she might have died by firelight with streamsong bearing her away. Or back on her beloved coast of Maine, there to forget herself in the lap and splash of the sea, in gull cries and the smell of salt air. I could have read to her there, we could have spoken when she wanted to speak, we could have sung like birds in the cage, and we and all those around her could have looked and listened for the very right thing, for the corroboration of earth and sea and sky, of the mind of nature that unites us all. Maybe the time will come when we will allow such deaths, such whole and beautiful deaths, for ourselves and those we love.

Death doesn't seem so frightening here. It seems a little thing, significant but small, like the nest of white bones I saw today in grasses by the canyon wall. Nothing here worries about its end. If I stayed long enough, death might come to seem only the next thing to happen, the next turn of the canyon, the river flowing into its future as it must and needs to flow. I can imagine a certain happiness—and maybe I even feel it, some slightest glow—in giving myself up to stones and coyotes, to the greatness of the desert sky. A happiness, a holiness, a remembering beyond measure.

But not yet, not nearly yet. I stumble into the night on my sore ankle and stiff legs to relieve myself, and the broad stripe of sky is a shock of smeared and scattered light. Great Milky Way, great smoky wheel, the specked and glittering trail of time . . . *Thou art that*, says the book, I am that light, I burn with the fire of all that is, and I need no lantern to find my way.

CHAPTER THIRTY-NINE

I̶t wasn't trouble with his parents that made him leave the cottage they had rented. No fighting, nothing bad going on, but the cottage was small and all the talking was between his parents and their friends, stories he had heard before, their laughter not a laughter he shared in. It was their place, not his. But outside was the North Carolina coast, the Outer Banks, the boom of breakers in the moist night air. He slipped out when no one would notice and walked north in shorts and t-shirt, striding fast but easily fast, his bare feet striking the sand heels first and leaving their prints behind, the longshore breeze blowing cool on his face, the Atlantic waves traveling unimaginable distances to rumble and spume in luminous glory.

The beach is his, his alone. The damp sand giving to his feet, a few stars scattered on the trail of night. At sea a single light wavers, lost, alive, and in a sudden strangeness it seems he has always been walking here. It is all so uncannily familiar that he cannot imagine himself not here. His real self has forever been part of the rumbling night, has always known this wind and sand, this scatter of stars, and only now, having left the cottage and set out walking, has he joined himself. Only now has he remembered who he really is.

His own night sky lights within him, in the thrilled emptiness where his breath tides in and out and his heart thuds fast and sure. It lights with more than he understands, almost more than he can feel. He senses his life extending behind him far down the beach and ahead of him at the same time, far north on the Carolina coast and the night's long trail, and though he cannot see or even sense the grown-up he will be and often wonders about, he knows that somehow he is that man, somehow he is his entire life, though twelve years of it is all he has lived. He walks outside himself somehow, his full completeness whatever it will be, and inside himself as the boy he is.

It is strange but so calmly strange, so clearly and certainly real, that he wants to walk and walk and never stop walking. Such a long, long way, he thinks to himself. Such a friendliness that there is a way, that there is this trail of sand and stars, the ghostly ocean alive and roaring and he alive to hear it and see it, to smell the moist wind and know for the first time who he is, though it's nothing he could say or explain. He knows that the boy who left his parents' cottage will turn around in the night and walk back there, but he also knows that the one he is, the one he remembered only this night, will not turn back. That one will go on walking beside the sea, will walk on in stars and the cool shore wind and will not stop walking, not tonight, not tomorrow, not ever.

In truth, I don't recall turning back that night. The memory is entirely of setting out, striding fast in a calm exaltation. How could I have lost it? How could I have forgotten till now that mystery of wind and stars, that singular strangeness of knowing, *knowing* who I was? I didn't forget it. The memory was with me, reduced and stored for travel. It came to mind less frequently over the years—

thirty-five years—as the busyness of living piled over it and made it a thing among many, a childhood toy, a piece of the clutter. I forgot how true it was, how eerily exciting it was to the boy. Maybe it took this particular rhythm of walking, fast but easily fast, to bring it back in its wholeness. And these rumbling waves, sliding up the beach in snowy foam, this breeze, this scatter of stars—it took all of this, and it took the boy. The boy who made me remember. The boy who remembered me.

He set out one night on the Carolina coast, and here I am on the Oregon coast still walking, still setting forth on the night's long trail and glad for the journey. A few pains of body and soul the boy didn't have—and a few he did—but still setting forth, my sky still lit with more than I know, still knowing what I cannot explain, still with a heart thudding fast and sure. Tonight I walk with sand and stars and the wind in my face on the brink of my home continent, on the border of all I know, exactly in the center of what I love. I walk fast and easy, dunes to one side, Pacific to the other, a strew of stars behind and before me, an Earth underfoot where it's good to be.

Tonight, somewhere, I'll stop and walk back again, and when I turn from the sea at last I will listen as I leave it behind. I will listen until I no longer hear the foaming slide of the waves, their withdrawing hiss and trill of pebbles. Until I no longer hear wavelets slapping and sloshing, brief veering currents jostling in the shallows. Until the pounding of breakers is muted by the dunes to a pulsing rumble almost quiet, both near and distant, a murmuring fierce and gentle —and by that sound I will know her as I must have known her before I was, when the anthem of her blood played round and bathed me in power I breathed and breathed until at last she could not hold me, until at last she opened and gave me the world.

CHAPTER FORTY

Every once in a while I'll say in my head, "Better go to the post office now," and then answer aloud, "Yeah, I think so too." I've always been more than one person. I remember distinctly sitting on my bed in our house in Maryland, ten years old or so, talking to someone named Bob—and Bob answering through my mouth. I was a solitary and sometimes lonely kid, and I suppose Bob showed up to keep me company. In a house of volatile tensions, he was a friend unfailingly genial and even-tempered. He was *normal*. We talked about ball games and fishing. We weighed the relative merits of biking to Cabin John to buy baseball cards or walking to Glen Echo Amusement Park to play miniature golf. We always got along.

The Inspector didn't have his title back then, but he too was around. I've always had a sense of being both a person who does things and a person who observes that person. When I batted a wad of tin foil high off the side of the house with a badminton racket, keeping it alive as long as I could, I was both the player—a well-known professional—and the TV announcer doing play-by-play. I don't know when the observer became so critically judgmental, but it must have been early on. You have to watch yourself (there he is) in an unpredictable household, and when things go awry the watcher is in a position to blame—to blame especially the one he knows best, the only one he might be able control. I wet the bed until I was ten or eleven. It was the Inspector, I see now, who made me say "I won't wet the bed" hundreds of times as I lay waiting to fall asleep, and it was the Inspector who bitterly upbraided me each time I awakened, too late again, to the moist warmth of my failure. He blasted me for being a coward when I hid in the house from the neighborhood bullies. He told me I was lazy and unworthy when I let a grade slip from A to B.

Once I was old enough to understand vaguely that having more than one self might be unhealthy, I kept Bob and the Inspector under pretty close guard. But they were very loyal in their way. Despite my inattention and contempt, they stuck with me. They inserted themselves, unexpectedly, into the writing of this book. I'm glad they did. I know them better now.

Bob, in particular, I've misjudged badly. I think it must have been in my dropout hippie days when I turned on the trusted cohort of my childhood and reviled him as bland and conventional. It must have been then that I gave him his surname, as great an insult as I could imagine in the late 1960s. Now I appreciate his strengths. His steadiness evens my ups and downs. He knows how to take a job of work and get it done. He's easy to please—this morning he bought an extension ladder, and he's been delighted all day long. And that, of course, is what I like about him most. He's happy. Bob is *happy*. I never dreamed that happiness would turn out to be something I so badly need, and that I'd find it in the oldest friend of my childhood.

The Inspector, on the other hand, isn't happy. It's not his nature to be happy, but he has eased up his scrutiny since I took that walk with him. Like anyone, he likes to be acknowledged. I think he appreciates the attention I've given him in this book. But it's the boy, definitely the boy, who deserves most of the credit for lightening the Inspector's mood. As I was hoping, the old man has been charmed. Some of his emptiness seems to have been filled. He fancies himself a kindly uncle when the boy's around. He tells stories, and listens to stories the boy tells him. He gets out of his room more. He's even straightened up his manner a little. He doesn't drink as much now that the boy is here, and he's cleaned the spots of dried oatmeal off his bathrobe.

In truth, we're all doing better since the boy arrived. It's good to hear his laugh now and then. He's a studious and self-reliant kid, as kids ought to be. Like me, he doesn't mind spending hours in a book. He likes to write poems. But there are times, of course, when he needs to go out and have fun. I'm learning to sense those times. I'll get a feeling and put down my pencil or book, say good-bye to the Inspector if I'm with him. I'll lean back in my chair gazing out the window, watching the birds at the feeder, watching nothing. And then we'll go.

If we're hungry we might drive to Burgerville—I don't usually go there, but the boy likes it—or to El Burrito Loco for *carne asada* tacos till they're coming out our ears. There are plenty of places to go, things to do. Sometimes he wants to head down to the river, the not-too-polluted Willamette, and throw rocks into its quiet current. Maybe look for blackberries, if it's summer. Mess around in the Riedel International yard, checking out the wooden spools of cable, the huge pieces of rusty equipment. If there's a baseball game or soccer match at the University of Portland, we might wander over to watch. Or if the boy has a hankering to play pinball—he's an old-fashioned kid, he doesn't like video games—I know a tavern down on Lombard where they'll overlook the boy's age and we can work the flippers and push the box to its tilt limit all day long.

If we're away too long the Inspector usually lets me hear about it, but he doesn't have his heart in it. I get my work done. If anything, I get more done than I did before. And I'm happier. The boy seems happy himself, all in all—especially when I take him backpacking. (The Inspector never comes along.) He skinny-dips, climbs rocks, catches lizards, gets scratched and grimy-handed and sometimes shouts for joy, surprising me. We stare into the fire at night, if we have one, as I used to stare into the fireplace beside my father. Once in a while, when I catch him unawares, I get the feeling that the boy looks up to me. I get the feeling that he's proud.

And when he's sad? Well, then he's sad, and I am too. Sadness isn't the worst thing. Sometimes it's a good time to write—sometimes it is fertile, as Thoreau claimed—and sometimes it's a good time just to do nothing. We might lie in the grass over in the park, looking into the trees, the sky. We might walk a while, aimless as the blowing leaves. Or we might stay home, where we're safe and comfortable. We might just sit with our sadness, or we might sleep, and when we sleep in sadness usually we dream. *I dreamed a horse,* one of us says, *a blue horse . . .* "Where?" *He was running on the plains . . .* We talk like that, and sometimes the sadness passes. And even if it doesn't, pretty soon it's time to fix dinner.

Marilyn has always loved the boy. She's glad to be seeing more of him. She says he takes after Bob, or Bob takes after him, and she's right. She likes Bob too, even though he doesn't do the laundry often enough to suit her and still hasn't tiled the closet floor. She compliments him on his cooking and never fails to thank him for the work he does around the place. The Inspector is harder for her to like, because she's seen what he does to me, and because she too has been the victim of some of his harsh and unreasonable judgments. If he's in one of his grouchy funks when she comes home, he might snap at her before I can stop him. "The Inspector's digestion is off," I'll tell her by way of apology. Sometimes she'll smile at this and allow herself to be kissed. And sometimes she'll say, "The Inspector is an ass, my dear, and so are you."

And so we get along. We have spats and differences, like any fam-

ily, but there's room for us all. I trust us, all of us, to be who we are
and to do what we need to do. I trust my dreams and visions. I trust
the pencil in my right hand, the little trails it makes across the page.
I trust myself to follow them. I trust my sadness, and I'm learning,
at last, to trust my happiness too. Many years ago, sometime in the
1970s, my mother wrote these words on a birthday card: "Each one
brings you nearer the harmony which you will achieve between
your selves, and diminishes the anguish, for you are learning love.
May your way become clearer."

I've got that card in front of me now, along with a few photographs, a few of her poems and meditations, a few of her colorful
dresses that Marilyn wants to make into a quilt. It's three in the
morning and I can't sleep, but tonight I don't mind. I woke with a
start an hour ago, remembering I hadn't set the garbage can out by
the curb for the morning pickup. I was lugging the can around the
corner of the house, in high-top sneakers and a rain parka over my
bathrobe, when I stopped short and laughed out loud. I sat on the can
in the pouring rain, looking at the sidewalk. It had come to me, finally, what I'd been missing in my vision of the roses. It was nothing
about the ring of roses itself but where the ring was, where it had
been placed for me to see as I opened the front door of the house. It
was on the parking strip next to the curb, just to the left of the bottom
of the front steps, the exact spot where once a week I place this garbage can—this vessel of husks and peels and empty containers, spent
coffee grounds and typewriter ribbons, the things whose good we
have taken and turned into our lives.

And so I came in here to my study, still laughing, to sit with the
sound of rain on the roof and look again at some of her spirited words,
look again at her canny and kindly and mischievous face. Soon I'll go
in and upstairs and slip back into bed with Marilyn, who will stir in
her sleep and murmur some glimpse of her dream. But before I go I
will do one thing. I have on my desk the antique travel clock my
mother inherited from her mother, a brass cabinet four inches high

with glass walls and a carrying handle on top. Not the ship's clock she missed and couldn't track down in memory, but a clock she had with her wherever she lived, a brass clock with elegant black hands and Roman numerals on a white face, a clock of a kind not made in the world anymore. It stopped—which day we aren't sure—at five minutes to eight, the hour of my mother's death. When I'm ready I will open the glass door in back, I will fit the key to the crank and wind the spring, I will leave the clock ticking behind me.

The Wilds of Home

I'm waist-deep in blackberry vines looking for a cat who isn't here. Or if she is, she has an acre to be hiding in and she's ignoring me. It's my fault either way. When the carpet layers arrived at 8:30 I put her on the deck, harnessed and leashed, to keep her out of their way. I brought her food and water and stayed a minute to soothe her ragged nerves, then drove to Dixie's Café for breakfast and the newspaper. When I came back, the leash was wrapped around a rosebush, and the harness, still buckled, lay empty in the grass. She must have un-peeled herself into freedom. A feline Houdini. No sign of fur or blood. No sign of cat.

And so I'm wading the tangled, thorny biota of our new home in the country, calling *Here, kitty kitty kitty* in a falsetto voice—the only way I know how to do it—embarrassed that the carpet layers might hear me and worried sick that I'm singing to a long-gone cat. Maybe she's taking a nap, my head argues hopefully. But my heart has a mind of its own, and my heart knows she's gone. She's fled the noise and confusion of this unsettled place to find the home she remembers, the home on Princeton Street in Portland where she was raised and for which she jilted her owner to move in with us. The home she defended from every tom and puss in the neighborhood with fierce screeches and deep, vibrant, business-meaning yowls. If my heart is right, she has a hundred miles to go and she won't make it. The farms around us all have dogs, many dogs, and around the fringes of the farms are coons and coyotes, and not much deeper in the woods are mountain lions.

And roads, of course. The instant I saw the empty harness I remembered in panic that I'd just seen a dead tabby on the way back from Dixie's—but it was two or three miles from here, and the body had already begun to bloat.

Here, kitty kitty kitty . . . I thrash ahead, listening for her odd, birdlike chirp.

Since her miserable, boxed-up trip from Portland, we've kept her mostly inside, letting her get to know the new house. As we cleaned and spackled and painted, she made her rounds. She sniffed meticulously, as high on the walls and lower cabinets as her hind legs would lift her. She rubbed her scent against corners and doorways of special cat significance. At a particular nail head along one of the joints of bare subfloor, something drove her delirious—she licked and pawed and rolled on her side in a frenzy of sensuous attention. She sharpened her claws on the subfloor and on the driftwood posts of my mother's old bed.

Once or twice a day, Marilyn or I would take her outside to let her acquaint herself gradually with the grounds. It was wonderfully absurd. A cat no more belongs on a leash than that French poet's lobster. She would creep along in slow motion, drawing out the retractable leash with no regard for the human at the other end, immersed in whatever intensities her eyes and ears and nose were bringing her, abruptly turning now and then to try to lick the har-

ness off her back. She crept, I now recall with sadness, inexorably
away from the house. And once back inside, especially after dark, she
would park herself by the screen door, listening into the night. She
pawed at the screen and tried to squeeze through where the former
owner's dog had torn it. We had to patch the hole with duct tape to
keep her in.

I stumble loose from our thicket into the neighbor's trees, and as I
turn around our new house startles my eyes. I've been glancing out
its windows for ten days but have hardly seen *it* in that time. A plain,
brown, slope-roofed, oblong box—and it's beautiful. It's almost sur-
rounded in Douglas firs over a hundred feet tall. "We live here," I say
out loud. Today the carpet, tomorrow our furniture and thousand
boxes of things. We're out of the city at last, good city though it was.
Maybe, just maybe, we've finally found our place. I'd be wildly
happy, I realize, if I hadn't lost our cat.

She could be ten feet away, of course, and I'd never know it. She
was relentlessly indifferent to my mother and well capable of the
same indifference to me and Marilyn. Many times I've called her
from the doorway late at night, wanting to get her in so I could go to
bed, only to spy her sitting not twenty feet away, absorbed in the
darkness beyond, not only uninterested in my vocalizations but utterly, entirely oblivious to me and to anything human.

Well, to hell with her. I trudge back to the house, scratched and
sweaty, itching with nettles, taking no solace from the buttercups I
walk through or the tiny pears on the pear tree. There's work to be
done if we're going to be ready for the movers tomorrow. I'm hoping
hard for the joke to be on me, for Spooky Houdini to have remateri-
alized by the front door, sleeping or idly licking a paw. But no cat. Inside, the carpet layers are tacking and slicing and gluing away,
finishing off our fresh and empty rooms.

In the cool of evening, with Jimmie Dale Gilmore crooning on the
boom box, I'm remounting switch plates on creamy fresh-painted

walls, enjoying the smell and feel of the new carpet. Its dusty rose color is just right. Even my tilework in the entryways, which in the mortaring and grouting looked like a major disaster, has turned out, with a little cleanup, to be a minor success. Marilyn is on her way from Portland, having watched the furniture into the Bekins truck and said good-bye to our old house. I can't wait for her to get here, to see the work we've done made whole. A fresh start in the country. A creamy white and dusty rose beginning.

I've placed saucers of milk at all the entrances, and occasionally I go out to call—loudly, now that no human being can hear me. All I get in response are frogs chorusing by the stream and the raucous, ratchety cries of guinea hens from across the road.

When I called Marilyn to tell her about the cat, I was surprised to find myself choking up. For a while I could barely speak. I realized after we hung up that I was crying for more than the cat. I thought I was over my mother's death. I thought I had grieved my way through. It's been two years since she broke her hip and went to the hospital and didn't come home. Long enough, my mind declared. She lived eighty-four years, and most of them on her own terms. She lived a full life, a beautiful life.

But I miss her. I miss her very much, I realize, despite my sharp memories of the tensions of those years. As I screw the switch plates to their boxes, sometimes tightening too hard and cracking the plastic, I tell myself that I did all right by my mother in her old age, I did what I could. I tell myself, and I think I believe it. But losing the cat has opened up the emptiness again, renewed the callings of grief. I keep thinking how much she would have liked this place—the birds, the blackberries, the big trees. The garden I'm going to plant.

I drop my screwdriver and turn off Jimmie Dale's infinitely injured voice, his songs that cry so beautifully of loss, and put on Beethoven's *Violin Concerto*—the music whose opening timpani beats will forever wake me into Sunday mornings as a boy, when the hi-fi sometimes issued an ordered serenity into our home. My father, in glasses and bathrobe, would be reading in his rocking chair, my mother on the sofa, the cloth of love they wrung and tore between them momentarily at rest. The music seemed to gather us into its stately wholeness. It was an unspoken communion, a kind of Sabbath we shared.

I open a beer and stretch out on the carpet to listen as Beethoven rises into the authority of his allegro, working up the necessary tensions so that Isaac Stern's fiddle can slip free of them, dancing in a sky where joy and sadness mingle. *My mother and father made a life together,* it keeps coming to me. Despite everything, they made a life, and even after they couldn't live together they made a life for Jim and me. Phrases from my mother's letters pass through me, letters she wrote my father in the 1960s. *They miss you . . . We're behind on John's orthodonture . . . Jim is taking courses at the community college . . . They came from Springfield in fine fettle, as always after visiting you . . . Thank you for the extra check . . . Sorry I bawled you out so hard . . .* His letters to her from that time don't survive, but I know their gist and tone from reading hers.

What is it that so moves me? Their marriage lay in ruins, they each had wounds that wouldn't heal, spites they couldn't control, grievances that could never be redressed—yet this earnestness, this faithfulness, this wealth of caring for my brother and me. As best they could, they kept the broken family whole, so that we might live and grow and go on in the world.

They paid everything their love exacted. They paid willingly and at great cost. I honor them for it. And both of them now gone, and almost all their friends, all my relatives of their generation except for three aunts in their eighties and nineties. All that composed the family cosmos for me as a boy, all the talk and smiles and shouting and tears, all the meals and travels, the touching of hands, all of that gone from the world and yet not gone, all of it as present and vivid as Beethoven's measured exultances, here in the bare rooms of an Oregon house where no mother or father or child of mine will walk through the door. Here in the mystery of memory, the rising of love. I see no end to love. And, forty-six years old, very shaky with a waking joy, I see no end of coming of age.

The slow movement in Beethoven is almost always my favorite, when he wins through his despondencies and turbulent triumphs to the blessed interval, that timeless transitory moment when the soul knows itself and needs no more. Writing scarcely can touch that moment; Beethoven found it many times. I listen outside on the deck, in the company of stars and tall shadowy trees, until something goes wrong in the boom box or the CD. A low, discordant groan crescendoes under the tuneful sweetness of Stern's violin. It takes me several seconds to realize that the sound is coming not from the boom box but from my cat, and that I am looking at her. She's crouched in the spill of light from the kitchen window, her fur puffed up like Halloween, issuing an ominous low yowl to a second cat who has encroached too far into our territory.

I ought to let the drama play out, but I can't stop myself from going to her. The other cat slinks away; my own glances at me with what might be annoyance. She won't be held—too tensed, her awareness too charged—and so I stand nearby until she settles a little and begins to chew a spear of grass. "Spookus, you've been out all day," I inform her, and she lets me carry her into the house. There are burrs and little sticks in her underfur. As I pick them out I remember hidden mushrooms I found while searching the brambles this morning, a blue wildflower I'd never seen before, the sweet and dark and berry-rich smell of the moist ground.

The cat laps up a saucer of milk and pads to the screen door, where she waits to be let out. I tell her I won't have it, and after a while she folds her legs and sinks down on the carpet where she is. She stares out through the screen as my mother used to stare through her sliding glass door, toward things beyond my vision. Beethoven wraps up his sprightly conclusion. The quiet of the night floods in. Soon Marilyn will be here with a few last pieces of our old life. The cat and I will be waiting. We'll let the night breathe in with its quiet stirrings, its stillnesses that verge on speech, its rumors of that deepest wild where my mother and father have gone. We'll breathe the air, we'll keep our eyes open as long as we can, we'll listen for everything the night can tell us of this home where we now live.

ACKNOWLEDGMENTS

First I thank Marilyn, who knew the beauty and burden of those four years and lived them with me again as I read her the chapters-in-progress of this book. Her suggestions, and the portions of her journal she opened to me, helped make it whole. She would tell the story in a different way, a way as true and necessary as this one. I thank her for the love, forbearance, and support that made my telling possible.

Margaret Daniel, Adelaide Karsian, Betty Wilson, and Jim Daniel—two aunts, a cousin, and my brother—put their memories to work and provided correspondence to the book's benefit, as did three labor movement comrades of my parents: Alice Cook and Philip and Miriam Van Gelder. I am grateful for their help, and grateful also to the memory of Booton Herndon, whose letters and anecdotes over the years enriched my knowledge of the man and woman I was born to.

Jane Crosen helped with recollections of my mother in her Findhorn and *WoodenBoat* days, and Gordon Barton, my mother's spiritual cohort and fellow traveler, kindly and patiently answered my questions. Sarah Holmes, faithful friend to my mother in her last years, illuminated life in the beautiful wild of Prasanthi Nilayam. Paulann Petersen told me the story of her mother, and Satish Kumar allowed me to quote from the story of his; their accounts helped me write this one. John Sterne, my oldest friend, knowledgeably informed me on things Vedic (with the gracious permission of his spiritual masters, Lenora Lynx and Billy Puma).

Dr. Tom Harvey brought smiles to my mother's face and the best health he could to her faltering body. He helped her live well, and Dr. Dan Gilden gave us advice that helped her die well when that time came. Both offered clarifying counsel on medical matters during the writing of this book. (Any medical inaccuracies and all unattributed opinions are strictly my own.) I'm grateful also to the Medicare Alzheimer's Project, the Columbia-Willamette chapter of the Alzheimer's Association, the Volunteers of America Interlink Center, and Providence ElderPlace. Those organizations helped the three of us manage while my mother was with us, and they gave me, through mailings and lectures and conversations, an education in senile dementia.

The inner path that led to the writing of *Looking After* was opened in many sessions with Elizabeth Hendricks, Psy.D., a Jungian genius of listening and questioning. She is truly a doctor of the soul.

The writing grew from a little seed of an essay Annie Stine asked me to write for *Sierra,* when she was an editor there. Tim Schaffner, then my agent, persuaded me to try a book-length memoir. Lisa Ross, now my agent, encouraged me and found the perfect publisher for the book-to-be.

Jack Shoemaker, Counterpoint editor-in-chief, knew what this book needed to be long before I did and long before he had a contractual interest in it. He gave discreet clues to guide me along the way and edited the manuscript with a sure hand. I thank Patricia Hoard, Carole McCurdy, Jane Vandenburgh, and Nancy Palmer Jones for their suggestions and support. David Bullen, best in the business, designed a beautiful book, and Becky Clark, Jessica Kane, and Nicole Pagano helped see it into the world.

In the 1980s I dreamed of being published by North Point Press. In the 1990s it is a dream come true to join the Counterpoint venture in its beginnings. I thank publisher Frank Pearl for making Counterpoint possible and for the enthusiasm with which he embraced my book.

Black bears and pileated woodpeckers heard the first readings of the early drafts of *Looking After.* (Their reviews were indifferent.) The time and solitude I needed to write my way into the book were provided in the form of the 1994 Margery Davis Boyden Wilderness Writing Residency at Dutch Henry Ranch in the Rogue River country. I thank Frank Boyden, Bradley Boyden, and PEN Northwest for the unique privilege and good action of that seven-month stay in a fertile meadow far from town.

In early 1995 I was able to advance the book while teaching at Sweet Briar College and living in the nurturing pastures of the Virginia Center for the Creative Arts. An Oregon Literary Fellowship arrived with uncanny timing near the end of the year, just when I needed it to help me finish the book. My thanks to the staff and benefactors of Literary Arts, Incorporated. I made final revisions while living in the Thurber House in Columbus, Ohio, and teaching at Ohio State University as the James Thurber Writer-in-Residence.

I am grateful to the Walter P. Reuther Library at Wayne State University in Detroit for access to my father's and mother's papers and for generous help with photocopying expenses. The Knight Library of the University of Oregon and Fern Ridge Library in Veneta either had or found the books I needed.

Finally, I would like to acknowledge four women who won't be expecting it, each of them flowering uniquely with the gains and losses of age: Margery Boyden, Dorothy Stafford, Mary Stegner, and Ann Zwinger. In each of them I sense my mother's spirit.

In writing my book I found important help in the work of these authors:

Wendell Berry. *Harlan Hubbard: Life and Work.* Lexington, Ky.: University Press of Kentucky, 1990.

Edmund Blair Bolles. *Remembering and Forgetting: Inquiries into the Nature of Memory.* New York: Walker, 1988.

John Burroughs. *Riverby.* Boston: Houghton Mifflin, 1894.

Joseph Campbell. *Historical Atlas of World Mythology.* New York: Harper & Row, 1988.

Mary T. Clark, trans. *Augustine of Hippo: Selected Writings.* Mahwah, N.J.: Paulist Press, 1984.

Paul Davies and John Gribbin. *The Matter Myth.* New York: Simon & Schuster/Touchstone, 1992.

W. S. Di Piero. "Notes on Memory and Enthusiasm." In *Memory and Enthusiasm: Essays 1975–1985.* Princeton, N.J.: Princeton University Press, 1989.

Gerald M. Edelman. *Bright Air, Brilliant Fire: On the Matter of the Mind.* New York: Basic Books, 1992.

Mircea Eliade. "Mythologies of Memory and Forgetting." *Parabola* (Nov. 1986).

Ralph Waldo Emerson. *Essays and Lectures.* New York: The Library of America, 1983.

James Hillman. *A Blue Fire.* New York: Harper & Row, 1989.

James Hillman. "A Psyche the Size of the Earth." Foreword to *Ecopsychology: Restoring the Earth, Healing the Mind.* Eds. Theodore Roszak, Mary E. Gomes, Allen D. Kramer. San Francisco: Sierra Club Books, 1995.

Robert A. Johnson. *He: Understanding Masculine Psychology.* Rev. ed. New York: Harper & Row, 1989.

C. G. Jung. *Memories, Dreams, Reflections.* Trans. Richard and Clara Winston. Ed. Aniela Jaffé. New York: Vintage, 1989.

Satish Kumar. "An Interview with Satish Kumar." *Timeline* (Sept./Oct. 1995).

Stephen Levy. "Dr. Edelman's Brain." *New Yorker* (May 2, 1994).

Alan McGlashan. "The Translucence of Memory." *Parabola* (Nov. 1986).

Sherwin B. Nuland. *How We Die: Reflections on Life's Final Chapter.* New York: Alfred A. Knopf, 1993.

Robert Ornstein. *The Evolution of Consciousness.* New York: Prentice Hall, 1991.

William Stafford. *Passwords.* New York: HarperCollins, 1991.

Laurence Stapleton, ed. *H. D. Thoreau: A Writer's Journal.* New York: Dover, 1960.

Eliot Wigginton, ed. *Refuse to Stand Silently By: An Oral History of Grass Roots Social Activism in America, 1921–1964.* New York: Doubleday, 1991.

Philip and Carol Zaleski. "Walking on the Waves: An Interview with Keiji Nishitani." *Parabola* (Nov. 1986).